Anglo-American Politics
1660–1775

Anglo-American Politics 1660-1775

The Relationship Between Parties in England and Colonial America

ALISON GILBERT OLSON

1973
Oxford University Press
New York and Oxford

Preface

Factio, factionis, f.g. a division of people in sundry opinions
... also a companie or bande of men, sometyme rychesse,
authoritee, or estimacion in a citee. Factionum principes, the
heades of rebellion or sedition. Neque nos tanta factione sumus,
neyther bee we of so great authoritee.[1]

Such, if they had bothered to look it up in *Eliotes Dictionarie*,
was the definition of 'faction' which the Elizabethans and their
early successors brought over to the American colonies. On political parties in any other sense, 'Pars, partes, ... a partee or
syde in contencion, a faction' was all the dictionary writer had
to offer, clearly thinking of them in far less specific terms than
he did of faction.

Here, by contrast, are Dr. Johnson's definitions near the
close of the colonial period:

Party: (1) A number of persons confederated by similarity of
designs or opinions in opposition to others; a faction.
Faction: (1) A Party in a state.
(2) Tumult, discord, dissention.[2]

Both Johnson and Eliot use the words 'faction' and 'party'
interchangeably; nevertheless they also distinguish sharply
between them. To both men party is defined by what it is, and
presumably can continue to be indefinitely; faction is defined
more by what it does. Implicit also is the assumption that societies can tolerate parties (they are at least peaceful) but not
factions (they are tumultuous and militant).

Thus far the writers agree, but note the difference in their
emphasis. Eliot is almost solely concerned with faction: he pays

[1] *Bibliothica Eliotal, Eliotes Dictionarie*, by Thomas Cooper the third tyme cor-
rected (London, 1559), no page given.
[2] Samuel Johnson, *A Dictionary of the English Language: in which the words are
deduced from their Originals and Illustrated in their different Significations by Examples from
the best Writers* (London, 1755), no page given.

little attention to party in a political sense; to him, as to the Elizabethans who read him, divisions in the body politic must almost inevitably lead to strife. Dr. Johnson is not so fearful: he gives equal weight to party, suggesting that his Augustan contemporaries had come at least to acknowledge peaceful parties as a fact of political life.[3] Dr. Johnson himself seems to have dated the change to about the end of the seventeenth century, or at least his illustrations would suggest this. His authorities for the use of the word 'faction' are, significantly, Shakespeare, Charles II, and Clarendon; his authorities for 'party' are Locke, Addison, Pope, and Swift, and the *Tatler* and *Spectator*.

There is one other difference worth noting. To Eliot there are two main kinds of faction, on the one hand a ruling oligarchy, a clique of wealthy office-holders—'rychesse, authoritee, or estimacion in a citee'—and on the other hand a group of malcontents—'the heades of rebellion or sedition'. To Eliot's Renaissance reader, aware of peasant rebellions, city-state politics, and the politics of ancient Rome, and, perhaps, aware of Machiavelli's interpretation of them, a division between rebels and ruling oligarchies was a natural one. 'The inferior sort against their superiors', as the author of *Nehemiah on the Wall* put it, represented at least a half-truth about politics. Assumptions about the dangers of faction, in fact, formed part of the seventeenth-century argument about extending the franchise. Republicans like Marchmont Nedham put forth as a virtue of popular government the fact that it eliminated the possibility of factions among 'standing powers'— the most dangerous kind in a state.[4] Opponents of democracy (John Cotton would have argued this way) opposed it on the grounds that it opened the way to irrational, diabolical popular factions.

By Augustan times Eliot's distinction had been forgotten; political divisions were no longer seen primarily in terms of class war. In a halting, uncertain, devious, complex, and fascinating way the idea of peaceful political parties had taken

[3] The contemporary debate over Edmund Burke's narrower but better-known definition—'Party is a body of men united by their common endeavour to promote some principle of government'—should not obscure the value of Dr. Johnson's definition.

[4] Marchmont Nedham, *The Excellence of a Free State* (London, 1656), pp. 28, 120.

hold. Indeed, Dr. Johnson comes remarkably close to the definition adopted in Webster's *New International Dictionary*, 1961:

> Party: (3a) A body of persons forming one side (as in a contest). A group united in opinion or action as distinguished from or opposed to a similar or larger group (as the rest of a community or association).
>
> Faction: (1) party, combination, or clique (as within a state, government, or other association). Often contentious, self-seeking, or reckless of the common good. (2) Party spirit or tumult, esp. as manifested in discord, dissention, or intrigue (or the irreconcilable conflict of parties).[5]

The American colonies produced no lexicographers like Eliot and Johnson, but it is clear from the language of colonial politics that the colonists, too, had developed a new set of assumptions about political parties over the years between the first settlements and the Revolution. To John Winthrop, George Calvert, William Bradford, factions were lethal threats to the community; they could hardly see them as anything else, and probably, in the circumstances, they were right. To Charles Carroll, John Adams, and Benjamin Franklin, parties represented groups of 'ins' and 'outs' often composed of competing 'interests', but quite distinct from the radical groups labelled 'factious' by English contemporaries. 'In a constitution like that of Great Britain [and the colonies, he might have added] there ever will be (I wish never to see the day when there shall not be) parties', wrote one colonist who certainly would have accepted Dr. Johnson's definition.[6]

The change from Eliot to Johnson is of more than literary interest. 'A living language', as Webster's *Dictionary* itself suggests in a quotation opposite the title-page, 'must keep pace with improvements in knowledge and with the multiplication of ideas' (Noah Webster); and the evolving definition of 'party' kept pace with the whole striking change from the Tudor conception of politics to the Georgian. The very fact that the

[5] *Webster's Third New International Dictionary of the English Language*, ed. Philip Babcock Gove (unabridged edn.; Springfield, Mass., 1961).

[6] Peter Van Schaak to Henry Van Schaak, 27 Jan. 1769. Henry C. Van Schaak, *The Life of Peter Van Schaak, L.L.D., Embracing Selections from his Correspondence and Other Writings during the American Revolution and His Exile in England* (New York, 1842), p. 11.

relationship between 'party' and 'faction' changed more in the two centuries before Dr. Johnson than it did in the two centuries after suggests, perhaps, that conditions conducive to the development of party were created as rapidly in the seventeenth and eighteenth centuries as they were in the period more frequently recognized as relevant by historians—the age of the French and Industrial Revolutions. The growth of legislative power relative to the executive, and the multiplication of interest groups seeking political outlets in the legislatures, the change in the nature of the issues over which men divided, a corresponding change in attitudes towards dissent, and the changing idea of government in relation to the community— all these were conditions vitally important to the acceptance of parties as part of the political process.[7]

This book is intended as an essay on what might be termed a still further condition—the development of the American empire. I hope through it to suggest some of the ways in which simply being in the Empire contributed to—even speeded up— the early American party divisions, and some of the ways in which the existence of the Empire did the same thing for English politics.

For colonial politicians faced with a hostile local government London came to offer an alternative source of power. Recognition in London gave safety, legitimacy, to opposition groups in the colonies who might otherwise have been suppressed: 'His Majesty's loyal opposition' was a concept more easily developed in an imperial context than a domestic one. London influence, sometimes complementary to, sometimes competitive with, that of local governments, could be used as a lever in local politics, and the search for London connections decisively affected the establishment of American factions. Moreover, colonial factions were often directly inspired by English ones. The very first generation of colonial governors lamented frequently that factions were 'spirited up' from England; the complaints a century later of Governors Cosby, Belcher, and their contemporaries were almost identical on this point, even to the wording. And Governors Bradford, Winthrop, and Calvert

[7] For a far fuller and quite different treatment of this topic see Caroline Robbins, 'Discordant Parties: A Study of the Acceptance of Party by Englishmen', *Political Science Quarterly*, LXXII (Dec. 1958), pp. 505–29.

would have had no difficulty at all understanding the complaint of an English politician in America on the eve of the American Revolution: 'How then, my Lord, can any conciliating measures take effect here till harmony is restored at home?'[8]

To English politicians out of favour imperial questions offered useful issues on which to attack the government, the colonies potential havens in case of domestic defeat, even areas for political experimentation. Moreover, there were even some writers who thought of a spillover from colonial parties to English politics. ''Tis in such bodies as [the colonies]', wrote the third Earl of Shaftesbury, 'that strong factions are aptest to engender.'[9] A half-century later some writers still echoed Shaftesbury's sentiments. When Henry Cruger wrote 'The opposition in the House of Commons flatter themselves that the confusion in your country will overthrow the ministry',[10] he was writing of the revolutionary situation, but his assumptions about the spillover of political divisions still had much in common with Shaftesbury's.

In a more general sense the mere diversity of the Empire—diversity of authorities, associations, interests, and issues—helped destroy the concepts of a monolithic political structure and a homogeneous political community, so hostile to the development of political parties in England and the colonies. It is with this growing diversity of authorities, associations, interests, and issues that I am concerned in this essay—with the way in which the first British Empire affected local political divisions in England and America, and, in turn, the way in which the emergent parties helped to bring the Empire together at first and to tear it apart in the end.

There will be, I expect, some important objections to this theme itself, and it may be well to suggest my awareness of some of them before I start. (After all, as Dr. Johnson said, 'It

---

[8] Commodore Hood to E. Temple, 2 Sept. 1769. *The Grenville Papers: being the correspondence of Richard Grenville, Earl Temple, K.G., and the Right Hon. George Grenville, their Friends and Contemporaries*, ed. William James Smith, Vol. IV (London, 1853), p. 318.

[9] Anthony, third Earl of Shaftesbury, *Characteristicks of Men, Manners, Opinions, Times*, 6th edn., Vol. III (London, 1732), p. 113.

[10] Henry Cruger to Peter Van Schaak, 3 May [1769], *Life of Peter Van Schaak*, p. 38.

is the fate of those who toil at the lower employments of life, to be rather driven by the fear of evil than attracted by the prospect of good. . . .')[11]

For one thing colonial historians accustomed to thinking of colonial politics as a matter of shifting, kaleidoscopic groups, banding together from time to time, then exploding into unfamiliar patterns, will challenge my very use of the word 'party' in interpreting colonial politics. To this I would reply, 'But the colonists, certainly by the eighteenth century, thought and spoke as if parties did exist. Should we not take their word?'

To this the critics would argue that the colonists may have used the word 'party', and even used it as Dr. Johnson did, but they never meant by it anything like a political organization in the modern sense. To read back into eighteenth-century Assembly groupings any modern conception of a complex political organization is to be anachronistic, and therefore quite misleading. But there are two answers to this. One is that, as it happens, colonial political parties stand up rather well when scrutinized by twentieth-century standards. The idea of an organization transcending its immediate membership they did not have, but extensive grass-roots support, policy differences presented to the electorate as platforms (programmes) and to the Assemblies as agenda, colony-wide concerns for patronage, continuity well beyond the life of one political generation—all these they did have. By the early eighteenth century there is evidence that candidates ran on slates,* pamphlets carried the equivalent of political platforms, and some colonial officials like Robert Hunter or James Logan were able to predict the partisan make-up of the Assemblies before they ever met. And where in modern America are there parties with the continuity of, say, the New Hampshire political interests in the century before the Revolution?

But all this is incidental to the larger point: is it not an anachronism in itself to hold up early English and American parties to twentieth-century standards, and to assume that, if they do not fit modern criteria precisely, they cannot be called parties at all? To read back twentieth-century terms is in some

[11] *Dictionary*, Vol. I, Preface.
* Slate = 'list of candidates adopted by a party organization before an election'.

way to assume that politicians in the eighteenth century were unconsciously working their way to a modern conception of party which they were too unsophisticated to see. To do this is to miss the fact that for their own less complex society a simpler organization was appropriate.[12]

One other objection, quite a fair one: colonial parties developed in different ways, at different speeds, and with different relationships to the mother country. To reduce them to one pattern is simplistic. Surely North Carolina's politics developed at a vastly different speed from Pennsylvania's, for example; surely New Jersey's Elizabethtown patentees looked at the uses of partisan politics in a way quite different from that of the Massachusetts land bankers. And surely 'Namieristic' studies—which I have not done—are essential to a definitive analysis of political parties in the colonies.

Very true, and I hope in future to test my hypotheses against such Namierist studies as are now being done. I have enormous respect for Namier/cum roll call studies of the colonial Assemblies—they are essential to our further study of colonial politics. But this book is meant as a suggestive essay, not a definitive study, far less a catalogue of Assembly divisions. My hope is to propose some aspects of the relationship between politics in the mother country and politics in the colonies; and in doing so to suggest further studies in the history of early American politics and the American Revolution.

Perhaps there may be a further use. In some ways the American colonial situation was unique as empires go: the mother country was underdeveloped and could not prevent its servants participating in local politics; the colonies were settled by men of the mother country so no 'native' organization developed. But in other ways the American empire represented an early experiment at building up a body of loyal support for the mother country among the provincial inhabitants. For a while (1689–1715) the English came near to

---

[12] It may also be suggested that men of the eighteenth century very often used the word 'party' in a pejorative sense. The English government warned prospective governors not to fraternize with colonial parties; colonial politicians charged their enemies with fomenting party spirit. There *was* opposition to the idea of party— a good deal of it. But the pejorative use of the word as often as not calls attention rather to the eighteenth-century manner of criticizing institutions and movements while accepting them as a way of life.

creating a political community with the colonies. Then they
failed. Perhaps historians of other, more modern empires may
find the American colonial experience of some interest.

Having devoted the first part of this preface to exploring the
distinction between the words 'party' and 'faction', I have myself proceeded to use them interchangeably. My excuses are
first, that Webster lets me (faction: party, combination, or
clique), and second, that many of my colleagues, remaining
unhappy at the organizational shortcomings of eighteenth-
century parties, are more comfortable with the word 'faction'
applied to that period.

Having also used the preface to suggest some of my uncon-
ventional ideas, I have later in the book made heavy use of
some very conventional citations. Clearly the number of
sources available for a study like this is endless; my footnote
citations are necessarily selective and on a number of topics I
have mentioned mainly traditional sources because their
general approach might make them more useful to a reader
following the broad interpretations.

I am immensely grateful for all the help I have received on
this book. The Folger Library, the American Council of
Learned Societies, the American Philosophical Society, and
the American Association of University Women have given me
generous financial assistance at various stages of the project.
Manuscript librarians all over the United States and England
have been wonderful: my thanks especially to those at the
Folger Library, the Library of Congress, the Bodleian Library,
the British Museum, the Institute of Historical Research, the
Huntington Library, the John Carter Brown Library, the University Libraries of Princeton and Harvard, and the Historical
Societies of Massachusetts, New Jersey, Maryland, New York,
and Pennsylvania. The Folger Library has, in addition to
everything else, given me an intellectual home for much of my
writing. My thanks are also due to Dame Lucy Sutherland and
to Professors Richard M. Brown, Michael Kammen, and John
Shy, who read this manuscript in its preliminary stages.

My children, who have played snowflakes with unnumbered
pages of manuscript, unwittingly torn up scratchings of great
ideas to make circus tickets, and even, I suspect, in the case of

the baby, eaten a page or two now and then, have remained an
inspiration to get the manuscript finished. To them and to my
husband, whose help was considerably more constructive, this
book is appropriately dedicated.

Contents

Abbreviations

A.H.R.	American Historical Review
B.M.	British Museum
Bull.	Bulletin . . .
Cal. S.P.	Calendar of State Papers,
Col.	Colonial
Am. & W.I.	Colonial, American and West Indies
Dom.	Domestic
Camden Soc. Pubs.	Camden Society Publications
C.O.	Colonial Office
Colls.	Collections of the
Mass. Hist. Soc.	Massachusetts Historical Society
N.Y. Hist. Soc.	New York Historical Society
Va. Hist. Soc.	Virginia Historical Society
Docs. re Col. Hist. N.Y.	Documents re Colonial History of New York
E.H.R.	English Historical Review
Evans	Evans Early American Imprint Series
Ga. Hist. Q.	Georgia Historical Quarterly
Jour. Br. Studies	Journal of British Studies
L.C. Transcripts	Library of Congress Transcripts
Mass. Hist. Soc.	Massachusetts Historical Society
Md. Hist. Mag.	Maryland Historical Magazine
M.V.H.R.	Mississippi Valley Historical Review
N.C. Hist. Rev.	North Carolina Historical Review
N.J. Hist. Soc.	New Jersey Historical Society
N.S.	New Series
Pa. Hist. Soc.	Pennsylvania Historical Society
Pa. Mag. Hist. & Biog.	Pennsylvania Magazine of History and Biography
P.R.O.	Public Record Office
Procs. Amer. Antiq. Soc.	Proceedings of the American Antiquarian Society
N.J. Hist. Soc.	New Jersey Historical Society
Pubs. Col. Soc. Mass.	Publications of the Colonial Society of Massachusetts
S.P.G.	Society for the Propagation of the Gospel
S.P.G.N.E.	S.P.G. in New England
Va. Mag. Hist. & Biog.	Virginia Magazine of History and Biography
W.M.Q.	William and Mary Quarterly

I 'The Public Peace' Background to 1660

In 1630, as the first settlers of Massachusetts Bay were establishing their colony, Captain John Smith of Virginia fame offered
them some public advice. Writing his *Advertisements for the
Inexperienced Planters of New England*,[1] which John Winthrop and
his associates almost certainly read, Smith argued that coloniza-
tion was an art to be studied: the settlers of Massachusetts Bay
should by learning about the experiences of earlier colonies be
able to avoid their principal mistakes. As Winthrop put it,
Virginia's example 'hath taught all other plantations to prevent
the like occasion'.[2]

To Smith, as to other adventurers who had led the infant
Virginia colony, one of the most critical dangers new colonies
faced was the development of factions. Factions were deadly;
they could tear the community apart. John Rolfe, one of
Smith's principal colleagues, blamed all Virginia's early
troubles on factional disputes:

... the begynning of this Plantacion was gouerned by a President
+ Council Aristocratycallie, the President yerely chosen out of ye
Councell, which consisted of twelve persons. This government
lasted above two yeres: in which tyme such envie, dissentions and
iarrs were daily sowen amongst them, that they choaked ye seedes
and blasted the fruits of all mens labors. If one were well disposed
and gave good advisement to proceed in the Business, others out of

---

[1] London, 1631, printed in *Travels and Works of Captain John Smith*, ed. Edward
Arber and A. G. Bradley, Vol. II (Edinburgh, 1910), p. 929.
[2] Winthrop Papers II, B7, quoted in Loren Baritz, *City on a Hill: A History of
Ideas and Myths in America* (New York, 1964), p. 11.

the malice of their hartes would contradict, interdict, withstand and dash all . . . in which confusion much confusion yerely befell them, and in this government happened all the mysery.[3]

Similarly the Dedication of Alexander Whitaker's *Good Newes from Virginia* blamed everything from bad harvests to deteriorating Indian relations on factionalism. The Virginians

. . . fell first into factions, and at last into plaine distractions, and so one yeare of misgovernment overthrew that body, which til then had prospered [and brought] the most disastrous accident that ever befell that business. [It] brought all to nothing for it hindered the building of houses, planting of Corne, nay it burnt up the houses and consumed the provisions . . . and which was worse, consumed the men. . . .[4]

Smith, Rolfe, and Crashawe, who wrote Whitaker's Dedication, were all referring only to the first few turbulent years of Virginia's existence. (Smith used the word 'faction' to mean specifically those people who wanted to go back home to England during his presidency in 1610.) But, as they and their contemporaries were well aware, factional division continued to threaten the stability of Virginia politics, long past the 'starving time'. Regrouping from year to year, but divided apparently between those planters who came to do well under the Virginia Company's administration and those who did not, Virginia factions disputed the very forms of provincial government, down to and after the open rebellion against Governor Harvey in 1635.[5]

Nor was Virginia the only infant colony to be nearly torn apart by factions. John Robinson warned the Pilgrims before they left England: '. . . be, I besheech you brethren, much more carfull, that the house of God which you are and are to be, be not shaken with unnecessarie novelties or other oppositions at the first setting thereof.'[6] But despite this, William Bradford soon

[3] John Rolfe, *A True Relation of the State of Virginia left by Sir Thomas Dale Knight, in May last, 1616* (New Haven, Conn., 1951), p. 34.

[4] Dedicatore by W. Crashawe (London, 1613), p. B2. In the same vein, see a sermon by Patrick Copland, *Virginia's God be Thanked* (London, 1622), p. 24.

[5] Secretary Kemp to Lord Baltimore, Jan. 1638, *The Calvert Papers*, Part 1, Maryland Historical Society Fund Publications, No. 28 (Baltimore, 1889), pp. 150–1.

[6] William Bradford, *Of Plymouth Plantation, 1620–1647*, ed. Samuel Eliot Morison (New York, 1952), p. 370, quoted with comment in George D. Langdon, Jr.,

complained of a difficult faction in the Plymouth settlement. The faction began with the arrival of 'particulars'—men who came over independently, unsupported by the Company of Adventurers in London and unwilling to compact with the Pilgrim Community. Led by the Reverend John Lyford and William Oldham,

> Some of those that still remained here on their Particular began privately to nourish a faction; and being privy to a strong faction that was among the Adventurers in England, on whom sundry of them did depend. By their private whispering they drew some of the weaker sort of the company to their side, and so filled them with discontent as nothing would satisfy them except they might be suffered to be in their Particular also; and made great offers, so they might be freed from the General.[7]

At first Bradford bought them off with easy terms. But soon after the same men were again acting in a faction against the governor, this time demanding the establishment of an Anglican Church. Lyford and Oldham were brought to heel and Lyford eventually banished, but not long afterwards the despairing Bradford was writing his London associates, 'We have rid ourselves of the company of many of those who have been so troublesome unto us; though I fear we are not yet rid of the troubles themselves.'[8]

To John Winthrop, then, one of the lessons most dearly taught by the experience of Virginia and Plymouth was the danger of letting factions develop. Not that factions were a uniquely colonial problem; it was common thought among Englishmen that factions were a disease affecting the organic society. But while factions were disruptive to any society, they were peculiarly devastating to infant colonies.

The problem with provincial factions was that disputes could not be kept within workable bounds. The colonists' various functions—farming, fighting, trading, attending church—overlapped so closely that a difference of opinion in one area could not but create differences in others. The Virginia settlers, for

---

Pilgrim Colony: A History of New Plymouth, 1620–1691 (New Haven, Conn., 1966), p. 24.

[7] Bradford, *Plymouth Plantation*, pp. 140–1.

[8] Bradford to Cushman, 9 June 1625, Governor Bradford's 'Letter Book', *Colls. Mass. Hist. Soc.*, Vol. III (Boston, 1794), p. 36.

example, were early divided into military companies; in these companies they not only drilled but attended church and marched to work in the fields. Company commanders were responsible for seeing that their men attended church and met their quota of agricultural production. At Plymouth also the citizens marched to church in companies of militia; significantly the faction of 'Particulars' not only demanded rights to farm on their own but also demanded the institution of Anglican Church services, and in the heat of the quarrels refused to show up for work.[9]

John Winthrop understood the implications of these arrangements well:

When brethren shall looke one at another as enemies and persecutors, etc. . . . how shall they joyne together in any publike service? How shall they cohabite and trade together? How hardly will they submit to such overseers? How will it hinder all affaires in Courts, in Townes, in Families, in Vessels at Sea, etc., and what can more threaten the dissolution and ruine of Church and Commonwealth?[10]

Now the problem of overlapping functions was certainly not unknown in contemporary England; the spirit of community in the early colonial settlements represented a return to the medieval communalism which England itself had not fully outgrown in the early seventeenth century. But in the early colonies the channels of authority were less clearly established; there was a flexibility but also an uncertainty about the manner of settling disputes; there was, moreover, a general uncertainty about the bases of local authority. In addition, the existence of vast acres of unsettled land meant that factious souls could

[9] On the general subject see Darett Rutman, 'Militant New World, 1607–1740: America's First Generation, Its Martial Spirit, Its Tradition of Arms, Its Militia Organization, Its Wars' (unpublished Ph.D. thesis, University of Virginia, 1959); Records of the Colony of New Plymouth in New England, ed. Nathaniel B. Shurtliff, *Court Orders*, Vol. I: *1633–40* (Boston, 1855), pp. 6, 14, 22, 38; 'For the Colony in Virginia Britania, Lawes Divine, Moral, and Martial', *Tracts and Other Papers Relating Principally to the Origin, Settlement, and Progress of the Colonies in North America*, coll. Peter Force (New York, 1947), Vol. III, Tract No. 2; Morrison Sharp, 'Leadership and Democracy in the Early New England System of Defense', *A.H.R.* L (Jan. 1945), 244–60.

[10] John Winthrop, *A Short Story of the Rise, Reign, and Ruine of the Antinomians, Familists and Libertines*, printed in David D. Hall, *The Antinomian Controversy, 1636–1638: A Documentary History* (Middletown, Conn., 1968), p. 299. A copy of this pamphlet, published under Thomas Weld's name in 1644, is in the Folger Library.

destroy a community by talking a majority of settlers into leaving, or by talking Company supporters at home into swamping the local authorities with hostile settlers. Bradford believed, and probably correctly, that the Adventurers intended to send over enough people from England to swamp the colonial government and destroy its original purpose.[11] Hooker's migration to Connecticut is the best-known mass departure of colonists already settled, but no colony was really free from the danger of losing numbers of its settlers. It was with only slight exaggeration that Secretary Kemp of Virginia wrote, 'The frequent and constant Reports this yeare of a Companye coming upon us doe at pr[e]sent much distract us, in so much that most are rather contriving how to desert the place then too loose any more Indeavour [here] when no stabilitye of their Affaires is to be expected';[12] and Thomas Cornwallis threatened to leave Maryland if Lord Baltimore did not give him special concessions:

... the best part of the trade would have been drawne out of ye territoryes by yr own Subjects whoe beeing thereby forst toe shelter themselves under another government and finding perhaps a Little Sweetnes in it, would quickly grow to such an Avertion against this supposed oprestion, as nothing would be more hateful toe them then you and yr Authority.[13]

Not only that, but provincial politics, far more than politics at home, were susceptible to outside pressure; colonial oligarchs consistently complained that hostile factions were motivated directly from England. Smith himself warned the New Englanders that 'indeed the cause of our factions was bred here in England',[14] a comment that was to be repeated by Governor John Harvey when he was about to be deposed by the Virginia councillors five years later: 'This faction I find great cause to suspect is nourished from England.'[15] In the same vein William

[11] Bradford, *Plymouth Plantation*, pp. 155–7.
[12] Secretary Kemp to Lord Baltimore, Jan. 1638, *Calvert Papers*, Part 1, pp. 150–1.
[13] Cornwallis to Baltimore, 16 Apr. 1638, *ibid.*, p. 177.
[14] *Works of Captain John Smith*, ed. Arber and Bradley, Vol. II, p. 931.
[15] Harvey to Windebank, Summer 1734, quoted in Nathaniel Claiborne Hale, *Virginia Venturer: A Historical Biography of William Claiborne, 1600–1677* (Richmond, Va., 1951). At the time Harvey wrote this, rumours were circulating in Virginia that Sir Thomas Hinton, London merchant and father-in-law of Harvey's leading

Bradford spoke of the Plymouth Particulars as 'being privy to a strong faction that was among the Adventurers in England'.[16] Once started, factions and rumours of faction were enough to discourage investment from England; moreover, as James Shirley wrote Bradford, 'I have heard it credibly reported, that some have said that til you be disjointed, by discontents and factions amongst yourselves, it boots not for any to go over, in hope of getting or doing good in these parts.'[17]

In a far deeper sense factions undermined the sense of mission so essential to the early colonial community. Virginian, Pilgrim, and Puritan alike shared the faith that colonies were settlements of chosen people, Israelites of the seventeenth century. 'What need we then to feare, but to goe up at once as a peculier people marked and chosen by God to possess it [Virginia]' quoted John Rolfe, exhorting his fellow settlers to stand stoutly for the 'Lordes Cause', commending the goodness of the Land they discovered to the faces of their opposers, '. . . as Caleb and Joshua in the very heate of the grudgings, murmurs, and assemblies of the children of Israel'.[18] Factions were indeed sent by the devil as the severest test he could offer an infant colony, in the same way the devil had created divisions among the children of Israel.

In quelling factions the Plymouth and Virginia oligarchies had used opposite methods: the Virginia Company had produced the Laws Divine, Moral, and Martial, with Sir Thomas Gates and the heavy-handed Sir Thomas Dale imposing martial law on the colony; Bradford had tried killing the faction with kindness by giving in to nearly all the economic demands of the Particulars. Later on he had to banish Lyford and some few others of the leaders. None of the methods worked; moreover, all the colonial leaders found themselves censured in England for the harshness they showed in handling their adversaries. Complaints against Dale came near to destroying the Virginia Company; for banishing some Particulars Bradford was warned

---

provincial opponent, was to replace him as governor. Extract from a letter of Captain Thomas Yong to Sir Toby Matthew, 1634, *Narratives of Early Maryland, 1633–1684*, ed. Clayton Colman Hall (New York, 1910), p. 61.

[16] Bradford, *Plymouth Plantation*, pp. 140–1.

[17] James Shirley to William Bradford, 19 Mar. 1629, Bradford 'Letter Book', *Colls. Mass. Hist. Soc.* III, pp. 71–2.

[18] Rolfe, *Relation*, pp. 40–1.

from the Company to 'take no advantage against any, for any disrespect, but rather wait for their mending amongst you, than to mend them yourselves by thrusting them away, of whom there is any hope of good to be had'.[19] It was a source of particular bitterness to colonial leaders that they had not only to face local opposition inspired from England but also to face English censure in dealing with that opposition.

It was against the background of factionalism in Virginia and Plymouth that John Winthrop made plans for Massachusetts Bay. His passionate belief in the covenant, his conviction that individuals who attacked the authority of magistrates were endangering the power of the State, and with it the possibility of salvation revealed through the community experience, owed much to Puritan theology, but they also owed much to Winthrop's realization, as an immensely practical administrator, that factional attacks on magistrates had nearly destroyed the earlier American colonies.

To Winthrop it was clear that Virginia's early problems with factions arose because the would-be settlers were not properly screened, and because the wrong kind of government was established. With a weak government, and settlers of doubtful intentions, there could be no covenanted community, so essential to stable settlement in the New World. But merely screening settlers and establishing a covenant with them would not alone be sufficient to hold a political community together, as the Pilgrim experience with the *Mayflower* compact had shown. Moreover, once the original community had begun to break into political divisions, neither the highhanded administration of martial law, or generous concessions, or even exile of the disaffected leaders, could heal the break; momentarily disoriented, the dissidents would regroup with new complaints. The problem in creating a new society, with no organizations of law enforcement, was to find long-run means of heading off factions before they started, rather than letting them start and then handling them with temporary expedients. To the enormously complex problem of keeping genuine differences of opinion from becoming the basis of seditious factions, John Winthrop constantly put his energies. What, he

[19] Shirley *et al.* to Bradford *et al.*, 18 Dec. 1624, Bradford Letter Book, *Colls. Mass. Hist. Soc.* III, p. 33.

repeatedly asked, are the means of achieving compromise, and the limits of a compromise settlement?

Carefully he screened applicants for passage, to eliminate potential malcontents. Once in the colony, he pressed for a law excluding settlers who would 'infect others with dangerous tenets'.[20] Equally to the point, removing the Company itself to Massachusetts eliminated the danger that factions in the London Company might inspire local factions in the colony, as they had done in Plymouth and Virginia. Moreover, Plymouth had suffered its greatest trouble from the Particulars, settlers who had a separate arrangement with the governor which made them only partly subject to the laws of the colony; Massachusetts' assumption that everyone in the Bay Colony was subject equally to the General Court, election to which was by approved Church members only, eliminated the possibility of a pressure group developing with interests only marginally identified with the State. And hopefully the uniform adherence to the Puritan Church would, as John Cotton put it, keep the

Commonwealth . . . [from] distractions and popular confusions. . . . Purity, preserved in the church will preserve well ordered Liberty in the people, and both of them establish well balanced authority in the magistrates; God is the author of [Purity, Liberty, and Authority] and neither is himself the God of confusion nor are his wayes the wayes of confusion but of peace.[21]

If difficulties over Church or civil policy did develop, they were to be reasoned out; failing this, they were to be contained as narrowly as possible. When the Watertown pastor advised his townspeople that the rates levied on that town by the Court were too high, he, the elder of the church, and other townsmen were summoned to the Court, where, 'after much debate, they acknowledged their fault'.[22] When Roger Williams questioned the colony's right to their land, John Endicott was sent to

<hr/>

[20] See 'A Brief Answer to a Certain Declaration' (Winthrop's 'Defense of an Order of Court made in the Year 1637'), in *The Hutchinson Papers*, Vol. I, Publications of the Prince Society (Albany, N.Y., 1865), p. 94.

[21] John Cotton to Lord Say and Sele, 1636, quoted in *Puritan Political Ideas, 1558-1794*, ed. Edmund S. Morgan (New York, 1965), p. 172.

[22] 17 Feb. 1631/2, John Winthrop, *The History of New England from 1630 to 1649*, ed. James Savage (Boston, 1853), quoted in *Puritan Political Ideas*, ed. Morgan, p. 97.

argue with him, and Williams, declining to be influenced by
Endicott's arguments, was given a month to change his mind.
Four years later when Williams tried to talk his congregation
into renouncing communion with the other Bay churches,
Thomas Hooker was sent to dispute with him. On 18 January
1635/6 Mr. Vane and Mr. Peter, 'finding some distraction in
judgment, and withall some alienation of affection among the
magistrates and some other persons of quality and that hereby
factions began to grow among the people', they procured a
meeting at Boston where, 'after the Lord had been sought,
Mr. Vane declared the occasion of this meeting a more firm
and friendly uniting of minds'.[23]

The meeting revealed another facet of Winthrop's approach
to politics, for the high point of the occasion was the announce-
ment that Dudley and Winthrop, the two magistrates who
disagreed most strongly on the issue, had already settled their
differences in private: it was essential that magistrates should
keep a united front in public—'the wise and the rich were prone
to faction and sedition but the fools and poor were easy to be
governed'. At the same meeting Winthrop urged that magistrates should keep their differences among themselves, avoiding
any discussion of 'the business of parties' in public. The following year several ministers came to discuss some court proceedings with Winthrop. He declined: had they 'come, in a private
manner, to acquaint him therewith, etc., it had been well
done; but to come, so many of them, in a public and popular
way, was not well'.[24] If after lengthy discussion of an issue one
magistrate or elder continued to disagree with his colleagues he
might post notice of his dissent, but without the reasons for it,
and without any attempt to rouse public interest.

In his own mind Winthrop was a lenient governor (Cotton
Mather's label 'Moderate' would have pleased him),[25] encouraging the reasoning-out of differences, the toleration of
divergent opinions as long as they did not lead to destructive
factions, and the imposition of extremely mild penalties on
those who unwittingly violated the law. It was the very conviction of his own leniency in dealing with potential divisions

[23] Ibid. pp. 104-5. [24] 3 June 1637, ibid. p. 108.
[25] *Selections from Cotton Mather*, ed. Kenneth B. Murdock (New York, 1926),
p. 63.

that made him particularly exasperated with Anne Hutchinson, for the Hutchinson case was exactly what Winthrop had all along been trying to avoid. With Roger Williams he disagreed, but Williams left the Bay Colony quietly and never was a threat to its stability. He had severed his connections with Salem congregation before the final dispute. This explains Winthrop's affectionate correspondence with Williams after Williams's banishment.[26]

Mrs. Hutchinson, on the other hand, carried dissent so openly 'as it could not stand with the public peace, that they should continue amongst us'.[27] Initially she had challenged some of the sermons preached by particular ministers, but her theological assumptions soon appeared to challenge the mercantile assumptions of the ruling elders, and she attached to herself the wealthy merchants of Boston. These in turn challenged the authority of the General Court when some of Mrs. Hutchinson's other followers were brought before it for questioning; when one of Mrs. Hutchinson's leading opponents was appointed commander of an Indian expedition her friends refused to serve.[28] Thus, uncontrollably, a theological controversy had become a mercantile, political, judicial, and military one. 'So in towne-meetings, military trainings, and all other societies, yea almost in every family, it was hard if that some or other were not ready to rise up in defense of them.'[29] In November 1637 the General Court finally had to banish Anne Hutchinson from the colony.

All the means devised to restrain factions had failed to narrow the limits of Mrs. Hutchinson's dissent;[30] all the lessons learned

[26] Similarly, Samuel Maverick, who differed from the Bay Colony authorities, but never really posed a threat to the stability of the community, wrote that Winthrop was one of only two men in the colony who had dealt fairly with him. Maverick to Winthrop, 1 Mar. 1640, *Colls. Mass. Hist. Soc.* 4th Ser. VII (Boston, 1865), pp. 308-9.

[27] *Puritan Political Thought*, ed. Morgan, p. 110.

[28] Emery Battis, *Saints and Sectaries: Anne Hutchinson and the Antinomian Controversy in the Massachusetts Bay Colony* (Chapel Hill, N.C., 1962), *passim*, but esp. Chs. XI–XIV.

[29] Thomas Weld's Preface to Winthrop's *A Short Story of the Rise, Reign, and Ruine of the Antinomians, Familists, and Libertines,* in Hall, *The Antinomian Controversy,* p. 209.

[30] In his account of the controversy Winthrop was at great pains to show the various stages of negotiation at which the Bay government had tried to reach a compromise with Mrs. Hutchinson and her followers. See, for example, his reasons

from Virginia and Plymouth had not prevented Mrs. Hutchinson's suffering the same fate as Lyford, and, ironically, Winthrop's also suffering criticism from home for his severity in dealing with dissent.[31] The very problem Winthrop had hoped to avoid by studying the Virginia and Plymouth experience had in fact confronted him. Appropriately in his *Wonder Working Providence* Winthrop's friend Edward Johnson entitled his chapter on Anne Hutchinson 'Of the cunning policy of Satan in that Machiavellian policy, divide and overcome'.[32]

At the same time that Winthrop was coping with Anne Hutchinson, Lord Baltimore was facing a variety of types of opposition in the infant colony of Maryland. He, too, had 'taken due prospect upon all those inconveniences, which a long time have hindered and of the measures which have helped forward other Plantations'.[33] But Baltimore's situation—Maryland was assumed from the beginning to have a substantial number of both Protestants and Catholics—was different from Winthrop's, and so was his approach. While Winthrop agreed with The Simple Cobbler that 'that state is wise, that will improve all pains and patience rather to compose, than tolerate differences of religion'.[34] Baltimore instructed his governor to 'be very carefull to preserve unity and peace amongst all the passengers on Shippboard, and that they suffer no scandall nor offense to be given to any of the Protestants, whereby any just complaint may heereafter be made'.[35] Baltimore's plan was simply to leave religion out of politics, thereby getting rid of religion as a source of contention.

---

against Wheelwright: 'The Court declared what meanes had been used to convince him and to reduce him unto the right way . . . the court hath used much patience toward him from time to time', *Antinomian Controversy*, ed. Hall, pp. 252–5.

[31] For the disillusionment of English Puritans see A. P. Newton, *The Colonizing Activities of the English Puritans* (New Haven, 1914), pp. 284–5.

[32] *Johnson's Wonder Working Providence, 1628–1651*, ed. J. Franklin Jameson (New York, 1910), Ch. XI.

[33] *A Declaration of the Lord Baltimore's Plantation in Maryland* (London, 1633); facsimile reprint (Baltimore, Md., 1929), p. 12. For a general discussion see Bernard C. Steiner, *The Beginnings of Maryland, 1631–39*, Johns Hopkins University Studies in History and Political Science, Ser. XXI, Nos. 8–10 (Baltimore, Md., 1903).

[34] *The Simple Cobbler of Aggawam in America*, 5th edn. (Boston, 1713), p. 8, in Force, *Tracts*, Vol. III, No. 8.

[35] 'Instructions to the Colonists by Lord Baltimore, 1633', *Narratives of Early Maryland, 1633–1684*, ed. Clayton Colman Hall (New York, 1910), p. 16.

But Baltimore's plans to 'preserve unity and peace' ran up against two types of opposition, one common enough to contemporary colonial situations, the other virtually unique. The first problem was represented by William Claiborne, the Virginia Puritan, who claimed Kent Island under the original Virginia patent, though it had been regranted to Lord Baltimore. Claiborne's claims were ultimately decided in Baltimore's favour, after long and quite uncertain litigation that made Kent Island a trouble-spot particularly attractive to later Puritan invaders and gave a geographical colouring to Maryland factionalism that was lacking in other colonies. But his opposition to Baltimore's Catholicism, to his commercial monopoly, and in fact to the entire proprietorship, meant that he, like Anne Hutchinson, John Lyford, and other dissidents 'could not stand with the public peace'.

In another sphere, however, Baltimore faced quite a new kind of opposition. The proprietor sent instructions to the first colonists; these they seem to have accepted without question, but when he subsequently sent draft copies of laws for ratification by the Maryland Assembly, a majority of the Assembly rejected them, and after acrimonious manœuvring passed an alternative set of laws curtailing some of the powers originally assumed by the proprietor.

As a result of the controversy a new faction evolved, led by Thomas Cornwallis, a Catholic, a merchant, a friend of Governor Calvert, and an erstwhile proprietary supporter. Cornwallis opposed, among other things, the proprietor's attempt to keep the Assembly from taking the initiative in legislation; he also opposed the proprietor's monopoly of trade, and wished the proprietor to be more generous in his support of Catholicism. But, significantly, he did not support the demands of Catholic priests in Maryland for more extensive privileges, he opposed the proprietor's monopoly of trade primarily because he himself wanted a share in it, and he let it be known that permission to share his Indian trade with the proprietor would certainly soften his opposition.[36] His followers therefore by no means constituted a Catholic faction or a mercantile one,

---

[36] For Governor Calvert's description of Cornwallis' opposition see his letter to Lord Baltimore, Feb. 1638, in William Hand Browne, *George Calvert and Cecilius Calvert* (Baltimore, Md., 1890), p. 77.

much less an overlapping Catholic mercantile regional one that threatened the form of government itself. Cornwallis was using his position primarily for patronage, and his opposition to Baltimore was far from creating the disruption that Anne Hutchinson and John Lyford had caused; for these reasons the faction which briefly developed around him represented something quite new in colonial politics. By 1640 Maryland had a novel if hardly stable form of dissent—the Assembly faction which opposed the provincial authorities on particular policies but not on fundamental principles.

But Cornwallis's experience was too brief and the experience of Matthews's faction in Virginia was too checkered to show most colonial leaders how areas of dissent might be so narrowed that certain sections of the population could oppose the government consistently on selected questions of policy. By 1640, despite attempts to learn from past experience, colonial politicians were still quite uncertain of the best way to deal with dissent. They had yet to understand the difference between the kind of dissent which could tear apart a community and the kind of political opposition which could exist within it.

In the absence of such knowledge the colonists still had no satisfactory way of dealing with dissent. Concessions, arbitration, banishment: all the existing means of handling dissent had failed to work. Dissenting groups once trimmed back grew up again like hardy perennials. For the moment, and indeed for another generation, colonial governments tried to fall back on forceful repression, as the only method of averting mortal blows to their communities.

(ii) THE ENGLISH SIDE

In the early years of settlement dissent was not a purely local problem, however, for colonial factions had characteristically been nourished from England. A variety of Englishmen with a variety of motives—dissident members of colonial companies, parliamentary leaders critical of royal charters, London merchants disappointed by the lack of profits, Privy Counsellors appalled by the lack of colonial co-operation—had encouraged dissident groups in the colonies. Faction after faction in the provinces had been 'spirited up from home'; in the eyes of colonial ruling groups English 'meddling' was one of the primary sources of local division. It stood to reason, then, that the logical accompaniment to repression in the colonies was a policy of isolation from the mother country.

What was true for the decades before 1640 was even more so afterwards. Before 1640 the English groups interested in the colonies were somewhat scattered and their resources relatively weak. Now the English civil wars, and the crises which developed in their wake, concentrated the hitherto scattered groups in one centre with considerable strength—the government. Successive British governments seeking recognition, partisan committees responding to factional appeals, wings within the various councils of state competing for colonial influence: any one of these might be a lethal threat to the stability of a colonial government. Understandably, the colonial oligarchs wanted to have as little to do with the mother country as possible.

On the colonial side the uncertain status of all the local charters, the changing appearance of support for particular politicians as friends or enemies rose to power in England, the dissatisfaction with incumbent governments that accompanied the shortage of supplies from England, inevitably led to the 'disturbance of the minds of the people and the publick peace'.[37]

Within five years of the outbreak of civil war there had been civil war in Maryland, and an entire turnover in both Chesapeake legislatures. Baltimore and the Maryland Assembly had reached a virtual impasse, which the Assembly attributed to 'mistakes and misinforments that your Honour is unfortunately subject to';[38] and Baltimore blamed '. . . the subtile Suggestions of some who ought rather to have assisted in promoting all fitting means of preserving a good correspondence, rather then to raise, or cherish any Jellousies or discontents betweene us, and the people there'.[39]

Massachusetts' problems were far less severe, but even here the impact of the English Revolution was clear enough in the case of Robert Child, a Presbyterian who was jailed after a

[37] Proceedings and Acts of the General Assembly of Maryland, Jan. 1637/8–Sept. 1664, *Archives of Maryland*, ed. William Hand Browne, Vol. I (Baltimore, Md., 1883), p. 335.
[38] Assembly to Baltimore, 21 Apr. 1649, ibid.
[39] Baltimore to Assembly, 26 Aug. 1649, ibid. p. 263.

dispute originating over the selection of militia officers in Hingham, Massachusetts. Child and his Presbyterian friends called the colony '. . . an ill-compacted vessel . . . for diversity of judgements amongst us, many being for Presbyterial government, according to the Reformation in England, others opposing it; some freemen, others not'.[40]

Faced with growing restlessness and an already recognized danger of English help for local malcontents, it was natural that governors in New England and the Chesapeake colonies should work to keep local dissidents from receiving help directly from England. How well they succeeded in maintaining their isolation depended, of course, on the approach of the politicians who dominated successive English governments from 1640 to 1660, and among them two different attitudes were uppermost from time to time. One tempted men to look at colonial political factions in terms of their usefulness to particular groups in England, and to encourage colonial dissidents if they could be helpful in a particular English situation. The other tempted them to sympathize with colonial ruling cliques seeking to avoid in their own domain the kind of factious opposition that doomed successive English governments at home.

In the conflict between these two temptations one can see the struggle for mastery at home affecting the English interpretation of colonial politics, and in particular the English attitude towards the colonial oligarchs and their opponents. One must look to London as well as the provincial capitals.

A. *'So many men, so many minds' : The English Civil Wars*

During the wars themselves the combination of colonial aloofness, uncertain alignment of colonial sympathies,[41] and obvious distractions in England discouraged both sides in the

---

[40] John Winthrop, *The History of New England, from 1630 to 1649*, ed. James Savage, Vol. II (Boston, 1853), p. 350.

[41] Only a few references for these generalizations can be suggested here.— See Richard Arthur Preston, *Gorges of Plymouth Fort* (Toronto, 1953), p. 270; W. F. Craven, *Dissolution of the Virginia Company, the Failure of a Colonial Experiment* (Gloucester, Mass., 1964); W. H. Browne, *George and Cecilius Calvert* (Baltimore, Md., 1890); Clayton Colman Hall, *The Lords Baltimore and the Maryland Palatinate* (Baltimore, Md., 1904); J. Moss Ives, *The Ark and the Dove* (London, 1936).

A different interpretation is suggested in Jack H. Hexter, *The Reign of King Pym* (Cambridge, Mass., 1941), and Valerie Pearl, *London and the Outbreak of the Puritan Revolution: City Government and National Politics, 1625-43* (London, 1961), p. 162.

mother country from attempting immediately to convert their American associates into active supporters. At Oxford the harried courtiers of the King, including Gorges and Baltimore, had almost no time to think about colonial problems, working as they were within earshot of enemy guns and eventually under their bombardment. Apparently they never developed any committee for handling relations with the colonies, though the King himself did continue to assert his personal authority over the colonies, by nominating some supporters to local office in Virginia and the West Indian Islands, and commissioning ships from the western ports to trade with the Plantations. In the colonies governors like Berkeley and Leonard Calvert, who sympathized with the Royalist cause, none the less included Parliamentary or Puritan sympathizers in their major offices, ignored inflammatory issues like the royal commission for the arrest of ships whose owners adhered to Parliament, and carefully kept the base of their government as broad as possible.

Nor were the Parliamentary leaders any more active in cultivating partisan support within the colonies. They did not refer to colonial problems in either of the documents they drew up to summarize and publicize their grievances—the Grand Remonstrance of 1 December 1641, and the nineteen propositions presented in June 1642. They did not create any committee of their own to handle colonial affairs until well after the first Civil War was under way; for the first year or so after the war began Parliament continued to leave colonial matters to the Privy Council appointed by the King.

On the provincial issue which did come before Parliament they declined to act decisively. Quite early in the Long Parliament George Sandys, son of a former president of the Virginia Company, presented a petition on behalf of some Virginia colonists for the restoration of the Company. The petition was referred to a committee of twenty-six, headed by the Parliamentary leaders Pym, Vane, and Hampden.[42] Apparently the committee recommended the petition favourably, indicating

---

[42] The committee included Vane, Pym, Colpeper, Erle, Vassall, Wheeler, Massam, Cholmeley, Roe, Fairfax, Pye, Hungerford, Rainsborow, Brooke, Whistler, Ash, Grimston, Parkhurst, Maynard, Mildmay, Purefrey, Bond, White, Cheeke, and Rainsford. Leo Francis Stock, *Proceedings and Debates of the British Parliaments respecting North America* (4 vols., Washington, D.C., 1924), Vol. I, p. 102.

that Parliamentary leaders were in favour of restoring the Company. But when the King chose not to respond to Parliament's vote, the leaders did nothing, and the matter was dropped.

Indeed, when they finally did set up a committee to handle colonial problems they did not take advantage of the obvious opportunity for partisan manœuvring which it provided. The Warwick Committee was created in 1643 to settle differences within and among the various colonies. It was empowered, among various things, to nominate and appoint governors, counsellors, commanders, officers, and agents to handle military affairs relating to the colonies, and to reduce colonies that did not recognize Parliament. Potentially the Committee had the power to influence local politics in the colonies through patronage, handling of appeals, and even military intervention. Many of the Committee members had worked together in old colonizing companies and on other Parliamentary committees. They could have looked at themselves as a committee delegated to develop the power of Puritan factions in the colonies. But they did not.

For one thing, in handling their new cases the Committee did not act as a homogeneous group of Parliamentary opponents with a uniform approach to colonial administration;[43] rather, their deliberations were affected by an immense variety of personal friendships with colonists and personal interests in colonial problems.[44] In 1644 the Committee decided that a part of the Narragansett country, claimed by Roger Williams on behalf of Rhode Island and by Hugh Peter on behalf of Massachusetts, should go to Rhode Island, and they granted Williams a charter to that effect.[45] In 1646 they heard Samuel Gorton's appeal against his persecution by the Massachusetts government, and awarded Gorton a charter for a part of the

[43] This interpretation is in contrast with that presented by Charles McLean Andrews in *British Commissions and Councils of Trade and Plantations, 1622–75*, Johns Hopkins University Studies in History and Political Science, Ser. XXVI, Nos. 1–3 (Baltimore, Md., 1908).

[44] This was as true after 1645, when the size of the Committee was more than doubled, as it was before. See Richard S. Dunn, 'John Winthrop, Jr., John Winthrop, Sr., and the Problem of Colonial Dependency in New England, 1630–1676' (unpublished Ph.D. thesis, Princeton University, 1955), p. 184.

[45] *Calendar of State Papers, Colonial, 1574–1660*, ed. W. N. Sainsbury (London, 1860), p. 325.

Narragansett country.[46] In 1646 the Committee considered a petition from Maryland settlers against Baltimore, but sent it on to Parliament, evidently because they could not agree.[47] While the cases were pending, Vane lobbied for his friend Roger Williams.[48] Warwick was a friend of Gorton's, Cromwell was close to Hugh Peter, who was appearing against Williams. Warwick lobbied for his friend Baltimore; Baltimore's enemies, led by Matthews and Claiborne, were well connected through their London merchant acquaintances, old friends in the Virginia Company.

Moreover, members of the Committee represented nearly every part of the spectrum of revolutionary views about English government, from Warwick, whose conservative political sympathies inclined him to encourage the colonists to continue to recognize the King, and also inclined him to support Presbyterians against the Massachusetts theocrats, to the radical Arthur Haslerig, soon to be the Republican leader, already probably unconcerned with the semblances of royal approval, and somewhat sympathetic to the Puritans of New England.

The Presbyterians seem to have held a slight majority in the Committee, but, if anything, the Committee's decisions were determined more by personal friendships than by political principles: when Peter, for example, tried to get Massachusetts a patent for the Narragansett country claimed by Williams, he was supported by the Republican radicals, and opposed not only by the conservative Warwick, but also by the radical Vane, who had personal objections to some of the leaders of Massachusetts Bay.

The variety of personal opinions probably kept the Committee from effectively working for colonial support in the first part of the Civil Wars. But even in the later stages, when men of such varied associations did not serve, the Committee was still reluctant to interfere decisively in colonial politics.

[46] Committee to Governor and Council of New England, Apr. 1646. B.M. Stowe MS. 184, f. 123.

[47] On the general question see Stock, *Proceedings*, Vol. I, pp. 183–4; James W. Vardman, 'The Baltimore Proprietary and the Growth of English Colonial Policy, 1630–1691' (unpublished Ph.D. dissertation, Vanderbilt University, 1957), pp. 95–100; Historical Manuscripts Commission, *Sixth Report*, Part I, *Report and Appendix* (London, 1877), 101 et seq.

[48] Ola Elizabeth Winslow, *Master Roger Williams, a Biography* (New York, 1957), pp. 183, 236.

In the spring of 1647 the second Civil War began, this time with the King and the Presbyterian members of Parliament allied against another part of Parliament and Cromwell's New Model Army. From this time on, the Warwick Committee was unable to meet. In July of 1647 about a hundred M.P.s went over to the Army, and about half of Warwick's Committee were among this hundred. The rest stayed with the Presbyterian parliament, but were too busy with the war to pay much attention to colonial problems. The Committee's last colonial decision had been made in 1646.

When his Committee began to break up Warwick took on more and more colonial administration himself. Warwick was a nobleman long interested in colonial enterprise and long a partisan friend of leading settlers in the Chesapeake area and New England (through his early activity in the Virginia Company, his subsequent responsibility for getting Massachusetts's charter, and his interest in the Providence Company); on his taking sole responsibility for colonial decisions, one might have expected the Committee to take a more active role in developing Parliamentary and Presbyterian support within the various colonies. There is no doubt that he had some inclination to do this. He had long been eager for the Committee to assume a wider authority over the colonies. Early in 1647 George Fenwick wrote John Winthrop that he was working hard to keep Warwick's hands out of Massachusetts politics.[49]

Now, however, in the last year or two of the Civil Wars, Warwick decided to reduce his Committee's jurisdiction, rather than extend it, for a number of reasons. For one thing, as Lord High Admiral, Warwick was actively in charge of the Parliamentary navy; his time and resources were taken up planning several successful Channel encounters with both royal and rebel ships. While he was glad enough to commission the occasional privateer for colonial trade, he was reluctant to spare any ships from the Parliamentary navy for reducing the colonies to immediate obedience.

Far more important, however, it was becoming clear by this time that in the second stage of the Civil Wars Warwick's Parliamentary forces were on the losing side. Deeply dis-

[49] 17 Mar. 1646/7, 'Winthrop Papers', *Coll. Mass. Hist. Soc.* 4th Ser. V (Boston, 1861), 141-3.

illusioned about the direction the wars were taking, Warwick lost heart for the responsibility of forcing the colonists to recognize parliamentary authority. In 1648 he wrote that the initial leaders of the Revolution now found themselves 'enslaved by a company of factious, seditious, and covetous persons'. Above all he was distressed by the deteriorating position of the King and the aristocracy.

. . . if the Commons of England be the supream power, then he that can make the best friends shall have what he desires, though it be to the ruine of [a whole] or many familyes. We are already satisfied that it is as dangerous a thing to be governed by Votes, as it is to be governed by Armyes, when especially in such a time as when [sic] so many men, so many minds.[50]

Warwick concluded by threatening to join the Prince of Wales if Parliament did not sign a personal treaty with the King agreeing, among its items, to the disbanding of the Army.

Indeed, by the time Warwick took over the sole administration of the colonies he was himself so disenchanted with the direction of the Revolution that he was in no mood to force the colonists to recognize new revolutionary leaders. He had no interest in creating Parliamentary factions in Royalist colonies, or in forcing legal recognition of Parliament by Puritan colonies. Above all, he wished to avoid dissension in the colonies to keep them as effective bulwarks against Spain, not weakened by the futile divisions which beset the mother country.

Thus he gave no help to local Puritan rebels against Baltimore's government in Maryland, and, *de facto*, recognized Baltimore's government, though the House of Lords had previously voted his patent void. Maryland's treatment might be regarded as exceptional, since Baltimore did turn coat pretty rapidly after the King's initial defeat. What was more remarkable was Warwick's letter to Virginia authorizing the colonists to elect their own governor. He suggested the Puritan Captain Matthews, as a candidate devoted to the colony's interests 'next to the Honor of God and His Majesty',[51] but only if the Virginians did not choose to elect their present governor, the

[50] *The Declaration and Resolution of Robert Earle of Warwick, Lord Admirall for the King, Parliament of England, and all the Officers, and Seamen Aboard His Navie touching the Personall Treaty* (London, 1648).
[51] B.M. Stowe MS. 184, f. 124, no date.

Royalist William Berkeley. Berkeley's Royalist sentiments should not be exaggerated—his nomination of the Puritan Claiborne to the Virginia treasureship, and his later easy dealings with the Commonwealth government and the Protector, make it clear that he was, in his own way, as much a Politique as John Winthrop (moreover, Warwick had a personal distaste for Matthews)—but Warwick's letters made it clear that he had no objections to the governor's Royalist ties as such.

Not only did Warwick co-operate with Royalist leaders in the Chesapeake, he also worked to keep local demands for religious toleration from destroying the unity of the New England colonies. As the English Civil Wars went on Warwick became increasingly convinced that the multiplication of religious sects—'so many men, so many minds'—was one of the causes of the prolonged upheaval. Increasingly he appreciated the argument of New England apologists that religious persecution was not directed towards establishing religious uniformity as an end in itself, but towards keeping 'the bond of peace'. The kind of argument put forth in Thomas Weld's pamphlet on the Antinomian controversy appealed to him. Antinomians worked,

... not only to disturb the churches, but miserably interrupt the civill Peace, and that they threw contempt both upon courts, and churches, and began now to raise sedition amongst us, to the endangering the Commonwealth; Hereupon for these grounds named, (and not for their opinions, as themselves falsely reported, and as our godly Magistrates have been much traduced here in England) for these reasons (I say) being civil disturbances, the Magistrate convents them.[52]

Warwick's conviction that civil peace, purchased at the price of religious persecution, was essential to the colonies explains his negative reception of petitions from Presbyterians like Robert Child in New England. After carrying his protest to the General Court Child ultimately took his case to Warwick, petitioning against both the religious and the political restrictions imposed by the colony. But Warwick, aware that Child's case threatened the military and political organization of the

[52] Thomas Weld's Preface to Winthrop's *Short Story of the Rise, Reign, and Ruine of the Antinomians*, in Hall (ed.), *The Antinomian Controversy*, p. 213.

colony as well as its religion, replied that colonial governments must have the final authority in deciding local disputes.[53]

Cases like Child's and Anne Hutchinson's made it difficult for Warwick to accept Roger Williams's passionate argument that the State could be run without reference to religious opinions, and the argument, deduced from the Old Testament, that religious dissension was, in fact, healthy for a community. Williams's 'Bloudy Tenant' was burned; to Parliamentary leaders like Warwick, Williams's argument just did not square with the needs of the colonial governments.

Warwick's rejection of Child's petition was in June of 1648. It was his last colonial decision. In the fall of 1648 the Army defeated the King and the Presbyterians. The Army and the radical M.P.s now negotiated with the King for a new constitutional settlement. They could reach no agreement, and in December 1648 Parliament renounced its allegiance to the King and voted to have nothing more to do with him. That month Warwick retired from public life.

B. *'We stand as two Armies': Politics under the Commonwealth*

Throughout the Civil Wars, therefore, the colonists were remarkably fortunate in being able to stay aloof from English politics. Neither Warwick nor his Committee sought to develop colonial support at the expense of the provincial oligarchies; they worked with and even strengthened the colonial governments, whether or not the men who ran them happened to be in sympathy with Parliament. The approach of the Commonwealth government, however, which ruled England from Charles I's execution in January 1649 to Cromwell's dissolution of Parliament in April 1654, was in striking contrast. The Commonwealth leaders, unlike Warwick, sought to build bases of support for themselves within the colonies. In so doing they interfered more aggressively in colonial politics than any other government of the Interregnum.

At first sight the Commonwealth leaders would have seemed incapable of pursuing an aggressive colonial policy. The govern-

---

[53] B.M. Stowe MS. 184, pp. 4–5, no fol. given. See also Major John Childe's *New England's Jonas Cast up at London* (London, 1647), in Force, *Tracts*, Vol. IV, No. 3; Richard S. Dunn's unpublished Ph.D. thesis, 'John Winthrop, Jr., John Winthrop, Sr., and the Problem of Colonial Dependency in New England, 1630–1676', pp. 180–205.

ment soon came to be run by an inner circle of Republican leaders, including Thomas Scot, Arthur Haslerig, and Henry Vane, some of whom were suspected of profiting handsomely from their position. The same group of men headed the executive committee—the 'Council of State', an unwieldy body with forty-one members and a vast complex of subcommittees. The leaders were neither popular nor united, and as the months went on, especially after the autumn of 1651, they became more and more concerned with factional infighting rather than with the development of constructive policy. Moreover, of the whole Council of forty-one members only seven had experience in colonizing companies or on Warwick's Committee.[54] The Council never developed a system for handling colonial affairs, and as one committee after another was created to deal with the colonies in general, or particular colonial problems, there was a great deal of overlap in functions. (The Committee of the Admiralty was the main body of reference for several months in 1650, and when the Council of State replaced it with a Committee of Plantations the Committee of the Navy continued to handle questions connected with issues it had previously considered.) Moreover, given the general accusations of corruption made concerning the Council of State, and given also the importance of personal 'connections' in determining the Council procedure, it is not unlikely that bribes were of great importance in determining which individuals the Council chose to serve as members of select committees on colonial matters.[55]

Considering, therefore, the general inexperience of the Commonwealth leaders in colonial matters, their disorganization, and their preoccupation with problems at home, one would have expected them to have left the colonies as Warwick left them. For the first two years after the King's execution they did so, but suddenly, after the battle of Worcester (1651), in which Cromwell defeated the army of Charles II, their inactivity came to an end. In just over a month after the news of Worcester reached London Parliament had passed the Navigation

[54] Rolle, E. Pembroke, Cromwell, Haslerig, Vane, Bond, Holland. For members see Wilbur Cortez Abbot, *The Writings and Speeches of Oliver Cromwell* (Cambridge, Mass., 1937), Vol. II, p. 14, n. 19.

[55] In addition, while the Council of State was the supreme administrative body, colonists dissatisfied with its decisions could appeal to Parliament over its head.

Act of 1651 (it had been proposed before the battle, but was not passed until after the results were known), and the Council of State had appointed and dispatched commissioners to subdue Chesapeake and Barbados rebels, had awarded part of Rhode Island to Christopher Coddrington, and had begun to consider revoking the charter of Massachusetts. Indeed, the autumn of 1651 is the high-water mark of Commonwealth energy in colonial administration. Why?

There were, of course, a number of reasons. One was that after the King's execution several colonies were openly defying British authority—a particularly crucial problem, since the Commonwealth government was at war with the Dutch. In Virginia Governor Berkeley had 2,000 troops ready to serve Charles II, and in Massachusetts there appeared to be some threat that the province would repudiate British authority altogether. Connecticut, Massachusetts, and Virginia were trading with the Dutch; with a Dutch colony at New York and with Dutch maritime strength increasing, the Commonwealth leaders had reason to fear a Dutch seizure of British colonies encouraged by colonists themselves. Colonies, therefore, took high priority in the allocation of Commonwealth resources.

Moreover, colonial defiance was particularly galling to a Council of State composed of ardent advocates of a strong Republican centralized government, established at the expense of local autonomy, in every part of the Commonwealth. Although many of Charles I's opponents had fought him to gain a more decentralized authority, with greater local autonomy, the Republicans were not among these, and they said explicitly that the colonies were to be subject to parliamentary law. The fact that on at least two occasions (2 March 1650 and 8 February 1651) the Council of State turned itself into a Committee of Trade and Plantations, and that on 6 June 1650 and 8 February 1651 a committee discussed 'Plantations', indicates that the Council of State may well have been considering a general policy for the colonies which the old Warwick Committee had had neither time nor inclination to do.[56]

As important as these reasons were, however, the particular struggles which developed between factions of Commonwealth leaders. The final defeat of the Royalist army released Crom-

[56] *Cal. S.P. Col., 1574–60*, pp. 335, 340, 349.

well from the preoccupation of military campaigns which had
kept him out of London in the months before. Now he returned
to take the lead in the growing criticism of the oligarchs who
were running the Commonwealth. In November 1651, just two
months after Worcester, Cromwell was at the head of the list
of a new Council of State elected by Parliament; from then until
it was dissolved in the spring of 1653 the Commonwealth
government was rent by the increasingly bitter dispute between
Cromwellian and anti-Cromwellian factions.[57]

The terror of the anti-Cromwellians over the return of their
sharpest critic, with vast military power, is one key to the
vigour of their attempt to establish a base of support in the
colonies: colonies were at worst a refuge, at best a base for a
counter-offensive, should Cromwell establish the military
dictatorship they feared. (In this assumption, perhaps, lies an
explanation for their insistence on saying in the Navigation Act
that the colonies were subject to 'such laws, orders, and regula-
tions as are or shall be made by the Parliament of England'.)[58]

But Cromwell's opponents were also divided among themselves, and the new-found strategic importance of colonies
meant that rival factions of Cromwell's opponents struggled
tenaciously against each other for predominance in the various
colonies. The role of particular individuals in the making of
colonial decisions is hard to trace, because the records of the
Commonwealth Council of State, like those of the Warwick
Committee, are scant. But it is clear from circumstantial evidence that the centre of every dispute was the head of the Admiralty Committee, the complex but consistent Sir Henry Vane.

On the one hand Vane was a passionate Republican who had
no desire to see the authority of Charles I simply replaced by
the authority of Cromwell. If necessary he could build up the
colonies as a base for Parliamentary operations against Cromwell.[59] On the other hand he loved and respected Cromwell

[57] Abbott, *Cromwell*, Vol. II, pp. 501–2.

[58] The Commonwealth Council of State also instructed the agent from New
England to notify the New England governments that they must keep legal
records in the name of the Commonwealth of England, and should take out new
charters from the Commonwealth government. But they did not actually send this
order directly to the New England governments, and only Rhode Island agreed to
comply. Dunn, 'John Winthrop', p. 281.

[59] See *The Memoirs of Edmund Ludlow*, ed. C. H. Firth (Oxford, 1894), Vol. I,
p. 347.

personally far more than any of his other colleagues on the Commonwealth Council: his fervent attempts at compromise between Cromwell and the Republican leaders, his last-minute effort to work out a satisfactory arrangement with Cromwell to perpetuate the Parliament, his remaining among Cromwell's friends even after the Republican government was overturned, all testify to his personal devotion to Cromwell.

By contrast, he rapidly developed contempt for men like Haslerig and Scot; Vane, an intimate friend of Roger Williams, passionate sharer of Williams's convictions on religious toleration, and himself a victim of the Massachusetts General Court's handling of the Antinomian controversy, threw his support to Williams, and soon to Baltimore's claims in the Chesapeake: a victory for Williams in New England and Baltimore in Maryland would assure him of friends in critical areas of the colonies. Scot, Haslerig, and their colonial associates inevitably took opposite stands.

At every stage of their handling, colonial problems were affected by the power struggles among these Republican factions in England. In 1649 and early 1650 colonial problems, mostly concerning the reduction of the Caribbean Islands and the Chesapeake, were referred to Vane's Committee of the Admiralty. By the end of 1650 the falling out between Vane and Haslerig had already become serious; the Council of State created its own Committee of Trade and Plantations, which gradually superseded Vane's parliamentary Committee. By 1651 the newer colonial issues concerning New England began to be referred to the Committee of Trade and Plantations, while the Admiralty Committee handled only problems held over from its earlier work. Now Vane himself shifted his influence to the Council of State; when he was able to outmanœuvre his opponents there on the issue of Williams's patent, Haslerig and Scot at least considered taking the question—and perhaps the management of colonial questions in general?—to the Rump Parliament as a whole.

Indeed, Williams's dispute with Christopher Coddrington over the patent for Rhode Island seems to have brought the factional quarrels of the Republic to a head. On 27 March 1650 Coddrington, a Newport merchant with rather limited support from some friends and fellow merchants, petitioned the

Council of State for two islands within the area given to Williams by his charter of 1644. Coddrington was a friend of Hugh Peter and Arthur Haslerig, and, apparently with Haslerig's support, he got a commission from the Council of State in the autumn of 1651 to govern Connecticut and Rhode Island. By the end of 1652, however, Vane and two associates, working through the Council of State, had somehow managed to get Coddrington's commission recalled and Vane's friend Williams temporarily given back his previous authority.[60] By April 1653, just before the Council was dissolved, Williams's charter had been confirmed by the Council, notwithstanding the efforts of Haslerig, his friends Colonel Fenwick, Mr. Winslow, and Mr. Hopkins, 'and all the friends they can make in Parliament and the country. . . . We stand as two armies.'[61]

Less clear are the factional divisions on the Chesapeake controversy between Maryland and Virginia. The evidence is circumstantial, not direct, but here, too, 'two armies' of Republicans, one certainly led by Sir Henry, manœuvred to affect the decision, and once again it was Vane who won.

On 13 October 1649 Virginia was still under Governor Berkeley, not yet having officially recognized the Commonwealth. The Council of State referred the case of Virginia to the Admiralty Committee, and on 4 December the Admiralty Committee was also directed to consider how the government of Maryland should be altered. On 28 December, and again on 9 January 1649/50, Vane's Committee listened to complaints of continuing Royalist support in Maryland from merchants trading to that colony, and after the hearings ordered the Attorney General to prepare a draft of a patent recognizing Maryland as included within the ancient boundaries of Virginia. Baltimore protested, so the Committee called the patent back to reconsider it. Three weeks later they decided to present to the Council, and from them to Parliament, the draft

---

[60] Winslow, *Roger Williams*, pp. 236, 244. Williams's friendship with Vane is mentioned particularly in his letter to John Winthrop, Jr., written 'From Sir H. Vane's at Whitehall 20/2/52', *Winthrop Papers, Coll. Mass. Hist. Soc.* W2.122.

[61] Williams to the Towns of Providence and Warwick, 1 Apr. 1653, *The Complete Writings of Roger Williams*, Vol. VI (New York, 1963), p. 254. See also 'A Letter Written to a Gentleman in the Country', by John Hall, 3 May 1653, quoted in Abbott, *Letters and Speeches of Oliver Cromwell*, Vol. II, p. 584.

of an Act vaguely described as 'settling Virginia affairs'; whether the Act took away Baltimore's patent or not is impossible to tell for certain; probably it did not, since some time during the hearings Vane himself, probably influenced by Maryland's Act of Toleration and Baltimore's welcome to Puritan exiles from Virginia, had come to support Baltimore's position. Vane's Admiralty Committee had thus come over to Baltimore's side in his struggle to keep Maryland separate from Virginia. The battle now shifted to the Council of State, which clearly was divided on the issue. Repeatedly the Council reversed itself on Maryland as the majority changed from meeting to meeting.

Meanwhile ship captains coming into London were reporting that Virginia and Barbados still openly refused to recognize the Commonwealth. On 6 June the Council of State referred to its own Committee of Plantations the general question 'What is to be done for reducing foreign Plantations?' Later in the summer the Admiralty Committee ordered the Attorney General to prepare a Bill for reducing these colonies to obedience. He did, in consultation with some Barbados merchants, and in September the Council of State, after further consideration, referred the Bill to Parliament; it was finally passed the following month. The Act was a sweeping one, cutting off trade to Virginia and the West Indies, empowering the Council of State to send ships to reduce the colonies and to nominate colonial officers, and stating categorically that Parliament had the authority to legislate for the colonies.

A year later[62] the Council of State sent Captain Robert Dennis, Thomas Stagg, Edmund Curtis, and Richard Bennett, along with Captain William Claiborne, the old anti-Royalist leader of the 1630s, to bring the Chesapeake colonies to obedience. Baltimore had got Maryland left out of the Parliamentary Act, but the Council of State now included all of the Chesapeake in the area the commissioners were to reduce. With Baltimore's old enemy William Claiborne appointed commissioner there seems no doubt that Scot and Haslerig had now convinced a majority of the Council of State that Maryland should be reincorporated into Virginia. The rank and file

---

[62] The appointments were made and instructions prepared 26 Sept. 1651. On 2 Oct. 1651 additional secret instructions were sent to Bennett.

members of Parliament, led by Vane, on the other hand, had now apparently begun to sympathize with Baltimore.

Meanwhile some of the original commissioners had returned to the Chesapeake area, and one of them, the Puritan Richard Bennett, had been elected governor by the Assembly of Virginia. Shortly after his election Bennett got information that Baltimore's governor was issuing official papers in Baltimore's name only, with no acknowledgement of the Commonwealth. At the invitation of nearly a hundred Maryland settlers, some of them Puritans whom Baltimore himself had introduced from Virginia, some of them Baltimore's 'professed friends' who had already betrayed him in the 1649 Assembly, Bennett deposed Baltimore's governor and took over the government of Maryland himself. He was officially acknowledged by a fragment of the Maryland Assembly, the faction which had in recent years been growing increasingly hostile to the proprietary government itself.[63]

It was the struggle between two wings of the Commonwealth government, then, that seems to have determined Maryland's official status throughout the Commonwealth period. Sir Henry Vane sought to shore up Lord Baltimore's authority; the commissioners sent by his English rivals deliberately developed and exploited the proprietary opposition. Maryland seems, in fact, to have been one of the clearest early examples of English politicians looking at colonial dissent in terms of their own advantage. Indeed, the Maryland experience may well have disposed the colonists to challenge the argument put forth on behalf of the Commonwealth by their English contemporaries —namely, that Republics by necessity prevent factions, since Republics represent the popular interest, and factions, by

[63] This interpretation of the handling of the Chesapeake colonies has been put together largely from the *Cal. S.P. Col., Am. & W.I., 1574–1660*, pp. 328–39, *passim*; Stock, *Proceedings*, Vol. I, p. 218; Bernard C. Steiner, *Maryland under the Commonwealth: A Chronicle of the Years 1649–58*, Johns Hopkins University Studies in History and Political Science, Ser. XXIX, No. 1 (Baltimore, Md., 1911), p. 54; Vardaman, 'The Baltimore Proprietary', pp. 107–17, *passim*; Thomas Birch, ed., *A Collection of the State Papers of John Thurloe, Esq.*, 7 vols., Vol. V (London, 1742), p. 486; Donnell MacClure Owings, *His Lordship's Patronage: Offices of Profit in Colonial Maryland*, Studies in Maryland History, No. 1 (Baltimore, Md., 1953), pp. 115–22; *Virginia and Maryland, or the Lord Baltimore's Printed Case, uncased and answered* (London, 1655), in Force, *Tracts*, Vol. II, No. 9, pp. 18–22; *Leah and Rachel, or the Two Fruitful Sisters Virginia and Maryland . . .* (London, 1656), Force, *Tracts*, Vol. III, No. XIV, pp. 24–6.

definition, exist only in defiance of that interest.[64] This was the argument of some of the Levellers; Baltimore and Vane, for two, could hardly accept it.

c. *Cromwellian Government*

On 20 April 1653 Oliver Cromwell entered Parliament and sent the members home for good; that afternoon he disbanded the Council of State. From then until his death in 1658 Cromwell was forced to experiment with a series of governments, none of which gave him any real power at home, hedged in as he was, first by the Army and later by the conservative Parliamentary leaders.

Given Cromwell's constitutional responsibility, first to the Council and then to Parliament, and given also his dependence upon a demanding Army or a demanding Parliamentary alliance, one might have expected his colonial policy to have been created successively by the Levellers who managed the nominated Parliament, the Army leaders who drew up the Instrument, and the Parliamentary party who drew up the Humble Petition and Advice; one would equally expect the arbitration of colonial affairs to be handled by the Council and by Parliament. But in fact this did not happen at all. During the Protectorate it was not the Army, the Parliamentary leaders, nor even the Council, but Cromwell himself who handled colonial affairs. It was Cromwell who personally appointed colonial officials from his own acquaintances or friends of his personal advisers[65] (not on the Council), Cromwell to whom colonial agents appealed directly in disputes under arbitration, Cromwell who decided upon leniency to the New England colonies in opposition to the wishes of the majority of his Council,[66] and above all Cromwell who decided after a year's

---

[64] See *A Declaration or Representation from His Excellency Sir Thomas Fairfax and the Army under his Command* (1647), in *The Leveller Tracts, 1647–1653*, ed. William Haller and Godfrey Davies (Gloucester, Mass., 1964), p. 58; and Marchmont Nedham, *The Excellence of a Free State* (London, 1656), p. 28.

[65] T. Povey to Searle, 27 Mar. 1658, and Povey to Richard Povey, 3 Apr. 1658, B.M. Add. MS. 11411, ff. 58–60, 62–3, show Cromwell deciding between Searle and a rival governor in Barbados, and considering Richard Povey's complaints about his job in Jamaica. Povey also wrote his brother William on 3 Apr. (ff. 55–7) that Cromwell was considering 'the differences concerning the judges place . . .'.

[66] This is indicated by the tellers on a Bill to prohibit tobacco planting in England. The division on the Bill was on 1 Apr. 1652; tellers for the ayes were

hesitation—during which the Parliamentary commissioners were at one time encouraged to continue subduing Maryland, and Roger Williams wrote 'We have report of a general governor'—that the established colonial governments should be left undisturbed. The Protector's personal influence on colonial administration must have been quite out of proportion to his influence on affairs in England. Why?

One reason is that while a very small number of members of the various Parliaments—Republicans like Haslerig and Scot in particular—had experience and interest in colonial affairs, they were preoccupied with institutional reforms at home. Even if the Parliamentary leaders had wished to extend at once their authority over the colonies they would have had difficulty in doing so, for Cromwell's parliaments simply did not last long enough to prepare satisfactory legislation or provide suitable facilities for arbitrating colonial disputes in Parliamentary committees.[67]

More important, by the time the Protectorate began, those political leaders who had been interested in the colonies at the beginning of the Civil Wars had largely passed from public life, and the Protector himself was one of the few men left in government who had any connections with the colonies. Warwick, and men like Manchester and Say and Sele who shared his desire to leave the ruling parties in the colonies alone, had gone into retirement when the King was executed, and refused to be lured back into Cromwell's government or even into his Upper House. On the other hand, Arthur Haslerig perpetuated the Republican hopes for an aggressive, divisive colonial policy (five years after Cromwell's accession Haslerig was still working on 'A General Plan for the Colonies').[68] But Haslerig was in opposition to Cromwell, and Vane was eventually imprisoned by him. Who, then, did this leave in the Protector's Council whose previous experience would make him competent in colonial affairs? Virtually no one but the Protector himself. There were seventeen members in Cromwell's

Vane and Haslerig, and for the noes Cols. Marten and Morley. Stock, *Proceedings*, Vol. I, p. 228.

[67] See Note 1 at end of chapter.

[68] Haslerig even continued his interest in Colonial reorganization as a member of Richard Cromwell's Council of State and the recognized leader of Richard's parliament.

Council.[69] Two of these—Edward Montagu, a nephew of the Earl of Manchester, and Nathaniel Fiennes, a second son of Say and Sele—were close relatives of Providence Company members. Two others—Henry Lawrence and Viscount Lisle— had served on committees in the Commonwealth Council of State which dealt with particular colonial problems. Lisle was interested in the Virginia–Maryland dispute; Lawrence was interested in New England and was a friend of Roger Williams. A fifth member, Sydenham, was eventually to serve on the Committee for America created in 1657, though he had no association with the colonies when the Protectorate began. None of the other army officers had any connections with the colonies;[70] conspicuously, Lambert and his fellow officers who drew up the Instrument of Government said nothing in it about the management of colonial affairs.

Cromwell, by contrast, had been a close associate of the colonizers in the Providence, Saybrook, and Massachusetts Bay Companies. His relatives Sir Thomas Barrington, St. John, and Hampden were active in the Providence and Saybrook Companies. No doubt he must have taken part in discussions about the colonies which had merged into discussions of Parliamentary tactics at Warwick House in the early 1640s; he had a friendly acquaintance with Warwick, who apparently continued to advise him after his official retirement from government. Cromwell had been a member of Warwick's Committee for Trade and Plantations, and had also been on the Commonwealth Council of State. Apparently he had considered emigrating to the colonies himself, once, and he had a deeply respectful correspondence with New Englanders like John Cotton.[71]

Because of his known association with the colonists and colonizers of New England Cromwell attracted to himself the leading colonists who returned from Massachusetts Bay to

[69] A. A. Cooper, Edward Montagu, Viscount Lisle, Sir Charles Wolseley, Francis Rous, Henry Lawrence, Philip Jones, Philip Shippon, Charles Fleetwood, John Asborough, Sir Gilbert Pickering, William Sydenham, Walter Strickland, Nathaniel Fiennes, Edmund Sheffield, Humphrey Mackworth, Richard Major; for a discussion of their backgrounds see Heath, 'Constitutional Essay', pp. 95 et seq.

[70] Colonel Tobias Bridges also served on the Committee for America in 1657.

[71] Cromwell to Cotton, 2 Oct. 1651, Thomas Carlyle, ed., *Oliver Cromwell's Letters and Speeches: With Elucidations* (2 vols., New York, 1845), Vol. II, Part I, pp. 9–10.

England to fight on the side of the Saints.[72] John Leverett, for example, served as a captain in Cromwell's regiment; Cromwell later sent him back to America briefly, to recruit troops from the Confederacy of New England to serve in the Dutch War.[73] John Winthrop's son Stephen fought in the Civil Wars (in Desborough's regiment) and served on Cromwell's Committee for America. Hugh Peter and William Hooke, New Englanders, were Cromwell's chaplains and George Downing his Scoutmaster General.[74]

Magnates of the colonizing companies, returned colonial émigrés, colonial merchants: Cromwell could draw on all of these for advice. He had one other source of information. Agents for various colonial interests, capitalizing on Cromwell's desire to make himself personally available to them, made a point of going directly to Cromwell, finding it harder to solicit individually the multifarious members of his Council than to appeal over their heads to the sympathetic and attentive Protector.[75]

And so, because of his experience, his access to information, and the brevity of his Parliaments, Cromwell became the final arbiter of colonial problems in his own government. Yet, for all the contrast between Cromwell's extensive colonial power and his limited power in domestic affairs, and, indeed, for all the contrast between Cromwell's own interest in colonial administration and his disinterest in the minutiae essential to the managing of his own Parliaments, Cromwell was as reluctant as the Earl of Warwick had been to interfere in the local politics

---

[72] For colonists in Cromwell's army see Sir Charles Firth, *The Regimental History of Cromwell's Army* (2 vols., Oxford, 1940), Vol. I, pp. 95, 179, 418–19, 579. The returned colonists were scattered throughout the Roundhead Army, but there can be little doubt of their personal loyalty to the Protector. As far back as 1644 Manchester accused Cromwell of favouring New England men. C. V. Wedgwood, *The King's War, 1641–1647* (London, 1958), p. 387.

[73] He then went on to serve as governor of Nova Scotia.

[74] John Beresford, *The Godfather of Downing Street, Sir George Downing, 1623–84* (Boston, 1925), p. 51. Returning colonists might have been expected to present the 'New England Case', but they were generally disillusioned with New England's isolationism and religious intolerance. See, for example, Stephen Winthrop to John Winthrop, Jr., 6 Feb. 1650/1, Mass. Hist. Soc. MSS., Winthrop MS. W. Au. 113; R. Williams to J. Winthrop, Jr., 20 Feb. 1652, Winthrop MS. W. 2.122; Roger Williams to John Winthrop, Jr., 2 July 1654, Winthrop MS. W. 2.122; Hugh Peter to John Winthrop, Jr., 4 Sept. 1646, *Colls. Mass. Hist. Soc.* 4th Ser. VI (Boston, 1863), p. 109; Thomas Sheppard to Hugh Peter, 27 Dec. 1645, Bodleian MS. Clarendon 26, f. 110 (at Oxford).

[75] See Note 2 at end of chapter.

of the colonies. After the vigorous colonial policy of the Republican oligarchy Cromwell's administration of the mainland colonies was indeed a return to the *laissez-faire*, noninterventionist, approach of Warwick's Committee. Despite the profound disappointment of some of his closest supporters, Cromwell refused to interfere in Massachusetts politics in order to procure settlers for Jamaica. Similarly, when the New Englanders seemed reluctant to respect the Navigation Acts, Cromwell did not interfere with their trade; when they refused formally to support his attack on New York, he acquiesced in their suggestion that he should recruit volunteers instead. And, despite the fact that most of Cromwell's advisers on New England were returned *émigrés*, hostile to the intolerance of the established governments, and despite Cromwell's own concern with religious toleration he made no attempt beyond personal remonstrances with friends to impose toleration on the Bay Colony.

Similarly, by the Protector's own decision, Lord Baltimore was ultimately supported in his own proprietary, as he had been by Vane and Warwick. When Cromwell became Protector the Commonwealth Commissioners were still in the Chesapeake area; with no new authority from Cromwell they claimed to be working for the Protector now, rather than the Republic, but their real sympathies clearly continued to lie with Haslerig and the overthrown Republican leaders. When Baltimore's governor, acting on the strength of a letter addressed to him as the proprietary governor, issued proclamations in the name of the proprietor rather than the Commonwealth, the commissioners had him arrested and themselves took over the local government. Baltimore at once complained to Cromwell, claiming that an independent proprietorship was from the Protector's standpoint the safest kind of government for the Chesapeake; Baltimore's enemies replied that a feudal proprietorship was incompatible with the nature of the Commonwealth.

Cromwell now made it clear that between a tolerant proprietor of Royalist background and orthodox Puritan commissioners of Republican background he preferred the proprietor. To the commissioners he wrote sharply criticizing these interferences in Maryland. Baltimore's complaint was referred to Whitelock and Widdrington of the Council of State, conservatives likely to favour Baltimore's claim, par-

ticularly at the expense of the commissioners. They reported
in favour of Baltimore in May 1655. Cromwell referred their
report to the Council of State, who referred it to the Council
of Trade; they also reported in favour of Baltimore. This report
the Council sent to Cromwell, though somehow the matter
returned once again to the Council and the Committee of
Foreign Plantations, and there it stayed.

Nearly a year elapsed. Nothing was done. Finally the Virginia commissioners appealed to Secretary Thurloe to get
something done, 'because of your inclination to take cog-
nizance to this business'.[76] Thurloe got nothing done. About
a year after the commissioners' plea to Thurloe, Matthews for
the commissioners and Baltimore for the proprietary government of Maryland signed Articles of Agreement which were
very favourable to Baltimore and restored his rights of government. The Agreement went into effect without further consideration by the Council or Parliament, which means that the
Protector must have given his approval, and that this was
sufficient to make the Agreement valid.[77]

In both New England and the Chesapeake the strong im-
pression one gets is that, despite the enormous discrepancy
between his imperial authority and his local power, Cromwell's
personal decision was invariably on the side of non-intervention
in colonial government. Why?

Given the demands of his foreign wars, there was possibly
little Cromwell could do to subdue recalcitrant or unco-
operative colonies—though the Commonwealth had managed

---

[76] Bennet and Matthews to Thurloe, 10 Oct. 1656, *Thurloe State Papers*, p. 482.

[77] Cromwell's handling of the Maryland controversy is treated in Steiner,
Maryland under the Commonwealth, Johns Hopkins University Studies in History and
Political Science, Ser. XXIX, No. 1 (Baltimore, Md., 1911), pp. 75 to end;
Cal. S.P. Col., Am. & W.I., 1574–1660, pp. 412–77, *passim*; Cromwell to Richard
Bennet, 12 Jan. 1654, and Cromwell to Commissioners of Maryland, 26 Sept.
1655, in *Oliver Cromwell's Letters and Speeches: With Elucidations by Thomas Carlyle*,
Vol. II, Part I (New York, 1845), pp. 132, 182–3; Edward Diggs to Cromwell,
29 June 1655, Bodl. MS. Rawl. A.27, p. 783, printed in *Thurloe State Papers*,
p. 596; Bennet and Matthews to Thurloe, 10 Oct. 1656; ibid. p. 482; 'A Paper
Relating to Maryland', ibid. pp. 483–6. Disappointingly, Bulstrode Whitelock
does not mention his own handling of the Maryland question (in his *Memorials of
the English Affairs from the Beginning of the Reign of Charles the First to the Happy Restoration of King Charles II* (Oxford, 1853), Vol. IV), suggesting that the important
decisions were not left to him but made by Cromwell. See also *Virginia and Maryland, or the Lord Baltimore's Printed Case, uncased and answered*, in Force, *Tracts*, Vol. II,
No. 9.

to subdue Virginia and Maryland while fighting the Dutch. Moreover, Cromwell was far more concerned with popular acceptance of a government: if Englishmen generally accepted the Protectorate, he argued in speech after speech to his Parliaments, then let not the members of Parliament waste time debating the form of government; if colonists generally accepted their local government, let not the Protector interfere with them. A more plausible explanation is that Cromwell was no more concerned with forms of government in the colonies than he was in England. Proprietorship, theocracy, government by commission, even the confederacy of several colonies within the Empire—this diversity in colonial governments was intolerable to Cromwell's Republican opponents and his Presbyterian advisers alike, who could not see how such various forms of government could breed equal loyalty to the mother country. But Cromwell seems to have felt for the colonies the same optimistic confidence in their loyalty that he had for each new Parliament of the Protectorate as it assembled—the feeling that, whatever their form of government, right-thinking Englishmen were capable of seeing the common good as Cromwell saw it, and of acting accordingly. The confidence in his colonies was only slightly better placed than that in his Parliaments.

Moreover, Cromwell was peculiarly in a position to appreciate the argument of colonial leaders that local divisions could quickly grow to the point of destroying the colonies themselves, for Cromwell thought of his own role in English politics much as the various colonial leaders thought of theirs. He had, as he lamented to Parliament, led the English, his own chosen people, out of the wilderness, only to see his world threatened by political divisions. Religious opinions—'mere notions'—held by individuals could not of themselves threaten the body politic; in a people newly creating political foundations, after years in slavery, political divisions could destroy the State. That he saw the parallel between the English and colonial situations is reflected in his profoundly significant warning to Rhode Islanders:

. . . his Highness has sent unto us an express command, to provide against internal commotions, by which his Highness noteth, that not only ourselves are dishonored and endangered, but also dishonor and detriment redounds to the Commonwealth of England: It is ordered that if any person be found by the examination of the General Court of Commissioners, to be a ringleader of factions or divisions among us, he shall be sent over at his own charges, as a prisoner, to receive his trial or sentence at the pleasure of his Highness and the Lords of the Council. . . .[78]

This is remarkably similar to the commands sent to Virginia on his behalf:

And if any person shall presume, by any undue wayes to interrupt the quiet, or hazard the safety of his Highness' people there, order will be taken . . . to make further provision, for securing of yo[r] peace.[79]

And so for all but a short part of the Interregnum the colonial oligarchies succeeded in avoiding direct English intervention. Friendship with colonial leaders, frustration arising from the turbulence of English politics, genuine fear of political divisions in any State, all combined to make most English governments reluctant to interfere in colonial politics. By 1660 the established colonial governments had weathered the challenges from local dissenters supported by factions among the councillors of the Commonwealth government, and probably the government of Richard Cromwell. But the conviction remained that divisions were as likely to begin in London as they were to begin in the colonies.

[78] Williams to the Court of Magistrates and Deputies assembled at Boston, 15 Nov. 1655, *Williams Letters*, Vol. XI, p. 294. This coincides exactly with Cromwell's sentiment expressed in his letter to the Maryland Commissioners of 12 Jan. 1654, *Cromwell's Letters and Speeches*, Vol. II, Part I, p. 132. Cf. Sir Henry Vane to Providence, 8 Feb. 1653/4, quoted in James K. Hosmer, *The Life of Young Sir Henry Vane* (Boston, 1888).

[79] Letter to Virginia, signed 31 Aug. 1658 (though presumably drafted earlier) by Henry Lawrence, by Order of the Council of State. *Journals of the House of Burgesses of Virginia*, ed. McIlwaine, p. 130.

NOTES

1. To arbitrate, or prepare legislation, Parliamentary committees needed to get information: they had to send for merchants from English seaports to testify, and send for fresh information from the colonies themselves. Merchants could not afford to wait around in London while Parliament put off their testimony during a constitutional crisis; more important, to cross the Atlantic took about two months each way, and when Parliaments lasted only a few months this meant it

was virtually impossible for them to have any assurance of fresh, reliable information when they were in session.

Thus from April 1653, when the Rump was dissolved, until September 1658, when Cromwell died, Parliament passed no colonial legislation—a striking contrast to the activity of the Commonwealth and even the Civil War periods. Only a very few times were particular matters from the colonies referred to Parliament—once in 1653, when the agent for Virginia appeared before the Nominated Parliament to urge that the new Parliament should recognize the authority of Virginia commissioners sent out by the Commonwealth; again in 1654, when the Council of State briefly referred the same matter back to Parliament, but soon recalled its papers. Later in 1659 Secretary Thurloe was accused in Parliament of selling a political opponent into slavery in Barbados. Significantly the Committee on Petitions did not follow through the first appeals, but referred the agent to the Council of State, and the last appeal, a rather contrived effort to get at Richard Cromwell through a personal attack on his secretary, was defeated in Parliament.

On only one possible occasion did Parliament itself seem to take any initiative in colonial administration. This was on 12 October 1654, when the House resolved to resolve itself into a Council of Trade every Tuesday. The resolution was presumably passed by a Republican–Presbyterian majority, and may have been part of a series of moves to limit the executive power of the Protector and Council under the Instrument. Ostensibly the committee was to consider trade; there is no way of telling whether it was also intended to cover Plantations, since the committee never did anything.

Parliaments, then, never got any appreciable share in colonial management, partly because of their short duration, and partly because some M.P.s were preoccupied with, and others were forced into, filling their time with discussions of institutional reform in England.

2. Appealing personally to the Protector was always a considerable gamble. In the interview Cromwell would be charming, listen with attention, and appear to be convinced by the facts and argument. The agent would depart satisfied, only to find that Cromwell later changed his mind and gave in to arguments of an opposing agent, or let matters ride without doing anything at all.

> I did in my last, by a Postscript acquaint you that his Highness, had confirmed the proceedings of the Councill and Assembly concerning the alterations and Judges and his Highness was then soe well possessed with that busyness that it seemed beyond all farther question or uncertaintie as I doubt not but you are perfectly informed by Colonel Draxe. . . . But as soon as it was understood by the Agents for Colon¹ Colleton, they instantly bestirr'd themselves and soe effectually, that his Highness seemed somewhat unsettled in his former Resolutions, and thought fitt to give some kind of Check to that letter, which upon the instance of Mr. Noell and Colon¹ Drax he had signed, for the confirming what the country had donn (Thomas Povey to D. Searle, 27 Mar. 1658, B.M. Add. MS. 11411, ff. 58–60).

Leverett corresponded directly with Cromwell when he was in New England. His letters to Cromwell are in the Bodleian Rawlinson MSS. (4 July 1654, Rawl. A. 16, p. 52; 8 Sept. 1654, Rawl. A. 18, p. 58; and 'Conclusions of Commissioners in New England 1654', Rawl. A. 16, pp. 54–5). These are published in *Thurloe State Papers*, pp. 425–6, 583–4, 419–20.

II The Restoration

A. *'Cry and not be heard'*

THE restoration of Charles II represented no abrupt change in colonial politics. The existing New England governments continued, Baltimore had already won back Maryland by negotiations under Cromwell, Berkeley had already been re-elected governor of Virginia; working with them were many of the same families whose names had surfaced from time to time in the Interregnum. And the continuity of leadership was matched, with other things, by the continuity in their approach to political dissent: 'And truly, where a Kingdom, State, or Government keeps or cuts down the weeds of destructive opinions, there must certainly be a blessed harmony of quietness',[1] wrote a supporter of the Maryland establishment. To Massachusetts leaders Urian Oakes preached in the same tone. 'Sad it is', he said, 'if there should be contentions and Divisions, sides and parties and factions in Courts and Churches, and almost all Societies amongst us. This is very much unbecoming a people in our circumstances.'[2] Eleazer Mather had spoken similarly: 'When a spirit of Division and contention in matters of God's worship, is the Spirit of the Times, and thence Religion turns into faction, that is an evidence that the Lord is a leaving of a people. . . . When Societies crack in pieces room is made for God himself to be gone.'[3] During the Interregnum the insecurity of governors, the ambiguity of their relations with legislatures, proprietors, and successive English governments had blunted their effectiveness; after 1660 they were determined to extend to the fullest their enormous legal powers to

---

[1] George Alsop, 'A Character of the Province of Maryland' (1666), in Hall, ed., *Narratives of Early Maryland*, p. 350.

[2] Urian Oakes, *New England Pleaded With* (Cambridge, 1673), p. 36.

[3] *A Serious Exhortation to the Present and Succeeding Generation in New England Earnestly Calling Upon all to Endeavour that the Lord's Gracious Presence be continued with Posterity* (Cambridge, 1671), p. 10.

deal with local opposition. Through the use of patronage, land grants, offers of legislative support, control of legislative procedure, the governors were able within a short time to build up powerful local organizations; through local laws against sedition they had the legal authority to punish their most outspoken opponents.

Sheriffs, J.P.s, county clerks, and militia officers were appointed by governors—often from members of the House of Burgesses or the Maryland Assembly,[4] and while, in Virginia at least, the governor could not remove the appointee for an adverse vote, there was usually a tacit understanding that such placemen would not consistently vote against them. In Virginia the governor could recommend councillors to the British government; in Maryland councillors were the personal appointees of the proprietor. In Maryland anyone who wanted land had to apply to a private land office run by Baltimore's friends; in Virginia they appealed to the governor. Not surprisingly, there was very little chance for an opposition to organize, especially one discredited by the downfall of the Puritan government in England.

To the proprietors of the new colonial areas went enormous colonial authority: they could determine the time and place the colonial Assemblies met, sponsor some laws and veto others, appoint provincial and county officials, appoint members of the governors' councils and militia officers, and in Carolina even grant titles. They had enough favours, distributed intelligently, to give them strong influence over provincial Assemblies, and the governor of New York did not even have to cope with an Assembly but ruled by decree instead.

Moreover, in nearly every colony, proprietary or non-proprietary, the governor had the legal authority to punish or suppress opposition. The governor of Maryland, for example could imprison or otherwise punish 'seditious people' at will, and though the other proprietary governors used their power with more restraint, they too took it for granted that political

---

[4] For Virginia see Patricia Holbert Menk, 'The Origins and Growth of Party Politics in Virginia, 1660 to 1705' (unpublished Ph.D. thesis, University of Virginia, 1945), esp. pp. 6, 40. Of thirty burgesses in 1666, six were colonels, two lieutenant-colonels, one a major, and fourteen captains in the militia; Thomas J. Wertenbaker, *Give Me Liberty* (Philadelphia, 1958), p. 77. For Maryland see Owing, *His Lordship's Patronage, passim.*

opponents who were too outspoken could be jailed, or that hostile petitioners whose language was too abusive could be fined. Similarly the governing oligarchies in Massachusetts and Connecticut had legal ways of putting down their opponents. In 1666, for example, the Massachusetts authorities summoned before the General Court several men who had signed a petition urging them to send agents to England.[5] In nearly every colony individual assemblymen could safely vote against measures that governors supported, but to oppose the governor systematically in the Assembly or to build up an opposition in the province was considered to be bordering on treason and hence punishable by strong measures.

Yet the creation of gubernatorial 'machines' produced an appearance of unity in colonial governments which was deceptive, for the fifteen years after the Restoration saw the emergence of new groups opposed to the government of every colony. New Jersey settlers who had obtained their land patent from New York found themselves accountable to a separate proprietary government they did not like; Dutchmen in New York found themselves under an English government because of the vicissitudes of war; Barbadian immigrants followed to Carolina the lure of proprietary appeals, only to meet proprietary discrimination against them in favour of more docile Virginia migrants; New England Puritans emigrated to New York, New Jersey, or New Hampshire, only to find themselves under non-Puritan, unsympathetic proprietary governments; newcomers in Virginia ran up against the real or imagined opposition of Governor Berkeley's Green Spring faction; merchant communities in New England ports found themselves at odds with the ideals of the Puritan governments.

Everywhere the movement of people and the expansion of

---

[5] The petitions are in the Danforth Papers, *Colls. Mass. Hist. Soc.* 2nd Ser. VIII, pp. 103–7. In the debate on the sending of agents to England, 14 Sept. 1665, Bradstreet, Dudley, and Stoughton were for sending the agents, Bellingham and Hathorn were against it (ibid. p. 101); see Herbert L. Osgood, *The American Colonies in the Seventeenth Century*, Vol. III (Gloucester, Mass., 1957), p. 191.

The debate over the way in which opposition should be handled pervades Massachusetts sermons of the 1660s and 1670s; see, for example, William Hubbard, *The Happiness of a People* (Boston, 1676; Evans Microprint No. 214); Eleazer Mather, *A Serious Exhortation* (Cambridge, 1671; Evans No. 162); Jonathan Mitchel, *Nehemiah on the Wall* (Cambridge, 1671; Evans No. 163); Urian Oakes, *New England Pleaded With* (Cambridge, 1673; Evans No. 180); John Oxenbridge, *New England Freeman* (Cambridge, 1673; Evans No. 181).

trade created pockets of settlers disaffected to the government under which they found themselves, but lacking any legitimate means to influence that government. The disaffected had few opportunities for legal protest, few legitimate outlets for their opposition, no place at all in the structure of colonial politics. In their distressed situation there was one power strong enough to help them—the British government. Colonial factions, as the previous decades had shown, needed assistance, or at least inspiration, from the mother country if they were to thrive. But in the years immediately after the Restoration successive ministries, first under Clarendon and then under the Cabal, gave little encouragement to disaffected groups in the colonies. The oligarchs of 1660 were left undisturbed, free to brand their enemies seditious and all local opposition illegitimate.

Why should this have been so? Why, in a period of strong, popular royal government should the colonial oligarchies have been left so much to themselves? It was not for want of English committees and merchant advisers convinced of the need to reduce the powers of the oligarchs: successive committees and merchant advisers like Thomas Povey and Benjamin Worsley argued just on this line. Indeed, the very apparatus for breaking the monopoly of colonial oligarchies was created by Clarendon himself soon after the Restoration. To investigate and report to the Privy Council on colonial problems Clarendon established a Committee of Trade and Plantations within the Council in July 1660, and for this he picked men representative of all political persuasions from Puritan to extreme Royalist.[6] No sooner had this Committee been established, however, than Clarendon began to consider creating an additional group of advisers, who were not members of the Privy Council but who did have some particular acquaintance with colonial affairs.

To this end the Council of Plantations was commissioned on 1 December. It had forty-eight members and illustrated, even more than the Privy Council Committee, Clarendon's determination to balance a variety of opinions. Every possible group interested in the colonies was represented. It functioned, though with declining vigour, until the spring of 1665, when the original Privy Council Committee took over its duties.

[6] See Andrews, *British Councils of Trade and Plantations*, Ch. IV.

Theoretically there was a regular order for the handling of colonial affairs: either the Privy Council Committee or the Council of Plantations or, more likely, a subcommittee of one of them,[7] would carry out the initial job of gathering information on a particular colonial problem. They would hear testimony from colonists and English officials, examine petitions, talk to ship captains recently arrived from America, and on the basis of the information they gathered would then submit to the Privy Council a recommendation that commissioners should be sent to investigate a colony, for example, or that a letter ordering compliance with English laws be transmitted, or that a particular individual be appointed governor. After the Privy Council as a whole had debated the matter the recommendations would be approved or disapproved by the King in Council.

Here, then, was a workable arrangement for handling colonial problems and checking the pretensions of the colonial oligarchs, a committee to whom colonial dissidents could appeal, and yet Clarendon chose to ignore the committee and work with the colonial authorities himself. Routine problems— like Governor Berkeley's reappointment to Virginia, the preparation of his Instructions, and the determination of his salary,[8] or like the measures to combat kidnapping of servants for the colonies[9]—Clarendon was content to leave to the committee channels. But on more controversial affairs, particularly those concerning New England, committees would spend hours of time preparing reports or recommendations, only to have the Chancellor make up his own mind without regard for their work.

[7] At its first meeting, 7 Jan. 1661, for example, the Council for Foreign Plantations appointed two subcommittees, one of Sir Anthony Ashley Cooper, Boyle, Sir Peter Leere, Sir James Drax, Col. Venables, Messrs. Waller, Povey, Diggs, Colleton, Noell, Kendall, Middleton, Jefferies, Watts, and Howe (or any four) to study Jamaica and New England; the other composed of Messrs. Denham, Waller, and Povey to write letters to Jamaica, Virginia, etc. *Cal. S.P. Coll.*, *1661–1668*, ed. W. N. Sainsbury (London, 1880), No. 3, pp. 1–2.

[8] These were considered in the summer of 1662; see *Cal. S.P. Col.*, *1661–68*, Nos. 332–4, 341, 345, 353, 358, 368.

[9] In 1664 the Council of Plantations studied petitions, referred the question to the Attorney General, and received his report, while the Privy Council Committee recommended that an Act of Parliament should be passed giving government the necessary powers to remedy the evils of 'spiriting away' people to the Plantations. The King set up a commission for James and others to examine people going to the Plantations to see if they had been kidnapped. *Cal. S.P. Col.*, *1661–68*, Nos. 769–72, 791–8.

In the spring of 1661, for example, the Council of Plantations recommended to the Privy Council that a letter should be sent to New England threatening the colony with persecution if it did not send authorized agents to England immediately.[10] Such a letter would unquestionably have given heart to the opponents of the Massachusetts establishment; the issue of sending agents was soon to become one of the most pressing questions of policy before the colony. But on the very day that the Privy Council took it up Clarendon announced that he was creating a special committee to consider the affairs of New England—implying that acceptance of the letter would be inappropriate. Accordingly, the Privy Council decided that such a letter would not be sent, at that time or ever, by the Council of Plantations.[11] On 25 September 1662 the Privy Council Committee again took up debate on the settlement of New England. But Clarendon stopped the discussion by announcing, evidently without any advance warning, that the King would send commissioners to that colony.[12]

Moreover, when Robert Mason, proprietor of New Hampshire, and Ferdinando Gorges, proprietor of Maine, complained of the encroachments of Massachusetts on their territory, the

---

[10] The letter had been drawn up by Thomas Povey and Robert Boyle; it was approved by the Council of Plantations on 29 Apr. and considered by the Privy Council on 17 May.   [11] Ibid., Nos. 87–8.

[12] Ibid., *1661–68*, No. 370. When John Winthrop, Jr., came to England to procure a charter for Connecticut, he managed to get a warrant for the charter a week before the Privy Council was scheduled to hear the case. The reason: Clarendon had already taken up the charter appeal of Connecticut and Rhode Island himself. Instead of being settled by the Council and its committees as was originally scheduled, the question was handled in Clarendon's quarters, with Clarendon himself present and Robert Boyle acting as mediator between the two agents on their boundary dispute. See ibid., No. 222. Winthrop's petition to the King is No. 229; on 12 Feb. 1662 the petition was referred to the Attorney General for his opinion, which was generally favourable. On 26 Feb. 1662 there was a full Privy Council meeting at which it was ordered that all persons with a commission from New England were to appear at the Board on 6 Mar. (P.R.O., MS. Entry Book of Papers Relating to New England, C.O. 5/903, p. 506). On 28 Feb. a warrant was issued to prepare a Bill for a charter of incorporation for Connecticut (*Cal. S.P. Col.*, *1661–68*, No. 246). The MS. Register of the Privy Council (P.R.O. PC 2/55, pp. 566–8) notes that action on New England was put off until 7 Mar. and then dropped. Clarke tried unsuccessfully to get a hearing before the Privy Council. When, on 7 Apr. 1663, five arbitrators decided on a boundary between Rhode Island and Connecticut which conflicted with the Connecticut charter, Clarendon himself decided that the boundary must be determined by a royal commission. Dunn, 'John Winthrop, Jr.', *W.M.Q.*, 3rd Ser. XII (Jan. 1956), p. 80.

Council of Plantations set a hearing in 1662, expecting Massachusetts agents to have arrived in England by that time. When they had not, the Council wanted to go ahead with hearings anyway; it was Clarendon who decided they should be postponed.[13]

Similarly, when Lords John Berkeley, Craven, and Carteret, and the Earl of Albemarle approached Clarendon with a proposal for a proprietary settlement in the Carolinas, Clarendon promised them his influence with the King, without ever consulting the established committees. And he concurred with the establishment, on paper at least, of a strong form of proprietary government in the Carolinas.[14]

Clarendon's leaving the New England governments alone, his support of a strong proprietorship in the Carolinas, combined with his support for Lord Baltimore's government and his reappointment of Governor Berkeley in Virginia, added up to a policy of *laissez-faire*, if not open encouragement, for the established colonial oligarchies, a policy quite at odds with that supported by his own committees. Why? There seem to have been a number of reasons.

One personal reason was that, like Cromwell, Clarendon temperamentally distrusted committee recommendations; he could not resist handling the details of administration, and he could not bring himself to delegate authority, even when it was patently necessary to do so. Thus he read over the New England papers himself before sending them on to Secretary Nicholas;[15] another minister would have sent them on unread and waited for the Secretary to prepare an abstract. Clarendon personally attended meetings of the Council of Plantations, examined financial accounts from the colonies,[16] and considered the appointment of colonial officers.

Far more important, Clarendon's experience in English politics led him to value consensus in the political community

[13] Percy Lewis Kaye, *English Colonial Administration under Lord Clarendon*, Johns Hopkins University Studies in History and Political Science, Ser. XXIII, Nos. 5–6 (Baltimore, Md., 1905), p. 42.

[14] Charles McLean Andrews, *The Colonial Period of American History*, Vol. III (New Haven, Conn., 1937), pp. 182–7. See also K. H. D. Haley, *The First Earl of Shaftesbury* (Oxford, 1968), Ch. XII, and Marion Eugene Sirmans, *Colonial South Carolina* (Chapel Hill, N.C., 1966), Ch. I.

[15] Clarendon to Nicholas (? 1661), *Cal. S.P. Col., 1661–68*, No. 207.

[16] Bodleian MS. Clarendon 82, ff. 275–8, includes Virginia's financial accounts.

and to discourage partisan divisions. He was the peacemaker of the Restoration; to this end he refused to create even a Royalist party in the Commons of England; to the same end he opposed anything that would accentuate divisions in the colonies; and for this reason he found himself quite out of sympathy with most of the committee members, who wanted to encourage opposition to the established colonial oligarchies in the colonies, and particularly in Massachusetts.[17] Significantly, he thought that the New England governments should be reassured of the safety of their charters, and allowed to continue unmolested in their religion and politics, as long as they established some minimal channels of communication with the English authorities by such methods as sending agents and allowing judicial appeals. Like Cromwell and Warwick before him, Clarendon held to the hope that Massachusetts, once reassured of charter rights, would prove a co-operative member of the Empire. And so, when the Committee recommended that a sharply-worded letter should be sent to Massachusetts in 1661, Clarendon apparently bypassed them and persuaded the King instead to write a conciliatory note to the governor of Massachusetts;[18] he also took the matter out of the Committee's hands by setting up still another committee, which included several men well known to have been sympathetic to

[17] They had various suggestions for going about this. One point of view, put forth partly by naval officers, urged that Massachusetts should be reduced by military action, that a relatively small fleet would do, but that it must be sent soon to head off a Puritan rebellion. See Captain Middleton's later testimony before the Council of Plantations. He was confident that Massachusetts could be curbed by a few of his Majesty's first-rate frigates (*Diary of John Evelyn*, ed. Henry B. Wheatley, Vol. II (London, 1906), under 3 Aug. 1671, p. 264).

A second view held that some kind of action would be required to bring the colony into line, but sought to find alternatives to military conquest. Some people, like Governor Nicolls of New York, who held this view urged restriction of New England's trade (Nicolls to Secretary Morrice, 24 Oct. 1666; *Documents Relative to the Colonial History of the State of New York*, ed. E. B. O'Callaghan, Vol. III (Albany, N.Y., 1850), p. 136). Others suggested that if New York were built up as a commercial rival to Boston, Massachusetts would ultimately be so weakened by the drain of trade that she would be unable to resist British authority. Still another group hoped that if Massachusetts were surrounded by royal colonies in Maine, New Hampshire, and New York, and loyal chartered colonies in Rhode Island and Connecticut, it would lose the incentive to maintain its 'city upon a hill' philosophy (F. R. Harris, *Life of Edward Montagu, First Earl of Sandwich*, Vol. II (London, 1912), p. 219. Sandwich also favoured limiting emigration to New England and encouraging settlers already there to move south; ibid. p. 221.)

[18] 15 Feb. 1661. *Cal. S.P. Col., 1661–68*, p. 11.

New England.[19] In addition Clarendon agreed temporarily to suspend the Navigation Act of 1661 in New England.

And in 1664, when the King, at the insistence of Clarendon, Arlington, and James, sent commissioners to investigate the attitude of the Massachusetts authorities, and also to try and settle various boundary disputes among the New England colonies, the commissioners were warned in secret instructions:

> Since it is very notorious that there are not only very great factions and animosities in one colony against the other but in one and ye same colony between persons of different opinions in religion, so it is very probable all discontented persons will make application to you according to their several humours and interest; it will concerne you to be very wary in your conversation, that being sent as persons equall to determine controversyes amongst them you may not bee thought to enclyne to a party.[20]

The discontented New Englanders did, in fact, flock to the commissioners; when this occurred Clarendon assumed the commissioners' interpretations of New England politics were unreliable.

In principle Clarendon was averse to encouraging factional opposition to the provincial governors; his personal connections reinforced this attitude in three different ways. First, Clarendon's personal friendships were with representatives of the dominant cliques; second, his mercantile and ecclesiastical advisers also numbered friends chiefly among the provincial oligarchs. Third, and equally important, perhaps more so, Clarendon was as susceptible to bribes as he was to good arguments, and the established provincial governments were in a position to offer more generous bribes than their opponents.

Clarendon numbered among his own political acquaintances Governor John Winthrop, Jr., of Connecticut, Governor Berkeley of Virginia, Lords John Berkeley, Carteret, and Craven among the Carolina proprietors. He did not, on the other hand, know the opponents of any of the governors, and when sea captains like Thomas Breedon testified on behalf of colonial minorities he considered them biased. He was also influenced in his colonial decisions by members of the Royal

[19] Anglesey, Say and Sele, and Hollis.
[20] Private instructions to Col. R. Nicholls, etc., 23 Apr. 1664, *N.Y. Col. Docs.*, Vol. III, p. 59.

Society and the Society for the Propagation of the Gospel in New England, both groups being inclined by connections to support the dominant colonial factions.

The Royal Society was founded by Charles II in 1660, and John Winthrop, Jr., one of the early members, was well acquainted with some of its leading members, like Henry Brouncker and Robert Boyle.[21] Most Royal Society members were inclined to have some scientific interest in the colonies; a clever diplomat-scholar like John Winthrop would not, therefore, find it difficult to enlist some interest and then secure some applications to the King and his Chancellor on Connecticut's behalf.

The S.P.G.N.E. had originally been established by Act of the Rump Parliament in 1649 to finance missionary activity among the New England Indians. Since Acts of the Interregnum were invalidated by the Restoration, the S.P.G.N.E. leaders applied for a new charter from Charles II. They got one, evidently with Clarendon's assistance,[22] and the Chancellor also helped to defend them against the claims of one Colonel Beddingfield, who claimed they had illegally bought his land as an investment during the Interregnum.[23] When the S.P.G.N.E. was reconstituted under its new charter, Robert Boyle[24] was Governor, Henry Ashurst[25] Secretary, and Clarendon and a number of other ministers were honorary members.

Nominally the group was Anglican—it had dropped some of its less acceptable Puritan members in 1660—but it certainly was not unsympathetic to the New England Puritan governments whose work, after all, it was to finance. And when New

[21] Raymond Phineas Stearns, 'Colonial Members of the Royal Society of London', *W.M.Q.* 3rd Ser. III (Apr. 1946), pp. 206–68.

[22] For the names of the new and old members see the order inscribing new names in the committee, 17 May 1661 (*Cal. S.P. Col., 1661–68*, No. 88). The Society's patent of incorporation is No. 223.

[23] The Company's petition against Beddingfield (2 July 1662) is in *Cal. S.P. Col., 1661–68*, No. 318.

[24] Robert Boyle (1627–91), chemist associated with Boyle's law, was governor of the Society from 1661 to 1689. He was also a director of the East India Company.

[25] Ashurst (1614–80) was a Lancashire Nonconformist apprenticed in London at 15. He became a draper, and soon accumulated considerable wealth through his wife's fortune and the death of his partner, who left him the entire business. See Rev. William Orme, *Life and Times of Rev. Richard Baxter, with a Critical Examination of his Writing*, Vol. I (Boston, 1831), pp. 302–3.

England agents came to London, the Massachusetts General Court asked the S.P.G.N.E. to help them out, both financially and through the influence of its leaders.[26] Agents like Bradstreet and Norton could borrow from the Society to meet their London expenses. And Boyle and Ashurst were willing to wait on Clarendon to help Massachusetts and Connecticut.[27] The Massachusetts General Court asked Boyle to intervene with Clarendon and the King to have the commissioners of 1664 recalled.[28] Boyle once wrote Ashurst that he had spent hours waiting to see Clarendon, in order to talk to him about New England, and added, 'And when I spoke civilly to my Lord Chancellor of your Friend Mr. Winthrop, His Lordship assented to the character I had given him.'[29]

Finally, colonial agents, knowing him to be both powerful and impressionable, cultivated the art of persuading the Chancellor both by argument and by financial contribution, for Clarendon, like many of his contemporaries, was not above accepting a financial 'arrangement' or a grant of land. (Bribetaking with regard to Barbados was one of the charges in his impeachment,[30] and the Carolina proprietors obtained his support by offering him a proprietorship in the colony.) Winthrop of Connecticut and Clarke of Rhode Island, for example, were both trying to get charters for their respective colonies in the early months of 1662. Winthrop succeeded in

[26] General Court to 'English friends', 25 Jan. 1661. The English friends were named individually, but all of them at some time or other were members of the S.P.G.N.E.; *The Hutchinson Papers*, Vol. II, Publications of the Prince Society (Albany, N.Y., 1865), p. 85. On 19 Oct. 1660 Governor Endicott wrote John Leverett, then in England, that he had asked Mr. Saltonstall and Mr. Ashurst to take care of the colony's business (ibid. I, p. 42).

[27] Boyle to H. Ashurst [n.d.], but describing a meeting with Clarendon, in Thomas Birch, *The Life of The Honourable Robert Boyle* (London, 1744), pp. 452–3; also, Governor, Deputy Governor, and Court of New England to Boyle, 10 May 1673, ibid. pp. 453–6. Boyle wrote an unknown correspondent in July 1674 that he had helped out Massachusetts with important members of court; *Hutchinson Papers*, Vol. II, p. 182.

[28] Massachusetts Governor and General Court to Boyle, 19 Oct. 1664, in Birch, *Life of Boyle*, p. 452.

[29] Boyle to Ashurst [n.d.], ibid. pp. 452–3.

[30] James Buck to Sir George Lane, 26 Oct. 1667, Historical Manuscripts Commission, *Calendar of the Manuscripts of the Marquess of Ormonde*, N.S. IV (London, 1904), p. 279. In *Clarendon's Life and Continuation of His History of the Grand Rebellion*, Vol. III (Oxford, 1827), p. 311, the Chancellor answered the charge only by saying that he had tried to convince the King that the colonies brought in a great deal of money.

May, far sooner than Clarke, because Connecticut was a wealthier colony than Rhode Island and Winthrop could offer higher bribes.[31] The Connecticut charter granted that colony some land claimed by Rhode Island; Clarke was eventually able to persuade Clarendon to submit the boundary dispute to arbitration.[32] Just how he managed this is not clear, but it hardly seems a coincidence that the Rhode Island Assembly voted the Chancellor a substantial piece of land.[33]

And so under Clarendon the provincial governments were left unmolested by the English ministers, and their local opponents were left without English assistance; for different reasons the five ministers of the Cabal who succeeded him in power also kept out of colonial politics. For one thing, it was inconceivable that a group as heterogeneous as the Cabal would share any strong views on the American colonies. There is, in fact, only slight evidence that the five members as a group discussed colonial affairs at all: once, in 1671, petitions of Mason and Gorges for the restoration of their proprietorships in New Hampshire and Maine were referred to the Committee of Foreign Affairs of which the Cabal were all members.[34] Other than that, there seem to have been no occasions on which all the ministers discussed colonial affairs together.

In the absence of either a leading minister or an expression of group opinion about the colonies, influence in colonial administration went by default to individual ministers who were interested in it, and these tended to be interested primarily because they had connections among the established provincial politicians. Clifford, a Catholic, was concerned mainly in getting his friends into office in Maryland. Arlington was a long-time friend of most of the Carolina and New Jersey proprietors, and himself was awarded the proprietorship of Virginia in 1672. He was a friend of Governor Berkeley of Virginia, with whom he exchanged letters full of news. And Shaftesbury, of course, was for many years chairman of the Carolina proprietors; he was probably also acquainted with Lord Baltimore and with Increase Mather of Massachusetts.

---

[31] Dunn, 'John Winthrop, Jr.', *W.M.Q.* 3rd Ser. XIV (Jan. 1956), p. 77.

[32] Ibid. p. 78.

[33] Cranfield to Blathwayt, 5 Oct. 1683; Colonial Williamsburg, Blathwayt MS. 2.

[34] The petitions are discussed in *Cal. S.P. Col., 1679-84*, Nos. 439 and 593.

But it was not only personal connections that inclined the Cabal to leave the colonial oligarchs entrenched in power; it was also their general approach to colonial administration. The two major supporters of the Council of Trade and Plantations of 1672 were Arlington and Shaftesbury, and neither was inclined to interfere directly in colonial politics. Arlington was a very lazy man, who spent a good deal of time on his country estate and left to his secretary most of his work; an unoriginal man, who would gladly offer his own lodging as a meeting-place for the Council of Plantations, but never consider how the Council should be organized; and a man of superficial enthusiasms, who pressed for a Virginia proprietorship, only to drop his interest in the project when he saw how difficult it was going to be. One must size up Arlington's role in colonial affairs as that of the absentee Secretary who occasionally dropped into his office to check the paper work and pursue one or two favourite projects, and used his powers of persuasion with James or the King in favour of randomly chosen projects, like the conquest of New Netherland, the sending of commissioners to New England, or the creation of a Council of Plantations. His potential influence was great, but it was largely untapped.

And Shaftesbury's main interest was not so much in colonial policy as in the procedure by which it was created. It was Shaftesbury, apparently, who supplemented the unwieldy Council of Trade and Plantations, set up after Clarendon's fall, with the workable Council of Foreign Plantations, established in 1670.[35] And when the Council was merged with the Committee of Trade in 1672, Shaftesbury prepared a commission instructing the Committee to correspond directly with colonial governors, and to study the colonial administration of other countries with an eye to improving the English approach. Under Shaftesbury's inspiration the Committee kept its small membership, its regular meeting hours in members' private homes (it met for a while at Shaftesbury's home), and thereby its chance for intimate discussion of colonial affairs.[36]

[35] Harris, *Life of Sandwich*, p. 211.
[36] Ibid. p. 221, App. C, pp. 306–7; Ralph Bieber, 'The British Plantation Councils of 1670–74', *E.H.R.* XL (1925), pp. 93–106; Andrews, 'British Committees', op. cit. pp. 103–4.

But Shaftesbury paid far more attention to the machinery by which colonial developments were to be studied than he did to the actual developments in the colonies, and the accomplishments of his Committee were remarkably small. After reopening the entire New England question in 1671, for example (as a result of three things: renewed claims from Sir Ferdinando Gorges and Robert Mason for Maine and New Hampshire, the refusal of New Englanders to contribute military assistance to the home government in the Dutch Wars, and renewed evidence of religious persecution), the Committee decided simply to send commissioners to investigate conditions in New England.[37] Notably the commissioners were, in Sandwich's words, to be men 'of esteem in that countrye and not averse to them'.

And so, for the first decade and a half after the Restoration provincial authorities were left free to suppress local opponents as best they could. Their opponents had a few legitimate means of influencing the colonial governments, and few channels of appeal beyond them to the mother country. They could not effectively and systematically organize opposition within the colonial Assemblies; they could not develop it 'out of doors'. They did not have useful connections in England, nor did they have the resources to bribe as generously as the established governments. English investigators were instructed not to take their side; English witnesses who testified on their behalf were considered biased; English ministers were indifferent or even hostile.

Opposition factions, therefore, had few legitimate means of operating effectively within the structure of imperial political institutions. In desperation many of them looked for help from colonies neighbouring on their own. Long Islanders petitioned the Privy Council to be annexed to Connecticut, for example. Settlers in western New Hampshire, led by William Vaughan and Richard Waldron, and disavowing the proprietors' claims, recognized commissioners sent from Massachusetts. The inhabitants of Elizabethtown, New Jersey, sought help from the governor of New York. Appeals like these at least gave the

[37] The meetings to discuss New England are listed in Andrews, 'British Committees', op. cit., App. 4, 'Heads of Business of Councils, 1670–74', pp. 135–42. Many of them are described in *Evelyn's Diary*, ed. Wheatley, Vol. II, pp. 260–92.

appearance of courting legal support; more questionable was the correspondence of Dutch congregations in New York seeking continued political guidance from the mother Church in Holland. In time, these appeals came to nothing; the disaffected were driven to other methods. On occasion they set up rival Assemblies of their own: the Barbados group tried this in the Carolinas; so did delegates from Elizabethtown and neighbouring New Jersey towns in 1672. But these were short-lived expedients: beyond them what could discontented colonists do? They could rebel (Virginians tried this shortly after the Restoration), or they could leave (so many settlers fled the Carolinas that the proprietary Assembly passed a law forbidding ship captains from carrying emigrant passengers).[38] More important, they could simply pay no attention to the decrees of proprietors or the acts of Assemblies. Some colonists were in geographical pockets where the governors' authority scarcely reached; they enjoyed a limited immunity from attack by the provincial government.

Momentarily some colonial dissidents were able to take advantage of the inability of provincial institutions to keep up with the problems of territorial growth. In the fifteen years after the Restoration of Charles II it was clear that colonial governments still had neither the machinery to suppress local opposition nor the sophistication to make it legitimate. The problem of dissent remained: how could dissenters win a recognized position in colonial politics? In the early 1670s few people could have anticipated that the legitimatizing of colonial discontent would be accomplished by the British government itself, and accomplished very soon.

B. *'Factious parties in old and New England'*

After 1675 the picture of colonial politics began to change, as factions in opposition to the local oligarchs slowly emerged into the open. This does not mean that the idea of political parties in opposition to the government became acceptable; far from it. (There was still the fear, quite justified by Bacon's rebellion, the upheavals of 1689, and the lesser revolts in between, that opposition to provincial authority would lead to civil war; and

[38] Sirmans, *Colonial South Carolina*, pp. 21-2.

the multifarious responsibilities of Jacob Leisler, for example, merchant, militia captain, elder of the Church, showed that religious, military, economic, and political issues still overlapped inseparably, so that differences on one issue were likely to spill over to others.) Nor does it mean that pockets of settlers were any less apt to ignore laws than to try to change them by gaining office: there was no idea that factions were capable of alternating in positions of authority.

Nevertheless, there was a noticeable change in Restoration politics beginning in the 1670s, as the growth of the colonies produced new interest groups thrusting forth for political influence, and as colonists who opposed the local magistrates began to look for—and find—allies among English officialdom to make their cause respectable. The major reason?—renewed British intervention in provincial politics.

The first such intervention came with the Navigation Act of 1673, which required the colonists to give bond at their port of departure in the colonies for the payment of customs duties in England, and also required that customs officials should be sent to the colonies to enforce the Act.

The Act was important as an additional affirmation of Parliament's right to regulate trade. But it was also significant for a number of other reasons. For one thing, in setting up a colonial customs service Parliament was interfering more directly in colonial administration than it ever had before. For another thing, by creating the position of customs inspector Parliament was placing in the colonies some royal officials who, along with the naval officers, were directly responsible to the King and his ministers, rather than to the provincial governor. They were thus providing potential rivals to the governors, royal officials around whom the governor's enemies could legitimately rally. In royal and non-royal colonies the new officials became possible rallying-points for the disaffected, and more than one customs inspector was in the thick of a rebellion against the local governor.[39] Since they were appointed directly by the

---

[39] Of the four Customs Collectors appointed before 1677, three—Giles Bland of Virginia, Christopher Rousby of Maryland, and Thomas Miller of Albemarle in the Carolinas—were involved in some way in a rebellion or other challenge to the governor's authority. For Bland's accusation that Berkeley was interfering with customs collections see Bland to Berkeley, 16 Sept. 1675, B.M. Egerton MS. 2395, ff. 511–14. On this general point see also Wilcomb E. Washburn, *The Effect of*

British government, they could not be dismissed from office by
the governors for openly opposing them, and it was a tedious,
often unprofitable process for governors to complain about them
to Whitehall. Moreover, it was exceedingly awkward for a
governor to fine or pillory a royal official, and it was equally
awkward to claim that he and his colonial associates were being
seditious or disloyal to England by undermining the gubernatorial authority.

Royal officials were by no means immune from local harassment, but if such harassment took place it was certain, as the
persecution of local politicians was not, to come to the attention
of royal authorities at home.[40] In these circumstances what was
more natural than for leading opponents of the provincial
governor to come knocking at the door of the royal customs
inspector seeking his support? One should not overestimate
their importance, but the sending of royal officials to the
colonies was one small way in which the government of Charles II
inadvertently contributed to the divisions within the colonies
and the weakening of the colonial governorship.

Similarly, what was more natural than using Anglican clergy
to give respectability to a political cause? In 1675 a new
Bishop of London was appointed: Henry Compton, an
energetic man with a serious interest in the colonies, and
a willingness, which his predecessors had not had, to accept
the supervision of the Anglican Church in the colonies as
part of his job.[41] Compton began convincing Charles, James,
and the Lords of Trade that the Anglicans were the most likely
members of each colony to favour close ties with the mother
country, and that if colonial administration was to work, the
Anglican Church must be given effective support. The Bishop
successfully urged an examination into the extent of his jurisdiction over the colonies,[42] inclusion in the Pennsylvania
charter of a guarantee that any group of settlers might have an

---

Bacon's Rebellion on Government in England and Virginia, Contributions from the
Museum of History and Technology, Paper 17 (Washington, D.C., 1962).

[40] For a good illustration of this point see Pascal, Proprietary North Carolina,
pp. 490–503.

[41] Philip S. Haffenden, 'The Anglican Church in Restoration Colonial Policy',
in Seventeenth-Century America, Essays in Colonial History, ed. James Morton Smith
(Chapel Hill, N.C., 1959), pp. 166–91.

[42] Minutes of the Lords of Trade and Plantations, 21 Jan. 1675/6, C.O. 391/1, f. 1.

Anglican chaplain if they wished,[43] and the introduction of the Anglican Church in such Puritan strongholds as Boston.[44]

The 'Anglican invasion' of the northern colonies was slow, but its potential effects were beginning to be evident before 1688. Who could give more safety to opposition than an obviously loyal minister of the Church of England? What could constitute a better nucleus for a political organization than an Anglican congregation, or a more respectable means of spreading a political programme than an Anglican pulpit?

By seeking out associations with customs officials and Anglican ministers colonial politicians were developing imperial connections to make their local activities appear legitimate. Settlers in proprietary colonies had even better potential connections—proprietary relatives, or even proprietors themselves when the colony was a group enterprise. Not without reason had Charles Calvert, governor of Maryland, written his father, Lord Baltimore:

> My stay in England will be but short . . . & I have great cause to feare, that I shall find much confusion at my returne, for as yr Lopp was please to write that it will best to make my Uncle Govern[o]r in my Absence on the side I know it to be very necessary & againe am very sensible how much he has disgusted all in generall & especially those that have beene ever faithfull to yr Lopp interest here & such as have shewne me anything of Kindnesse since my Coming into this Province. He has soe much by Instruments employed by him threatened what he'le doe when the power comes againe into his hands as he gives out an other yeare it necessarily must in regard he und[e]rstands yr Lopp has a desire I should goe for England, next shipping, that the people doe dread nothing more especially such as I say'd afore had beene yr Lopps friends. . . .[45]

In 1672 the settlers of Elizabethtown, New Jersey, who had refused to pay quitrents to the proprietary governor, Philip Carteret, claiming that a land patent given them by the governor of New York exempted them from payment to the Jersey proprietors, called an Assembly in defiance of the governor, and elected in his place his nephew Captain James

---

[43] Minutes of the Lords of Trade and Plantations, 22 Jan. 1680/1, C.O. 391/2, f. 249.
[44] Haffenden, 'Anglican Church', op. cit. p. 186.
[45] Calvert to Lord Baltimore, 27 Apr. 1664, *Calvert Papers*, Vol. I, p. 251.

Carteret, a son of one of the proprietors. Fifteen years later the settlers of Carolina overthrew the proprietary governor and replaced him with another proprietary appointee who had just moved to the colony.

Dissident colonists, then, sought out English connections who would give respectability to their local resistance. At the same time a push to develop transatlantic connections was coming from the English government itself, as Kings and ministers undertook to bring the colonies under a much tighter administration and looked for colonists who would actively support its new approach. For the second half of the Restoration era saw the most far-reaching attempts to reform and reorganize colonial administration ever undertaken by the British government in the seventeenth and eighteenth centuries.

Indeed, the adventurousness of the second half of the Restoration era is in striking contrast to the hesitation of the first. How did this come about? It is tempting to explain these rapid changes as being part of some sweeping new plans developed by Charles and James to tighten their executive control over the colonies as well as England. Alternatively, one could look to the new and vigorous Committee of Trade and Plantations created in 1675, and suggest that they put forth new plans in order to strengthen their own direction of imperial administration. But neither of these explanations is really satisfactory. There is no evidence at all that either Charles or James ever developed any general scheme for the parallel reorganization of government in England and the colonies, and the Lords of Trade, however energetic and able they might have been, never put forth any recommendations for colonial reform that were really new or differed fundamentally from those put forth repeatedly by previous Committees and Councils of Trade.

If the Kings on their own did not come up with any basically new ideas about colonial administration and the Committees of Trade did not either, then the new approach cannot be traced solely to either one. It can, however, be sought in a new relationship between the two. After years of letting their leading ministers bypass the Committees' recommendations for a tighter imperial structure and a more vigorous colonial policy, Charles, and then James, finally began to consider the recommendations themselves and to take action upon them. The question to be asked is why the flighty, erratic Charles II, and later his brother James, began to take a personal hand in running the colonies, and why they were receptive to the Committees' recommendations.

Part of the explanation is that after 1675 there were no powerful ministers of state—no Clarendons, Arlingtons, or Shaftesburys—who came between the Committees of Trade and the King, and watered down the Committees' proposals for reform. Danby, the leading minister and most natural adviser, had no personal concern for the colonies. He dutifully read the abstracts on colonial affairs prepared by the Secretaries of State,[46] occasionally attended to some detail like arranging the salary for a colonial official,[47] and attended Charles's inner council of advisers, which discussed colonial problems several times during his ministry, but on no important issue did he show any profound interest at all.

Soon after he was appointed Lord Treasurer, Danby abolished the Council of Trade and Plantations and replaced it with a committee of the Privy Council, not on grounds that the old Council was doing a bad job (though he was, in Evelyn's words, 'no friend to [the Council]'),[48] but on grounds that they were too expensive. (The Council of Trade and Plantations had been salaried, while the new committee was not.) Nominally Danby himself was a member of the new committee, but he rarely attended; as a rule he showed up only when French trade—not the Plantations—was being discussed.[49] Colonial affairs seemed to bore him, compared to the fascinating building of his political organization at home.

If Danby could not advise him on colonial affairs, then

[46] Coventry Papers, Library of Congress, 78 ff. 1, 2, 26. Commissioners to Berkeley, 2 Mar. 1676 (f. 1), Berkeley's answer to the commissioners, 7 Mar. (f. 2), extracts of papers sent for Lord Treasurer's inspection, n.d. (f. 26). Also Ludwell to Coventry, 14 Apr. 1677 (ibid. f. 40), indicates that Coventry was preparing abstracts for Danby.

[47] Coventry Papers, 78 f. 144, Culpeper's notes of a meeting of the Committee of Foreign Plantations, 9 Dec. 1677.

[48] *Evelyn's Diary*, ed. Wheatley, Vol. II, 23 June 1673, p. 292: 'To London to accompanie our Council, who went in a body to congratulate the new Lord Treasurer, no friend to it, because promoted by my Lord Arlington, whom he hated.'

[49] Minutes of the meetings, including attendance, are in C.O. 391/1 and 2, Journals of the Lords of Trade.

the other advisers to whom Charles might logically have turned were the Secretaries of State, Henry Coventry and Sir Joseph Williamson, whose offices handled a good deal of colonial business. Both men had friends in the colonies, long experience in colonial administration, and in general knew their business well. But they did not come to have much influence over Charles, mainly because neither had a personal following great enough to put him in the front rank of English politicians, and neither had the knack of appealing personally to the King.[50] The same was true for Sir Leoline Jenkins, who succeeded Coventry in 1679.[51] The Secretaries of the following decade, Lords Sunderland and Middleton, had very little interest in colonial affairs at all.[52]

Without any ministers important enough to gain his confidence, or interested enough in the colonies to have strong opinions on them, Charles found himself forced to take colonial affairs directly into his own hands in the last years of his reign. From Danby's appointment up until the Exclusion crisis Charles seems to have made the major colonial decisions himself. This is most evident in the handling of Bacon's rebellion in 1676. The rebellion was of particular interest to the British

[50] Rarely did Coventry or Williamson intercede with the King to water down the recommendations of the Committee of Trade, nor did they exert any influence in the Committee for Foreign Plantations, of which they were both members. Coventry's hand, for example, cannot be seen directly in any of the King's decisions on the handling of Bacon's rebellion, though Coventry himself, as Secretary in charge of the Southern colonies, handled the papers; see Coventry Papers, MS. 78, *passim*. Similarly Williamson, though known to be a friend of the leading Massachusetts Puritans, offered no opposition to the *quo warranto* proceedings against the Massachusetts charter.

[51] Jenkins attended the Lords of Trade with great regularity—far more often, indeed, than any other Restoration Secretary. Between 1680 and 1684 Jenkins attended 78% of the meetings, whereas Coventry had attended 56% of them between 1675 and 1680, and Williamson attended 75% of the time between 1675 and 1679. Sunderland attended 34%, 1679–81, and 62%, 1683–88 (Ralph Bieber, *The Lords of Trade and Plantations, 1675–1696* (Allentown, Pa., 1919), App. B). William Penn claimed that Jenkins was instrumental in getting the Pennsylvania charter for him, but beyond this it is hard to track down any influence of Jenkins on major colonial decisions.

[52] Middleton rarely attended the Committee of Trade and Plantations; Sunderland attended slightly more than half the meetings after 1683. Sunderland corresponded with colonial governors; he may have had some influence in keeping his friend Penn's charter from being taken away, but on the whole he had very little concern with colonial affairs until 1688, by which time James's own ideas of colonial administration were already set. See Winfred J. Root, 'The Lords of Trade and Plantations', *A.H.R.* XXIII, No. 1 (Oct. 1917), p. 33.

government, because it was directed against one of the King's most loyal, capable, and heretofore popular governors, and because a disruption of the colony's trade even temporarily could cause a serious loss of customs duties which made their way into the English Treasury.

The King got his news of the rebellion through Secretary Coventry, and he did discuss it with ministers at the Council of Foreign Plantations before deciding to send out commissioners to inquire into the grievances behind the rebellion and troops to put it down. But as the crisis wore on Charles seems to have made more and more of the decisions himself, on the recommendations of the Lords of Trade. When, in December 1677, Lord John Berkeley prepared a defence of his brother Governor Berkeley, it was apparently the King alone who decided that no notice should be taken of the defence.[53] Disillusioned with Governor Berkeley's handling of the rebellion, the King determined that in future he would approve the appointment of colonial governors himself. In 1679 he personally interviewed Edward Randolph before sending him to New England as customs inspector.[54]

For several years Charles showed a flurry of energy in colonial administration, but his determination to make the major decisions by himself did not last long. More and more he turned to his brother James and the 'French party',[55] as James became a new leading minister and a new adviser on colonial problems. James's influence over his brother had been growing ever since the Restoration. He had shown himself an exceptionally capable Lord High Admiral in the 1660s, and when as a Catholic he was forced to resign office, after the Test Act was passed in 1672, he remained in Charles's inner cabinet and continued as the King's confidential adviser. During the Exclusion crisis Charles had to send his brother out of the country temporarily but James soon returned, and the crisis itself,

---

[53] A month later the King—in Council, but apparently making the decision himself—decided to accept a Council recommendation to the Virginia Assembly providing suitable punishment for Bacon's followers (Wilcomb E. Washburn, *The Governor and the Rebels; a History of Bacon's Rebellion in Virginia* (Chapel Hill, N.C., 1957), pp. 145–7).

[54] Michael Garibaldi Hall, *Edward Randolph and the American Colonies, 1676–1703* (Chapel Hill, N.C., 1960), p. 45.

[55] Lovejoy, 'Charter of Liberties', *W.M.Q.* XXI (1964), p. 511.

in which Charles's authority was threatened by the attempts to keep James from being eligible for the throne, brought the two brothers closer together than ever. For the last four years of Charles's reign James's influence was paramount, not least in the sphere of colonial administration.

It was James, for example, who began the attack on the chartered colonies, and then decided what kind of government Massachusetts should have once its charter was invalidated. (He made the decision to issue writs of *quo warranto* against the charters of Maryland, Connecticut, Rhode Island, and New Jersey, and decided not to allow Massachusetts a representative Assembly.)[56] James also worked personally with William Penn on Penn's claim to the three lower counties of Pennsylvania.[57] It was also James who made the appointments to the important colonial governorships. He got Sir Percy Kirke appointed first governor of the Dominion of New England, and sent Lord Effingham to replace Lord Culpeper in Virginia.[58] When in 1683 James succeeded to the throne, William Blathwayt wrote Lord Effingham that he was sure James would continue him as governor of Virginia, because James had obtained his appointment in the first place.[59] Blathwayt's remark applied to James's entire colonial policy as to appointments, once he was King himself, had he made them. James began his own reign determined to make all decisions himself. He attended the Lords of Trade, hurried the courts along on their *quo warranto* proceedings, appointed and dismissed colonial governors, and himself made the final decisions on which colonies were to be included in the Dominion of New England. By 1686 James was so busy with other matters that he had to limit the time he spent

---

[56] Hall, *Edward Randolph*, pp. 92–4. On this particular issue James felt so strongly that when in a cabinet meeting the Marquis of Halifax defended the right of Massachusetts to an Assembly against the arguments of James's own supporter Baron Jeffries, James took it personally and momentarily urged the King to dismiss Halifax. (Bieber, *Lords of Trade*, p. 33; H. C. Foxcroft, *Life and Letters of Sir George Saville, Bart., First Marquis of Halifax*, Vol. 1 (London, 1898), p. 428; Barillon to Louis XIV, 7 Dec. 1684; Rt. Hon. Charles James Fox, *A History of the Early Part of the Reign of James the Second, with an Introductory Chapter* (London, 1808), pp. vii–ix.)

[57] Joseph E. Illick, *William Penn the Politician; his Relations with the English Government* (Ithaca, N.Y., 1965), p. 58.

[58] Effingham and Culpeper sent James news from Virginia but he also had his personal correspondents there.

[59] 26 Apr. 1685; Colonial Williamsburg, Blathwayt MS. XIX.

on the colonies, but even as late as 1688 colonial agents like Increase Mather found it fairly easy to see the King in person.

Important and not so important decisions, then, were being made by Charles and then by James. But this still does not altogether explain why they favoured tighter colonial administration as recommended by the Lords of Trade. Why were they personally inclined now, as they had not been at an earlier date, to agree with the Lords of Trade?

For one thing, after 1675 the Stuarts enjoyed a period of international peace; they were allied by treaty with Louis XIV of France—the one power in position to threaten the mainland colonies—and they had made good the ouster of the Dutch from New Netherlands. So there was now no longer a danger—as there had been before 1673—that colonists faced with tighter imperial control might look to French or Dutch support.

For another reason, both Charles and James became genuinely disgusted with the results of their colonial administration, particularly in New England and Virginia. Fifteen years of endless argument over whether New England should be starved out, surrounded by Royalist colonies, subdued by force, or left alone had produced no policy and had no effect. The Massachusetts agents sent in 1675 were no more willing than John Leverett had been in 1660 to make concessions. Fifteen years of confidence in Governor Berkeley's abilities to keep Virginia loyal had been shattered, not only by Bacon's rebellion but also by Berkeley's alleged failure to cooperate with royal commissioners sent over after the rebellion. As if this weren't enough, in 1677 the customs collector in North Carolina was imprisoned as a result of a successful rebellion against his efficient methods, and four years later the customs collector for Maryland was murdered by the president of the Council there.

These colonial disturbances were bad enough for their reflections on British authority, but Charles and James had even more reason to fear them, since the government stood to lose about £200,000 in customs duties annually if colonial resistance prevented their collection. And £200,000—the returns expected from Virginia and New England—was indispensable to the King's revenue, especially after the Exclusion crisis began and Charles and James were forced to live without further parliamentary grants.[60] It was essential to the King's financial security at home, therefore, that they should strengthen their colonial administration.

Moreover, both Charles and James must have begun to share with the Lords of Trade the growing confidence that in every colony there was a substantial number of people who would genuinely welcome some reforms in colonial administration that would bring them in closer touch with England, and also enhance their position in their colonies by weakening the local authority of adversaries. They were beginning to have, in other words, a conviction that an easy-going colonial administration was tending to leave local politics to the wrong people, and to penalize a large group of loyal Stuart supporters in the colonies.

This conviction developed partly from the fact that by the end of the Restoration period there really were more Englishmen moving to those colonies that were determined to remain loyally within the Empire; but more important, it also came because the government now had far more extensive information about political alignments in the colonies than they had ever had before. In the early years of the Restoration the British government simply did not know how much loyal support it could count on in the colonies. Much of their information had been coming from the discontented colonists returning to England to complain of treatment in America: commissioners, like Carr and Cartwright and Maverick, whom most of the Plantations Committees did not trust, and the occasionally well-connected ship captains, like Middleton, who reported to their friends in the government when they returned home from a trip. With such scanty information, much of it of dubious accuracy, ministers and Lords of Trade simply did not know enough to take the initiative in determining the political struggles within each colony. All they could do was to try to sift the evidence for each issue impartially; they could only

---

[60] W. Harbord to E. Essex, 17 Dec. 1676: 'Ill news from Virginia and New England doth not only alarm us but extreamly abate ye customs so y^t not withsta^d all ye shifts Treasurer can make this Parliament must set.' *Selections from the Correspondence of Arthur Capel, Earl of Essex, 1675-77*, ed. Clement Edwards Pike, Camden Soc. Pubs., 3rd Ser. XXIV (London, 1913), p. 57. The £200,000 represented £100,000 each from Virginia and New England; see Washburn, 'Effect of Bacon's Rebellion', op. cit. pp. 146-9.

look upon themselves as judges, as detached arbiters of particular controversies which arose.

In the 1670s, however, for the first time the British government began to have enough information about the colonies to understand their domestic politics in some detail. For one thing, they began to use agents more than they had previously done.

Ever since the beginning of the Restoration period, when British authorities had asked that the governor of Virginia should instruct any planters who might be coming to London whether they would be willing to look after the colony's affairs from time to time,[61] the British government had encouraged the colonies to send agents. After 1675 they began pressing considerably harder. The Pennsylvania charter was the first to contain a requirement that the colony should keep an agent in London. At the urging of the Committee of Trade the King told the Massachusetts agents who wanted to go home in 1677 that they would have to stay as long as he wanted them to,[62] and Lord Baltimore, serving as agent for Maryland, felt compelled to offer profuse explanations when he left England for a visit to the colony in 1681.[63]

The Committee's attitude about exactly what role the agents should play was as yet not fully developed. Should they be ambassadors, errand boys, or something in between? In 1676 the Committee went more than half way in co-operating with agents sent from Virginia to obtain a royal charter, indicating its willingness to negotiate in good faith with agents empowered to reciprocate.[64] Repeatedly the Committee demanded that the Massachusetts agents should be authorized to negotiate about alterations in their charter. Yet in 1677 the King angrily told Bulkeley and Stoughton, the two Massachusetts agents then in London, 'that His Majesty did not think of treating with his own subjects, as with Foreigners, and to expect ye formality of powers; but having resolved to do all things that were fit for them, and consistent with his service, they might, from time to time, intimate the same to their Principals . . .'.[65]

---

[61] Draft of Instructions to Virginia, n.d. [1660] (B.M. Egerton MS. 2395, f. 336).

[62] 27 July 1677; Journal of Lords of Trade, C.O. 391/2, f. 97.

[63] Baltimore to Cousin Gilbert, 14 July 1679, *The Calvert Papers*, Maryland Hist. Soc. Fund Pubs., No. 2, p. 318.

[64] See Wilmington MSS., Vol. I (L.C. Transcripts), *passim*.

[65] 27 July 1677; Journal of the Lords of Trade, C.O. 391/2, f. 97.

This ambivalent attitude on the part of the government was to plague colonial agents from the Restoration to the American Revolution. But despite the uncertainties of the job, colonists by the 1680s were slowly beginning to recognize the value of having agents at Whitehall, not only to represent colonial interests but also to represent provincial parties in the appeal for growing colonial patronage. Virginia established its first permanent agents soon after 1680, and it is significant that the Massachusetts Puritans, long the most obstinate opponents of the agency, themselves sent Increase Mather to London to appeal against the government of Sir Edmund Andros in 1688.

In addition to the agents the government had other sources of information. In 1675, for example, the Committee of Trade and Plantations sent a circular letter to royal governors asking about the condition of their provinces, and saying that thereafter they should send journals of occurrences there; and these reports and journals began trickling in. In 1680 one Richard Chamberlain was sent to New Hampshire as Secretary to the Council to report details of discussions in that body.[66] Edward Randolph was repeatedly sent to gather information about New England politics, and in the aftermath of Bacon's rebellion three commissioners were sent to Virginia. With customs and naval officers in addition to royal governors in the colonies; with more and more English mercantile companies setting up branch offices in colonies, from which they regularly received information; with English officials like Williamson and Coventry assiduously developing their correspondence with personal friends and official acquaintances in the colonies; with so much information, indeed, that for the first time two full-time clerks and assistants from the Privy Council office were needed to handle the volume of colonial papers[67]—with all

[66] Osgood, *American Colonies in the Seventeenth Century*, Vol. III, p. 340.

[67] The four clerks of the Privy Council rotated in serving the Committee, and in addition there were two clerks for the Plantations office. Later an extra clerk was appointed (Bieber, *Lords of Trade and Plantations*, p. 43). The importance of these clerks can hardly be overrated. On the lowest level, minor and not-so-minor colonial officials used them as delivery boys, as Randolph used Blathwayt and Commissioner Moryson used a clerk in the Privy Council Office, to see that their mail reached the appropriate offices (Gertrude Jacobsen, *William Blathwayt* (New Haven, Conn., 1933, p. 111); Coventry Papers, MS. 78, f. 48, p. 750). Officials like Blathwayt corresponded directly with colonial officials, sending them news of

these, the government necessarily felt safer about its understanding of colonial politics than it had before.

It was the achievement of Edward Randolph, in particular, to point up to the government that within the New England colonies there was extensive support for reform among certain so-called 'submerged majorities'—the Anglican mercantile community and even some Puritan moderates, and that with patronage and direction these heterogeneous groups might be capable of working with royal officials to put the reforms into effect in the colonies.[68] Thus the government came increasingly to favour the moderates against Puritans in Massachusetts, the proprietary supporters against the pro-Massachusetts leaders in New Hampshire, the New York merchants against the Long Islanders, and the nebulous group of Virginians who favoured Jeffreys and Culpeper against Governor Berkeley's 'Green Springs' faction, and to believe that with help these groups

London, abstracting their reports to the Lords of Trade, and forwarding directives to them (Colonial Williamsburg, Blathwayt MSS., *passim*; Dongan to Blathwayt, 11 Aug. 1685, *N.Y. Col. Docs.*, Vol. III, p. 363). By their patience the secretaries could keep a particular matter before the Lords of Trade or the Secretaries of State and prevent the relevant papers from being lost or neglected. It is hardly surprising, in an age when administrative procedure was still terribly chaotic, and the same report could start out with the Lords of Trade, the Committee on Foreign Plantations, or the King himself, so that even the best informed colonial administrators did not know where to send them, that the secretaries were immensely powerful. It was often up to them whether requests from colonial officials received speedy attention or no effective attention at all. Some governors even thought William Blathwayt could keep them from being dismissed (Dongan to Blathwayt, 2 Mar. 1686 Colonial Williamsburg, Blathwayt MS. XI). Hence the secretaries were known as men whose friendship was worth cultivating. See Stephen Saunders Webb, 'William Blathwayt, Imperial Fixer: From Popish Plot to Glorious Revolution', *W.M.Q.* 3rd Ser. XXV (1968), pp. 3–21.

[68] In 1681, for example, Randolph wrote Secretary Jenkins that every New England colony was divided against itself. He admitted that the extreme Puritans outnumbered the moderates, but added that the moderates were superior in character and estates (30 Apr. 1681, *Cal. S.P. Col. 1674–76*, No. 91). See also Randolph's 'Narrative of the State of New England', July 1670 (ibid., No. 357); '. . . the inhabitants of Massachusetts have been misrepresented by a factious party, being generally desirous to be under the King's government'. See Michael G. Hall, 'Randolph, Dudley, and the Massachusetts Moderates in 1683', *New England Quarterly*, XXVII (1956), pp. 513–16. Possibly another similar argument which influenced the King and the Committees was that King Philip's War had broken up the Confederacy of New England, assuring the government that Massachusetts would no longer be aided actively by Connecticut and Plymouth (see Douglas Edward Leach, *Flintlock and Tomahawk; New England in King Philip's War* (New York, 1958), p. 244 et seq.). As it was, Plymouth and Connecticut offered sympathy, but no help, when the Massachusetts charter was invalidated.

could become powerful and co-operative enough to make colonial reforms effective.

Randolph's interpretation and its acceptance by British officials marked a new approach to colonial politics. In 1676 Randolph wrote Secretary Coventry: 'The Governm[en]t of this Place consists of a Gov[erno]r, 11 Magistrates & a Sec[reta]ry all yearly chosen; most of them are inconsiderable Mechanicks packed by the prevailing party of ye factious Ministry who have a fellow feeling both in the command & Profit.'[69] Later he answered a query from the Lords of Trade and Plantations: '[Some magistrates] with some few others of the same faction keep the country in subjection and slavery.'[70] And shortly after this the Commissioners sent to investigate Bacon's rebellion in Virginia implied that it was basically a rebellion of 'the people' against Sir William Berkeley's faction. Of Berkeley's plan for building forts '. . . the People gave out . . . that it was merely a Design of the Grandees to engrosse all their Tobacco into their own hands'.[71] Of Berkeley's party, only a few stood by him during the rebellion: '. . . the rest (whome the hopes or promise of Plunder brought thither) being now all in hast to be gone to secure what they had gott'.[72]

Taken together, the reports of Randolph and the commissioners gave a new meaning to the idea of faction in the American colonies, and with it a new approach to the rise of party by the British colonial administration. No longer were 'factions' simply the diehard opponents of the local authorities alone; now the oligarchs themselves constituted a faction. No longer were factions composed necessarily of men united on life-and-death issues; by the new definition factions could be held together by the spoils of office. No longer should the British government shore up the colonial oligarchies by forbidding, among several things, royal officials to meddle in local factions: no longer would it risk suicidal unpopularity to encourage the opponents of local oligarchs; now, according to Randolph and the commissioners, the British government should capitalize on, rather than play down, divisions in the

[69] 17 June 1676. Robert Noxon Toppan, *Edward Randolph*, Vol. II (Boston, 1898), p. 206. [70] 11 October, 1676. Ibid. p. 254.
[71] 'A True Narrative of the Late Rebellion in Virginia, by the Royal Commissioners, 1677', in *Narratives of the Insurrections, 1675–1690*, ed. Charles M. Andrews (New York, 1915), p. 108. [72] Ibid. p. 135.

colonies. To tighten the colonial ties with England would be popular; to appoint enemies of the local governors to office would be the beginning of a popular, pro-English, administration. Thus Randolph and the commissioners took an approach to colonial political divisions completely different from that of Clarendon and the Cabal. Doubtless they were influenced by the steadily growing number of colonists hostile to the theocracy in Massachusetts (though there were not yet very many of them), and the surprising extent of Bacon's support in Virginia. They were also influenced by the change in English politics, for they were witnessing the birth of a new form of party struggle in England, quite unknown in the days of Clarendon and the Cabal. In the earlier days a country gentleman's charges of court favouritism to a faction of grandees were met by embarrassed disclaimers of the existence of any faction;[73] by the Earl of Danby's day the existence of a corrupted court faction was beginning to be taken for granted. For Danby's extraordinary creation of a Court Party through royal patronage gave a new emphasis to partisan politics, and contributed to a growing debate on the nature of political parties which could not help influencing both British and American attitudes to colonial parties.[74]

[73] Debate in the House of Commons, 22 Feb. 1672, in *Debates of the House of Commons from the Year 1667 to the Year 1694*, coll. Anchitell Grey, 10 vols., Vol. I (London, 1753), pp. 5, 53. See also, Harris, *Life of Sandwich*, Vol. II, App. G, pp. 315–17; *Cal. S.P. Dom., 1668–69*, pp. 541–2.

[74] See Andrew Browning, 'Parties and Party Organization in the Reign of Charles II', *Transactions of the Royal Historical Society*, 4th Ser. XXX (London, 1948), pp. 21–36, esp. p. 34. Browning discusses Clarendon's Court Party, the 'Court Party' faction of the Cabal, and the political rivalry of Danby and Shaftesbury. See also Browning's biography, *Thomas Osborne, Earl of Danby and Duke of Leeds, 1632–1712*, Vol. I (Glasgow, 1944), p. 173. See also E. S. de Beer, 'Members of the Court Party in the House of Commons, 1670–78', *Bull. Institute Historical Research*, XI, pp. 1–23. Marvell wrote, regarding the King's relationship in the city:

> But a market, they say, does suit the King well
> Who the Parliament buys and revenues does sell
> And others to make the similitude hold;
> Say his Majesty himself is bought, too, and sold.
> ('The Statue in Stocks Market', *The Poems and Letters of Andrew Marvell*, ed. H. M. Margoliouth (Oxford, 1927), Vol. I, p. 129.)

The same theme appears in 'The Statue at Charing Cross', p. 191. The older interpretation by no means died out, but continued in tandem with the new one, and was given new force by the Exclusion crisis, as the writings of court apologists

Thus long before Bolingbroke and the other opponents of Sir Robert Walpole began publicizing similar sentiments the American colonists were already reading charges against corrupt local oligarchies—oligarchies maintained at the expense of the public interest—and these charges were prepared not by opponents of the government but by British colonial administrators themselves. Aware of contemporary developments in British politics, and at the same time attempting to convince their superiors of the need to curb the autonomous powers of the provincial governments, Randolph and the other colonial investigators introduced the idea of the corrupt ruling faction into the colonial vocabulary as early as the Restoration era.

Clearly, however, the Americans did not yet fully accept the idea: the colonists had not yet abandoned the concept of a group of rebels, 'conspirators', or 'agitators'. One can see the ambiguity of their approach in Cotton Mather's various writings. To Mather it was the Massachusetts moderates and their English allies who were the 'Harpies'. But Mather also made a comparison between contemporary political parties and feuding Italian families of the Renaissance. On the one hand, such families differed on no significant principles; they fought only for power, status, and office. On the other hand, they were on occasion perfectly capable of destroying the city-state in their struggles for survival.[75]

Such a comparison showed how well Mather had begun to pick up current English thinking about party. And the colonists were well aware that the new approach to faction was in some measure an English importation.[76] It was but a short step, as early as the 1680s, to look upon corruption itself as an English importation.

On the English side the new ideas were important for their impact on colonial administration. For one thing, in the existing royal colonies the government began investigating far more

---

like Dryden and L'Estrange testify. For the traditional interpretation of party as composed of 'seditious men' see *Mr. Sidney his Self Conviction or, his Dying Paper Condemned to Live, for a Conviction to the Present Faction, and a Caution to Posterity* (London, 1684).

[75] Kenneth B. Murdock, ed., *Selections from Cotton Mather* (New York, 1926), p. 68.

[76] See, for example, *A Memorial between Jest and Earnest*, a London pamphlet reprinted in Philadelphia in 1691.

closely the behaviour of the royal governors and the cliques they supported.

It is not surprising that the Lords of Trade gave considerable thought to the problem of controlling colonial governors. They approached the solution in three ways. First, they began requiring considerably more information from the governors about conditions in their colonies than previous Committees had demanded. In the autumn of 1675 the Committee of Trade sent a circular letter to the governors of royal provinces asking for a report on the laws, offices, defences, and trade of their colonies, and demanding that governors should continue to send over periodically a journal of occurrences.[77] William Blathwayt, secretary to the Committee, sent governors regular gazettes from London and wrote them news; in turn he expected a regular correspondence with each, and forwarded their reports to the Lords of Trade. The government also sent out special investigators—commissioners like Jeffreys, Berry, and Moryson, who went to check on Berkeley in Virginia, and roving reporters like Edmund Randolph and Robert Quarry. Through reports from lesser officials—Blathwayt corresponded, for example, with the Treasurer of Virginia, the Secretary of New Hampshire, and the Secretary of Massachusetts—the Lords of Trade conscientiously tried to check up on the behaviour of governors.

Moreover, the Lords made it clear that they were ready to reward disobedience, greed, or simple incompetence with disciplinary action, in the form of censure, annulment of acts, or dismissal. All of these weapons were used in the aftermath of Bacon's rebellion, for example. Governor Berkeley was dismissed and recalled by the King before the Lords of Trade took up the issue. Once the Lord began to review the rebellion, they recommended that Berkeley's decision to limit the application of the royal pardon to the rebels should be annulled, that the Virginia governor, Council, and Assembly should be censured for passing an Act of Attainder against one of the rebels, that all laws contrary to the King's proclamation of 27 October 1676 should be annulled, and they struck out of the Council members who were complained against by the investigating

---

[77] In 1680 they began demanding that governors should send over journals of their provincial Assemblies along with papers and reports of debates.

commission. In addition, as the government became better informed about patronage possibilities in the colonies, and distrustful of the governors' ability to use them wisely, some councillorships, militia offices, Justiceships of the Peace, Attorney Generalships, and so on began to be distributed from Whitehall, with an eye to developing colonial support.

Some of the revisions in governors' instructions, such as the addition of a requirement that governors should submit nominations for colonial councillorships to Whitehall for approval, must have been developed to this end. When Lord Culpeper's instructions as governor of Virginia were drawn up, for example, they included appointments to the Virginia Council; in making the appointments the Lords of Trade consulted the commissioners sent to Virginia after Bacon's rebellion, and with their advice struck out the names of incumbent councillors who had been too closely associated with Berkeley's failure to cooperate with the commissioners.[78] With the approval of the Lords of Trade, Lord Howard dismissed two Berkeleyites from the positions of Surveyor and Collector and tried to replace them with some of Berkeley's old opponents, or 'Baconians'.[79] When the Massachusetts charter was annulled and an interim Council set up to rule the colony, Edward Randolph nominated the councillors and quite naturally picked moderates like Joseph Dudley. Randolph also submitted nominations for militia officers in Massachusetts, Connecticut, and New Hampshire. And in New Hampshire, which became a royal colony by arrangement with Mason, the new royal governor in 1682, Lionel Cranfield, began building a political machine out of the old proprietary party.[80]

In patronizing those groups of colonists whom they assumed to be most loyal the government was usually building up the weaker, less organized, group in each colony.[81] There already

[78] Thomas J. Wertenbaker, 'Virginia Under the Stuarts, 1607–1688', in *The Shaping of Colonial Virginia* (New York, 1958), p. 216.

[79] See Menk, 'Virginia Parties', op. cit. pp. 41–109. It is not impossible that Danby had something to do with the original repudiation of Berkeley. Berkeley was a friend of Arlington, whom Danby would gladly have undermined in any way he could.

[80] Osgood, *American Colonies in the Seventeenth Century*, Vol. III, pp. 340–57.

[81] Michael G. Hall (*Randolph*, p. 105) disagrees with this conclusion for Massachusetts, for he concludes that the Moderate Party actually disintegrated under the Dominion.

was a strong Puritan faction in Massachusetts, in Connecticut, and in New Hampshire, while the moderates in these colonies were disorganized and hence weak, and Governor Berkeley had built up a powerful 'Green Springs Party' in Virginia by 1675. What the government was doing, therefore, was to even the balance between factions in each of the colonies that came directly under its administration.

The tactic of using patronage to build up loyalist support in some of the colonies was not originally developed by the English Tories to build up Tory support in the colonies although it later came to look that way. The technique as applied to the colonies began not with Danby but with Randolph, the commissioners, and the bi-partisan Lords of Trade; and in the beginning, certainly up to 1682, they were not inclined to look at colonial politics as either Whigs or Tories. The Committee which recommended *quo warranto* proceedings against the Massachusetts charter, for example, was evenly balanced between members of Puritan and Royalist backgrounds and the relevant meetings were attended equally by both groups. The same was true when Governor Berkeley's supporters were struck off the list of Governor Culpeper's Council in 1678. It is true that none of Shaftesbury's close followers were on the Committee until 1679, but there is no definite evidence that when they did get on the Committee they contemplated any effort to slow down the building of loyalist parties in the colonies. Moreover, in 1680, after Shaftesbury and his associates had been turned out of the Committee, the Lords of Trade voted to reinstate Christopher Rousby as Customs Collector of Maryland, even though Rousby was known to be a Shaftesbury supporter and Baltimore's enemy. And one of the members Lord Baltimore counted on most heavily for support was the Earl of Anglesey, staunch friend of Puritans like Mather, who themselves were in sympathy with Shaftesbury.

Clearly, then, the Lords of Trade were thinking not oɪ partisan politics but of both individual friendships and more efficient administration when they began building up the less organized Royalist supporters in the American colonies. But when, after 1682, the Lords of Trade and the British ministers became predominantly Tory, their colonial supporters inevitably became so too. And equally inevitably, as certain colonial leaders found themselves in the political wilderness as a result of royal patronage to rival factions, they came to assume that their only hope lay in a victory of the King's opponents in England, especially the Earl of Shaftesbury and the Duke of Monmouth.

When James inherited the throne in 1685 the desperate Whig leaders joined in a hopeless rebellion to put Charles's illegitimate son, the Duke of Monmouth, on the throne. There is no evidence that either Monmouth or the Earl of Shaftesbury who had directed the Whigs during the Exclusion crisis of 1679–1681, had consciously tried to create any colonial sympathy for the Whig cause. It is true that Shaftesbury's follower Henry Capel tried to obstruct the payment of Governor Culpeper's expenses in Virginia,[82] but this was about the only important thing Capel did, and he and Shaftesbury's other supporters on the Lords of Trade hardly attended the Committee at all. Shaftesbury was chairman of the Carolina proprietors, but even there he did not attempt to sponsor a group of Whig supporters in the colony.

But despite Shaftesbury's and Monmouth's indifference to colonial alliances there was considerable support for the Whig cause in the colonies. In 1681 Randolph urged proceeding against the Massachusetts charter to cut off the correspondence between 'factious parties in old and New England'.[83] In 1683 Increase Mather, one of the foremost Puritan leaders in Massachusetts, wrote to an acquaintance in Holland lamenting the death of 'that Great friend of God's cause the Earl of Shaftesbury' in exile, and the murder of two of his followers, Lords Essex and Russell, in the Tower.[84] Edward Randolph wrote home that the Puritans and even some moderates in New England generally favoured the Whigs in the mother country. And a substantial number of Virginians—probably in the Berkeleyan or 'Green Springs Party', which opposed James's Catholic governor Lord Effingham within the colony—were known to be sympathetic to Monmouth's rebellion.[85] In Mary-

---

[82] Culpeper to Coventry, 28 Dec. 1679, Coventry Papers, 78 f. 430.
[83] Randolph to Sir Leoline Jenkins, 30 Apr. 1681, *Cal. S.P. Col., 1674*, No. 91.
[84] Bodleian MS. Tanner 32, f. 187 (L.C. Transcripts), '3rd of 10th, 1683'. Mather to Mr. Gouge, minister of the English Church in Amsterdam.
[85] 'There were many in the colony who favoured the party of Monmouth as King and when news came that he had risen against James, they were open in

land Lord Baltimore's leading opponent told the colonists that during the Exclusion crisis the King and Parliament were at war; therefore anyone could criticize the proprietor and not be guilty of treason.[86] In May 1679 a rumour swept the colony that it was being said in Bristol, England, that Lord Baltimore was a traitor and Monmouth was the true proprietor of the country.[87]

Thus in the last decade and a half before 1690 British intervention created a new pattern of colonial politics. Everywhere colonists opposed to provincial oligarchies were finding support in Whitehall and London and Fulham Palace. Their personal identification with Englishmen in London and in the colonies, men whose loyalty to the Empire was unquestioned, made it difficult for opponents to brand them seditious. Their picture of British officials as representative of a populace outraged by the self-seeking of the established oligarchies destroyed the older image of the oligarchies themselves standing for the whole community.

The change was rapid and it was overwhelming. For the moment the established colonial governors and governments struggled to hold on to powers and procedures which they claimed by law; the increasing discrepancy between their authority as it existed on paper and the power they actually wielded resulted in a new violence in colonial politics. Over the longer run the association of colonial political leaders with Whig and Tory leaders in England drew attention to the parallel development of political parties on both sides of the Atlantic, and the contribution of English party rivalries to the development of factions in the colonies.

---

their sympathy' (Wertenbaker, *Government of Virginia*, p. 52). The party was led by Beverley and Ludwell. See also *William Fitzhugh and his Chesapeake World*, ed. Richard Beale Davis (Chapel Hill, N.C., 1963), pp. 28-31. Lord Effingham wrote of Monmouth's supporters in Virginia 'that their tongues ran at large and demonstrated the wickedness of their hearts, til I secured some and deterred others from spreading such false reports by my Proclamation' (P.R.O., C.O. 5, 1357-80. Quoted in Wertenbaker, *Virginia Under the Stuarts*, pp. 243-4).

[86] Andrews, *Colonial Period*, Vol. II (Settlements), p. 347, quoting *Maryland Archives*, Vol. XV, pp. 269; Vol. XX, p. xiii.

[87] Ibid. p. 348, quoting *Maryland Archives*, Vol. XV, p. 250.

III 'Create parties in the Commonwealth'

In February 1718 Cotton Mather bemoaned the existence of political parties in Massachusetts. The lamentation began with traditional expressions: 'One of the best Things that can be done for my poor Countrey is, to extinguish as far as tis possible, that cursed, and senseless Party Spirit, which is now among us, in a most abominable Operation. Lett me contrive to do all that I or others can towards the Extinction of so comprehensive a Mischief.' But he went on in terms that would have startled colonists of the Restoration: 'I procure an Interview with a member of the Assembly this Evening on that Intention.'[1] Mather's entry illustrates a combination of attitudes characteristic of colonists and Englishmen in the generation after the accession of William III—a dislike of political parties, but a recognition of their existence as a fact of life, a criticism of party as irrational, but not a fear of it as dangerous. What Mather, like so many of his contemporaries, recognized was that the violence was gone from the politics of the older colonies, at least.

In the Restoration era British attempts to bring the various colonies under tighter imperial administration had been just effective enough to weaken the authority of dominant colonial factions and give legitimacy to the aspirations and organization of their opponents, but not effective enough to settle the real disputes that divided the colonies. The result had been violent divisions within nearly every colony. After 1689 the reins of British administration were tightened, and the result was that the violence of colonial politics began gradually to subside: the

[1] 13 Feb. 1717–18, 'Diary of Cotton Mather, 1709–1724', *Mass. Hist. Soc. Colls.* 7th Ser. VIII (Bóston, 1912), p. 515.

uncompromisable local issues that had driven colonial communities to war were drawn off to imperial settlement, leaving colonial politics a matter of spoils and interests rather than tenaciously-held beliefs. The eyes of colonial politicians came to focus increasingly on London rather than the provincial capital, as the local oligarchs were drawn into the orbit of imperial politics; the explosive disputes between or within colonial communities came to be replaced by the far less tempestuous manœuvring of colonial factions for imperial favours and connections useful in local politics.

The most noticeable change was in the question of appeals to England. Previously colonial minorities had found it difficult to appeal to England against local decisions, partly because they could not get their side heard there, and partly because British politicians had been reluctant to take time to consider colonial appeals. Now, however, colonial politicians found it increasingly easy to meet English connections willing to bring their case before Parliament or Whitehall: now, with better information, better apparatus for considering colonial problems, and a greater interest in colonial affairs, English politicians were willing to spend increasing amounts of time on colonial disputes.

In the year after the Revolution, for example, a substantial number of M.P.s showed that they were willing to take up a colonial issue formerly left without question to the King, when they introduced and passed a motion to restore the New England corporations to their status in 1660. The motion was thrown out by the House of Lords; moreover, Parliament also declined a chance to state its colonial authority categorically, by excluding mention of the colonies from the Declaration of Right, and refusing to enact as parliamentary law some royal Orders in Council on master–servant contracts which applied to the colonies. But, taken together, the action in one case and inaction in others showed that Parliament would be willing to consider the possibility of acting upon colonial questions one by one as they arose.

When Parliament did not choose to act upon a colonial appeal, the Board of Trade, established in 1697, the Privy Council, the leading ministers, or the monarch himself might do so, and while William and Anne were less interested personally in the colonies than their predecessors had been,[2] the ministers and lesser officials who served them were immensely ambitious to obtain power over colonial affairs. Ostensibly most of the colonial problems could be handled by the Board of Trade, a small workable group (seven members) of gifted people who would—unlike the old Committee of Trade— become colonial experts and make the Board a clearing house for colonial problems.[3] But in addition a growing number of ministers were also eager to influence colonial appointments or handle other colonial affairs in their own departments. Somers, Halifax, Stamford, Addison, Sunderland, Scarborough, and possibly Marlborough and Argyle among the Whigs, and Nottingham, Leeds, Weymouth, Pembroke, Somerset, Rochester, Cutts, Orrery, and William Blathwayt among the Tories, were all interested in colonial affairs. And two sets of officers in particular—the Secretaries of State and the First Lords of the Treasury—emerged as more powerful than the others, and inevitably began to expand their own authority over colonial

[2] Advised by one or another of his English administrators, particularly by his Secretaries of State, William did at times intervene personally in the affairs of one of the colonies. He made the final decision on some disputed provisions of the new Massachusetts charter, granting the royal governors power to appoint judges and approve the election of councillors. He allowed Mather to nominate the first royal governor for Massachusetts. William once vetoed a nominee for the governorship of Maryland as incompetent. He personally advocated putting Pennsylvania under the administration of New York in 1692. And he himself appointed the first Board of Trade, though the idea of having such a Board was not his. But these were merely random interventions; in general, William's interest in the colonies was not nearly as great as James II's had been, nor as great as the interest William himself had in foreign affairs. He knew every British ambassador to the Continent personally, for example, something which certainly could not be said for the colonial governors.

What was true for William was even more so for Anne. Like William, she left the nomination of most of the colonial governors to her ministers, and Anne even let the ministers nominate the Board of Trade. Once in a while she took a hand in appointments (she appointed Robert Hunter governor of Jamaica, before he finally went to New York in 1709), and once in a while a particular issue, like the appointment of a bishop for the colonies or the arrangements of a military mission, caught her interest. But more often Anne was happy to leave colonial affairs to any ministers who were interested in them.

See *Cal. S.P. Col., 1689–92*, Nos. 1500, 1570, 1574, 1596, 1606, 1631, 1650, 1665, 1669–70, 1675, 1705, 1706, 1710, 1724, 1758, 1769; Jacobsen, *Blathwayt*, p. 309; Charles Worthen Spencer, *Phases of Royal Government in New York, 1691–1709* (Columbus, Ohio, 1905), pp. 14–18.

[3] See I. K. Steele, *Politics of Colonial Policy: The Board of Trade in Colonial Administration, 1696–1720* (Oxford, 1968).

administration. Both Godolphin at the Treasury and Sunderland as Southern Secretary, 1706–10, were typical administrative empire-builders, who wanted to add colonial affairs to their jurisdiction.[4] Moreover, the cabinet itself, just evolving from 1689 to 1715, discussed questions concerning colonial defence and proprietary charters.

What all this added up to was that the monarchs, M.P.s, ministers, and members of the Board of Trade could and did take up colonial affairs, and that all of them, with the exception of the monarchs, were more capable and more interested in colonial problems than they had ever been before.

As a result some of the powerfully divisive colonial issues were handled quickly across the ocean, and eventually removed from the forefront of colonial politics. The obviously vindictive exclusion of Dissenters from the South Carolina Assembly and the confiscation of Leislerian estates in New York were disallowed. The question of the Massachusetts charter was settled by the issuing of a new charter within two years of the Revolution.[5]

Other major issues, and particularly the old ones of proprietary rights and the new one of paper money, were not worked out at all before 1715. The lines of authority in England were unclear, decisions by one board or minister might be appealed to another, colonial agents who feared adverse decisions could stall almost indefinitely by failing to produce evidence, and ministers caught between the conflicting pressures of British and colonial interests would hesitate to offend either by producing definitive decisions. But the fact that the

---

[4] Dora Mae Clark, *The Rise of the British Treasury: Colonial Administration in the Eighteenth Century* (New Haven, Conn., 1960), p. 4. The Board had to request Sunderland to keep them informed of his decisions about the colonies; *Cal. S.P. Col., 1706–8*, No. 1067. They also criticized Sunderland for holding up decisions on some of their recommendations (ibid., *1709–10*, No. 294).

[5] The most important issue was the establishment of reasonably strong, freely elected Assemblies, for only in an Assembly with a reasonable amount of independence and authority would safe and legal opposition to the governor be possible, and the violent, extra-legal proceedings of Restoration politics be reduced. Decisions by the British government immediately after the Glorious Revolution, and proprietary concessions in the decade or so following, generally insured the recognition of responsible Assemblies. On religious questions see the interesting interpretation of Timothy L. Smith, 'Congregation, State, and Denomination: The Forming of the American Religious Structure', *W.M.Q.* 3rd Ser. XXV (Apr. 1968), p. 176.

issues were not settled now (or ever, as in the case of the Elizabethtown proprietors) did not affect the importance of moving the issues to England. The very process of appealing to an authority that was far away (and slow to act) took some of the immediacy out of local issues.

The issues themselves often remained as the basis of partisan politics, giving colonial parties more constant and consistent sources of difference than had Whigs and Tories in England, but the sting was taken out of them. It is hardly a coincidence that the issue of religious toleration, which was essentially settled in England, and hence in the colonies, by 1715, ceased to be the basis of most factional disputes in the colonies after that, but the proprietary and monetary issues, which were handled but never settled in England, were in fact the basis of many local partisan divisions.

The removal of life-and-death issues from the immediate sphere of colonial politics made way for the common acceptance of legislation passed by the colonial Assemblies; it also made way for the rise of a new type of political division within the Assembly, a division over patronage and profit which joined, if it never fully replaced, the division over issues. On the one hand, the colonial assemblymen ceased to be the spokesmen for rough groups of settlers whose way of life was at stake, and became instead the local aristocrats to whom patronage and profits in the governors' command were particularly attractive; on the other hand, the governors, lacking either a strongly partisan majority in the Assembly or the resources to do without an Assembly altogether, found themselves after 1689 having to bargain with assemblymen in order to get support for their administration. As a result, colonial factions were shaped by the changing relationship of the governors to the Assemblies.

The new breed of politician who appeared after 1689 in many of the colonies was a man whose wealth was beginning to set him apart from his neighbours, to give him local influence, to make him aware of countless possibilities for investment in his growing colony, and aware that the best way to tap these possibilities and enhance his social and political prestige was to get into the Assembly. In Virginia he had already appeared during the Restoration; there were about fifty planters like Byrd, Beverley, or Ludwell by the time of the Glorious Revolution.

In South Carolina, families like the Bulls were making their fortunes only towards the end of Queen Anne's reign; the North Carolina aristocracy developed even later. But in most of the colonies the leading families in early-eighteenth-century politics were getting their start in the quarter century after 1689: the Belchers, Wentworths, Waldrons, Sherburnes, Livingstons, de Lanceys, Carrolls, Dulaneys, and the like were making their fortunes at the turn of the eighteenth century. Just below these magnates were lesser merchants and planters, whose fortunes, already sufficient to give them considerable local standing, were also rising in this period.

In part the new aristocrat went into politics because he was genuinely concerned about certain issues facing the colony. But he also went in to protect and enlarge his estate, to develop his control of local offices, to enhance his local prestige, and perhaps to join the charmed circle of the provincial governor. Active participation in the Assembly might, for example, head off attempts to regulate the quality of his tobacco for export, or move the county courthouse away from his home town; it might get a warehouse or a wharf built near his farm or his business, it might also let the assemblyman get to know the governor, and through him to get patents for undeveloped lands and appointments to local offices.

Individually, the assemblyman was out for local patronage; together, in groups of friends and relatives, the assemblymen were out to get the chief political plums—the provincial offices which carried extensive patronage, control of the courts, or money-lending opportunities—for one of their group. Whether one of their friends got a militia commission or was made Justice of the Peace they did not much care; but whether he became provincial secretary (with as much patronage as the governor in some colonies), Speaker of the House and provincial treasurer (offices often combined), with great opportunities for surreptitious money-lending, or Chief Justice (with the determination of the most important provincial lawsuits), was a matter of paramount importance.[6] Secretaries and Chief Justices were appointed in England, but the governor could

---

[6] In Virginia the chief plums were the posts of Secretary, Receiver General, and Deputy Auditor. See Dodson, *Spotswood*, p. 158. The Deputy Auditor (appointed by the Auditor General of the Plantations) was also an important colonial officer.

make nominations; Speakers were chosen by the Assemblies, with the concurrence of the governor; and treasurers also came increasingly to be chosen in the same way. If a governor vetoed the Assembly's choice of one of their friends for a major office, or if he refused to make the desired nomination, the connection might consider an appeal to England. If he consistently blocked their private applications for grants, they might think of holding up revenue for a year. Little by little they would, like the anti-Leislerian faction under Bellomont, begin meeting together in taverns or homes during, and even between, sessions of the Assembly, planning measures to whittle away the governor's prerogative or unseat him by an appeal to home. If the faction found itself just short of a majority in the Assembly, they would look for an issue on which they could propose expanding the Assembly's power at the expense of the governor, and hence appeal to the uncommitted members of the Assembly.

If, however, the governor did support their application, they would be inclined to support him on the most important, though by no means all, issues before the Assembly. And a clever governor or governor's manager could build up quite a strong governor's party in the Assembly.

Thus, in all but Connecticut and Rhode Island, the crucial liaison between English and provincial politics was the governor. It was his job, by a judicious distribution of favours among family, religious, or old factional groupings, to create a 'court' party, which would serve at least to vote the revenue for his administration. In colonies like New York[7] and New Hampshire,[8] where the Leislerian and Massachusetts issues died hard, governors had the sturdy remains of pre-1689 factions to play

[7] Spencer, *Phases of Royal Government, passim*; Jerome Reich, *Leisler's Rebellion: A Study of Democracy in New York, 1664–1720* (Chicago, 1953), p. 128 et seq.; Lawrence H. Leder, *Robert Livingston, 1694–1728, and the Politics of Colonial New York* (Chapel Hill, N.C., 1961), pp. 57–240, *passim*; O'Callaghan, *New York Colonial Documents*, Vols. IV–VI; *Journal of the Votes and Proceedings of the General Assembly of the Colony of New York* (2 vols., New York, 1764–6); *Journal of the Legislative Council of the Colony of New York* (2 vols., Albany, 1861); Champante Papers, Bodleian MS. Rawl. A. 272; B.M. Add. MS. 15895, ff. 39–40; 349; C.O. 5/1047–1050.

[8] New Hampshire divisions can be followed in Nathaniel Bouton, ed., *Province Papers of New Hampshire*, II, vols. 1–3 (Manchester, N.H., 1868–89). For this period the secondary sources remain Jeremy Belknap, *The History of New Hampshire*, Vol. II, 2nd edn. (Boston, 1813); and William Henry Fry, *New Hampshire as a Royal Province* (New York, 1908).

off against each other. In Pennsylvania the kaleidoscopic divisions among the proprietary clique, the urban and rural Anglicans, the Quakers and the Turnerians, meant that governors, using the proprietary clique as an ever narrowing base, had to create coalitions from among the other factions;[9] New Jersey governors bargained mainly with the West Jersey Society proprietors and the Quakers, and left them to create their own coalitions from among the East Jersey Society proprietors, the Monmouth settlers, and independents.[10]

In Maryland and Massachusetts the sudden removal of the most crucial issues of the eighties—the proprietorship in one (Maryland was administered as a royal province in the quarter century after 1689) and the charter in the other—temporarily disoriented politics, and left individuals, rather than issues, the key to political factions. In both colonies the old oligarchies functioned as factions into the new reign: Elisha Cooke took some of the old political leaders with him in Massachusetts, and 'the friends of Lord Baltimore' were still considered a force in Maryland, even when the colony had a royal governor.[11] In these colonies particularly it was up to the governors to build

[9] For an excellent discussion of Pennsylvania politics in this period see Gary B. Nash, *Quakers and Politics: Pennsylvania, 1681–1726* (Princeton, N.J., 1968). It is possible to gain some idea of the shifting majorities in the Pennsylvania Assembly from Gertrude MacKinney, ed., *Pennsylvania Archives*, 8th Ser. II (Philadelphia, 1931); see also Roy N. Lokken, *David Lloyd, Colonial Lawmaker* (Seattle, Wash., 1959), pp. 27–162; and 'Correspondence between William Penn and James Logan', ed. Edward Armstrong, *Memoirs of the Historical Society of Pennsylvania*, IX–X (Philadelphia, 1872).

[10] Richard P. McCormick, *New Jersey from Colony to State* (New York, 1965), pp. 64–5, *The History of Voting in New Jersey, a Study in the Development of Election Machinery, 1664–1911* (New Brunswick, N.J., 1953), pp. 37–42, and 'The Province of East Jersey, 1609–1702', *Procs. N.J. Hist. Soc.* LXX (1952), pp. 81–96; Gordon B. Turner, 'Colonial New Jersey, 1703–1763', *Procs. N.J. Hist. Soc.* LXX (1952), pp. 229–45; John E. Pomfret, *The Province of East New Jersey, 1609–1702, the Rebellious Proprietary* (Princeton, N.J., 1962), pp. 276–331, and *The Province of West New Jersey, 1609–1702* (Princeton, 1956), *passim*; Russell E. Frances, 'Proprietary West New Jersey, 1674–1702', *Procs. N.J. Hist. Soc.* LXX (1952), pp. 163–72.

See also William W. Whitehead, ed., *Documents Relating to the Colonial History of the State of New Jersey*, 1st Ser. III, IV, XIII (Newark and Trenton, N.J., 1881–1890); *Journals of the Governor and Council of New Jersey*, Vol. I (Trenton, N.J., 1890); Sonmans to Dockwra, 10 Feb. 1710/11, 27 Mar. 1711, 30 May 1711, B.M. Add. MS. 14034, ff. 118–19, 135–42; C.O. 5/969/70.

[11] A list of Baltimore's friends is in the Bray MSS., Sion College. On 10 June 1707 Governor Seymour wrote the Board of Trade that the Assembly was 'wholy buoyed up by a gainsaying and restless party', and on 10 Mar. of the following year he complained that 'Baltimore's land interest continued to influence many

their own parties; a reasonably strong governor like Dudley or Hart could build up an effective, if temporary, personal party.[12] Only in North Carolina and Virginia did some form of 'court' party and 'country' party fail to appear. North Carolina, with the rival Assemblies of Glover and Cary, and the continuation of fundamental religious differences leading to civil war in 1710, had not emerged from the primitive stage of Restoration politics.[13] Virginia, with an established aristocracy fairly uniform in its outlook on economics and religion, proved to be a colony in which it was impossible for governors to create a court party. Nicholson, Andros, and Spotswood in turn found that there was no basis for one outside the oligarchy which dominated the country anyway.[14] Nicholson first tried a

---

assembly men.' William Hand Browne, ed., 'Proceedings of the Council of Maryland', *Archives of Maryland*, Vol. XXIII (Baltimore, Md., 1905). See also J. Thomas Scharf, *History of Maryland*, 3 vols., Vol. I (Baltimore, Md., 1879), Ch. XIII; Matthew Page Andrews, *History of Maryland: Province and State* (Garden City, N.Y., 1929), pp. 192–220; Charles B. Clark, 'The Career of John Seymour, Governor of Maryland', *Md. Hist. Mag.*, XLVIII (1953), pp. 134–159; Steiner, ed., 'Unpublished Manuscripts from Fulham Palace', ibid. XII (1917), pp. 115–41; William Hand Browne, ed., 'Proceedings and Acts of the General Assembly of Maryland', *Archives of Maryland*, Vols. XIX, XXI, XXIV, XXVI, XXVII, XXIX (Assembly) (Baltimore, Md., 1899–1909).

[12] See Perry Miller, *The New England Mind from Colony to Province* (Cambridge, Mass., 1953), pp. 164–371 *passim*, esp. p. 175. An excellent study of Massachusetts politics as they related to the agency is Charles L. Sanford, 'The Days of Jeremy Dummer, Colonial Agent' (unpublished Ph.D. thesis, Harvard University, 1952). William De Witt Metz, 'Politics and Finance in Massachusetts' (unpublished Ph.D. thesis, Wisconsin University, 1945), deals mainly with a later period, but the first 125 pages cover the period from the Glorious Revolution to 1715. See also 'Diary of Samuel Sewall, 1674–1729', *Colls. Mass. Hist. Soc.* 5th Ser. V (Boston, 1878), pp. 245 et seq.; 'Letter Book of Samuel Sewall', ibid. 6th Ser. I; Everett Kimball, *The Public Life of Joseph Dudley* (New York, 1911), Ch. X; Thomas Hutchinson, *The History of the Province of Massachusetts Bay*, Vol. II (London, 1767), *passim*; Cotton Mather to Lord Hatton, 26 Nov. 1703, and Increase Mather to Lord Nottingham, 6 Dec. 1703, B.M. Add. MS. 29549, ff. 109, 111; Belknap Papers, F. L. Gay MSS. and Miscellaneous Bound MSS., Mass. Hist. Soc.; C.O. 5/855–66 cover Massachusetts and New Hampshire.

[13] Hugh Talmadge Lefler and Albert Ray Newsom, *The History of a Southern State: North Carolina*, rev. edn. (Chapel Hill, N.C., 1963), pp. 53–6; Alonzo Thomas Dill, Jr., 'Eighteenth-Century New Bern: A History of the Town and Craven County, 1700–1800', Part III, 'Rebellion and Indian Warfare', *N.C. Hist. Rev.* XXII (1945), pp. 295–7.

[14] The most reliable interpretation is still David Alan Williams, 'Political Alignments in Colonial Virginia Politics, 1698–1750' (unpublished Ph.D. thesis, Northwestern University, 1959), pp. 1–208, *passim*; see also H. R. McIlwaine, ed., *Executive Journals of the Council of Colonial Virginia*, Vol. II (Richmond, 1927), and Vol. III (Richmond, 1932), *passim*. For Nicholson's quarrel with The Virginia

popular appeal, which simply antagonized the aristocracy; when he, and later Spotswood, tried to build up support among the aristocracy by developing their own aristocratic clique in opposition to the Blair–Ludwell 'core', they soon discovered that men like Robert Carter could be won for a session, but sooner or later would be lured back by the more enduring charms of the Ludwell group. Against the clique, with their combination of provincial influence and influence at the Virginia Coffee House in London, which controlled the important offices, the governors could create no stable base. When Spotswood tried still another device—creating forty tobacco inspectorships in the House of Burgesses—he ran up against the successful opposition of the aristocracy. Never did these governors succeed in breaking into the planter oligarchy.

And so, except for Virginia and North Carolina, the governors usually came to associate with particular factions in the colonies. But they also owed their appointment to political patrons in Britain and the Whig or Tory parties with which they associated. Thus they became liaisons between parties in England and the colonies,[15] serving further to tighten colonial associations with the mother country.

With a few notable exceptions like Lord Cornbury, who was appointed in New York in 1702, the colonial governors were

Council see also Louis B. Wright, 'William Byrd's Opposition to Governor Francis Nicholson', *Journal of Southern History*, XI (1945), pp. 68–79. For Spotswood see Leonidas Dodson, *Alexander Spotswood, Governor of Colonial Virginia, 1710–1722* (Philadelphia, Pa., 1932), 'The Official Letters of Alexander Spotswood', *Collections of the Virginia Historical Society*, N.S. I, II (Richmond, Va., 1882–5); and Jack P. Greene, 'The Opposition to Lieutenant Governor Spotswood, 1718', *Va. Mag. Hist. & Biog.* LXX (1962), pp. 35–42. N. Spencer to Lords of the Privy Council, 29 Apr. 1689, 'Letters, 1689–1846', *Va. Mag. Hist. & Biog.* XXII (1914), pp. 269–70.

[15] For varying interpretations of English parties in this period see Robert Walcott, Jr., *English Politics in the Early Eighteenth Century* (Cambridge, Mass., 1956); Keith Graham Feiling, *A History of the Tory Party, 1640–1714* (Oxford, 1924); and William Thomas Morgan, *English Political Parties and Leaders in the Reign of Queen Anne, 1702–10* (New Haven, Conn., 1920); James Olin Richards, 'English Parliamentary Elections and Party Propaganda in the Early Eighteenth Century' (unpublished Ph.D. thesis, University of Illinois, 1962), *passim*; and Robert Walcott, 'The Idea of Party in the Writing of Later Stuart History', *Jour. Br. Studies*, No. 2 (May 1962), pp. 60–1.

Walcott attacks Feiling's interpretations, and is in turn attacked by J. H. Plumb, *The Growth of Political Stability in England, 1675–1725* (London, 1967), and Geoffrey S. Holmes, *British Politics in the Age of Anne* (New York, 1967). See also Dennis Rubini, *Court and Country, 1688–1702* (London, 1967).

third-rank followers of British politicians.[16] They were not necessarily political followers or even politically-minded men: they belonged in that group of 'connections' which included relatives, friends, neighbours, military subordinates, and intellectual associates of political leaders. Governor Dudley, for example, was a relative of Lord Cutts; Governors Hunter of New York and Spotswood of Virginia were military officers who served under Lord Orkney. They were appointed when their patron had influence with the government or was actually in the government. And since certain leaders within each party were more interested in colonial affairs than their associates, it was their supporters who tended to get the colonial offices. Among the Whigs were Somers, Halifax, Stamford, Addison, Sunderland, Scarborough, and possibly Marlborough and Argyle; among the Tories were Nottingham, Leeds, Weymouth, Pembroke, Somerset, Rochester, Cutts, Orrery, and, of course, William Blathwayt. As Whigs and Tories alternated in office, patrons associated with the party in power were alert for colonial openings where they could press the claims of their candidates. With few exceptions, therefore, colonial governors represented the political persuasion of the party in power at the time they were appointed.

In the mixed ministry of 1689–90 William Phips, urged by the Whig Lord Wharton,[17] and Lionel Copley, apparently supported by the Whig leader Lord Somers, were appointed to the governorships of Massachusetts and Maryland. In addition Francis Nicholson, at that time under the patronage of Nottingham and Leeds, both Tories, was given Virginia.[18] As the government became more and more Tory between 1692 and 1694, Sir Edmund Andros, backed by Leeds, Nottingham, and Blathwayt, received the governorship of Virginia (Nicholson was transferred to Maryland),[19] Benjamin Fletcher, through

[16] On this, see Evarts Boutell Greene, *The Provincial Governor in the English Colonies of North America* (New York, 1898), pp. 46–7; Leonard W. Labaree, 'The Early Careers of the Royal Governors', in *Essays in Colonial History presented to Charles McLean Andrews* (London, 1931).

[17] Phips was originally suggested by Mather, who was receiving help from Wharton and Devonshire (Kenneth Ballard Murdock, *Increase Mather, the Foremost American Puritan* (Cambridge, England, 1925), Chs. XIV and XV).

[18] Jacobsen, *Blathwayt*, p. 142.

[19] John Oldmixon, *The British Empire in America*, Vol. I, 2nd edn. (London, 1741), p. 396; Jacobsen, *Blathwayt*, p. 142.

Sir Robert Southwell, Nottingham, Blathwayt, and the Earl of Athlone,[20] was appointed governor of New York and Pennsylvania, and Samuel Allen, through Blathwayt, was allowed, as claimant to proprietary rights, to be governor of New Hampshire, with John Usher as his deputy.[21]

When the Whig Junto came to predominate in 1694–8, many of these appointments were reversed. In Virginia Andros was replaced by Nicholson, but this time Nicholson, who had been thoroughly annoyed with the Tories in 1692 for sending Andros to supersede him, got his job from Whig patrons—Locke and the Bishop of London in particular.[22] Fletcher was replaced as governor of New York by Bellomont, a friend of all the Junto Lords,[23] who was also given the governorship of Massachusetts and New Hampshire (in New Hampshire Richard Partridge, put forth by the Whig Sir Henry Ashurst,[24] replaced Usher as lieutenant-governor). Nathaniel Blakiston, supported by the Earl of Scarborough, replaced Nicholson in Maryland.[25] The new appointees and their patrons were Whigs.

Again, during the increasingly Tory period of William's last years, and during Anne's first Tory ministry, Nicholson was replaced by Edward Nott. Blakiston retired and was succeeded by John Seymour, brother of Sir Edward Seymour and the Duke of Somerset. Bellomont died, and was ultimately succeeded in New York by Lord Cornbury, son of the Earl of Clarendon (New Jersey, newly under royal administration, was also put under Cornbury's jurisdiction). In Massachusetts Bellomont was succeeded by Joseph Dudley, patronized by

[20] Jacobsen, *Blathwayt*, p. 312.

[21] George H. Guttridge, *The Colonial Policy of William III in America and the West Indies* (Cambridge, England, 1922), p. 125.

[22] Nicholson wrote, 'I think . . . I [was] kicked . . . out of Virginia . . . by my Lord Nottingham and it is much wondered at in these parts of the world that Sir Edmund Andros and Colonel Fletcher should keep their governments, when they came in upon such interest' (Jacobsen, *Blathwayt*, pp. 307–8). See also Blair to Locke, 20 Jan. 1697/98, 8 Feb. 1698/99, Locke MS. C. 4, ff. 8–11; Carpenter, *The Protestant Bishop*, p. 266.

[23] See Spencer, *Phases of Royal Government*, pp. 18–22; J. A. Doyle, *The English in America: The Puritan Colonies*, 2 vols., Vol. II (London, 1887), p. 430; G. P. R. James, ed., *The Shrewsbury Correspondence: Letters Illustrative of the Reign of William III from 1696 to 1708*, 3 vols., Vol. I (London, 1841), p. 239; O'Callaghan, *New York Colonial Documents*, Vol. IV, pp. 259–61; Bellomont to Locke, 26 and 29 May, Locke MS. C. 7, ff. 128, 130.

[24] Doyle, *The Puritan Colonies*, Vol. II, p. 426.

[25] Jacobsen, *Blathwayt*, 309n.

Lord Cutts,[26] with Usher again lieutenant-governor of New Hampshire. William Penn, trying to win support from the Tory ministers, appointed John Evans, who was soon to become a close friend of Cornbury's,[27] governor of Pennsylvania; the proprietors of the Carolinas, who had been predominantly Whig in the previous decade, and had appointed a series of Dissenter governors, now became, by a gradual change in membership, largely Tory, and appointed as governor in 1702 the Tory Nathaniel Johnson.[28]

Finally, when the Marlborough–Godolphin ministry became Whig in 1706, Robert Hunter, supported by Marlborough, Addison, Argyle, and Somers,[29] replaced Cornbury in New York and the Jerseys, Alexander Spotswood went to Virginia as deputy for Orkney,[30] William Gookin replaced Evans in Pennsylvania, and the Carolina proprietors, once again predominantly Whig, recalled Johnson and let the council of deputies rule the colony for a while. In 1712 they finally sent one of their own members, Charles Craven, to govern the province. Craven was the only new governor appointed to the American mainland colonies before Queen Anne's death in 1714.

Even if the governor had no experience in the colonies he would still probably incline to one party before he left England.

---

[26] Hutchinson (*History of Massachusetts Bay*, Vol. II, 64n.) says that Dudley applied to Leeds, Sidney, Blathwayt, and Cutts for support. Kimball (*Joseph Dudley*, pp. 174–5, 180) includes the Bishop of London among Dudley's supporters.

[27] James Logan to Penn, 24 July 1708, *Memoirs of the Historical Society of Pennsylvania*, Vol. X, p. 277.

[28] McCrady, *History of South Carolina*, p. 389. In this period North and South Carolina were under the same administration, but the governor often lived in South Carolina and appointed a deputy of his own political persuasion for North Carolina. Samuel A'Court Ashe, *History of North Carolina*, 2 vols., Vol. II (Greensboro, N.C., 1908), Chs. XII–XV; Sirmans, *Colonial South Carolina*, Chs. IV, V.

[29] Peter Smithers, *The Life of Joseph Addison* (Oxford, 1954), pp. 298, 379; Jordan D. Fiore, 'Jonathan Swift and the American Episcopate', *W.M.Q.* 3rd Ser. XI (Oct. 1954), pp. 425, 426–33; Spencer, *Royal Government in New York*, pp. 22–3; Samuel Bustall to his wife, 1 Nov. 1716, *New Jersey Archives*, 1st Ser. IV, pp. 262–4; Hunter had earlier been rumoured as governor of Massachusetts to succeed Dudley (25 Mar. 1707, Narcissus Luttrell, *A Brief Historical Relation of State Affairs*, Vol. II (Oxford, 1857), p. 152) and had actually been appointed governor of Virginia, though he was captured by the French on his way to the colony and never took over its administration.

[30] Spotswood was well acquainted with Blakiston and Popple, and through them may have come to know more influential Whig politicians. Like Hunter and Orkney (the governor of Virginia) he had served as one of Marlborough's officers (Dodson, *Alexander Spotswood*, Ch. VII).

Since the governors were rarely politicians themselves, they probably did not support Whig or Tory principles as such, nor did they consider themselves Whigs or Tories. On the other hand, the fact that it was clearly in their interest to have their patron remain in a position of influence meant that they did have some stake in English party struggles.

Generally the governors knew very little about colonial policies before they were appointed to office. One or two 'professional' governors, like Nicholson, had formed opinions about factions in their colony from some previous experience in another colony (Nicholson, who had been lieutenant-governor of New York during that colony's rebellion of 1689, deserted Coode's faction in Maryland because they, too, had been rebels in that year).[31] And when colonists themselves were appointed governors, like Phips and Dudley of Massachusetts and most of the governors of the Carolinas, they often had a previous association with one faction or group, and of course proprietary governors would generally, but not always, depend on the support of their faction. The rest of the governors, however, were not very well informed.

Knowing this, leading colonial politicians and their friends in England would assiduously begin to court a new gubernatorial appointee before he left England. Provincial leaders would send him letters of compliment. The colonial agents would probably be at the new governor's doorstep the very day his appointment was announced. Richard Partridge, for example, was almost certainly influenced against Usher's party in New Hampshire by his conversations in London with Sir Henry Ashurst,[32] and few agents worked harder than John Champante did in his efforts on behalf of the Leislerians to soften up Robert Hunter before he went to New York.[33]

Moreover the agents tried to make sure the governor met the 'right' people upon first landing in his colony. Jeremiah Dummer, for example, a supporter of former Governor Dudley, made arrangements for Governor Shute to stay at Paul Dudley's house his first night in Massachusetts.

[31] Bernard C. Steiner, ed., 'Unpublished Manuscripts from Fulham Palace', *Md. Hist. Mag.* XII (1917), pp. 122–3.

[32] See Marguerite Appleton, 'Richard Patridge, Colonial Agent', *New England Quarterly*, V (1932), p. 294.

[33] Champante to Hunter (Nov. 1710), Bodleian MS. Rawl. A. 272, ff. 261–4.

Then, too, roving officials, like Robert Quarry, with experience in several colonies might call upon a new governor if they happened to have an interest in the colony to which he was appointed. So there were many pressures on a governor to align himself with particular political groups before, or at least soon after, his arrival in the colony. The incautious governor might rush into an arrangement and later change his mind; ordinarily the governor would wait as long as he could before committing himself. He might hold out a long time, as Spotswood did, in a colony where there were neither divisive issues nor intense family feuds, but sooner or later he would find himself having to build support for his administration in the midst of factional differences where he had to take a stand, or in the midst of demands from a faction with which he could not comply by reason of his instructions.

Just how the uncommitted governor made up his mind is not always easy to tell. But unless he had a very short term he found himself working with one faction or another. In some colonies the fact that the governor built up one provincial faction and was in turn supported by a faction back home made no difference to the colonists' approach to English politics. This was true in Virginia, where Governor Nicholson's opponents appealed home to the Tories and a few years later were using their personal connections with Whigs to get local offices. It was slightly less true in the proprietary colonies. But in the other colonies the transatlantic political connections of the governors tended to reinforce the connections suggested by the colonial agents: the factions which were to be supported by 'Whig' governors tended also to be those whose agents sought help mainly in Whig circles.

In Massachusetts Governor Phips, patronized by Lord Wharton, gave his patronage to the 'old charter' party who had received Whig support in their efforts to get their charter back. So did Governor Bellomont, whose patrons were Whigs; but Joseph Dudley, a Tory who had been a moderate in Massachusetts before he entered English politics, was supported by his old friends in an essentially personal party throughout his administration.[34] In New York the Whigs

[34] 'Diary of Samuel Sewall, 1674–1729', *Colls. Mass. Hist. Soc.* 5th Ser. V

Bellomont, Nanfan, and Hunter allied with the Leislerian party; the anti-Leislerians supported Ingoldesby, Fletcher, and Cornbury.[35] After the Jerseys were taken over by the royal government in 1702 they were placed under the governor of New York: the Basse party supported Cornbury, the Hamilton party, Hunter.[36]

Maryland politics were similarly consistent, until 1702. The Whig-oriented Coode party supported John Copley and Blakiston and opposed Nicholson. But their position briefly changed with the arrival of John Seymour. Seymour's connections were undoubtedly 'high Tory', yet in the beginning of his administration the governor seems to have had the support of Coode's party—partly because he managed to win the recommendation of Blakiston, partly because he strenuously opposed the financial claims of Sir Thomas Laurence. By 1706, however, Seymour seems to have broken with Coode's party. Much to the anger of 'a malitious faction' he moved the capital of Maryland from St. Mary's, which apparently was convenient to the Coode faction, to Annapolis, which was far more satisfactory to Lawrence's party.[37]

(Boston, 1878), p. 245 et seq.; 'Letter Book of Samuel Sewall', ibid. 6th Ser. I; Kimball, *Joseph Dudley*, Ch. X; Hutchinson. *History of Massachusetts*, Vol. II, *passim*; Cotton Mather to Lord Hatton, 26 Nov. 1703, and Increase Mather to Lord Nottingham, 6 Dec. 1703, B.M. Add. MS. 29549, ff. 109, 111; Belknap Papers, F. L. Gay MSS. and Miscellaneous Bound MSS. Mass. Hist. Soc.; C.O. 5/855–66 cover Massachusetts and New Hampshire.

[35] Spencer, *Phases of Royal Government, passim*; Reich, in *Leisler's Rebellion*, p. 128 et seq.; Leder, *Robert Livingston*, pp. 57–240, *passim*; O'Callaghan, *New York Colonial Documents*, Vols. IV–VI; *Journal of the Votes and Proceedings of the General Assembly of the Colony of New York* (2 vols., New York, 1764–6); *Journal of the Legislative Council of the Colony of New York* (2 vols., Albany, 1861); Champante Papers, Bodleian MS. Rawl. A. 272; B.M. Add. MS. 15895, ff. 39–40, 349; C.O. 5/1047–1050.

[36] William A. Whitehead, ed., *Documents Relating to the Colonial History of the State of New Jersey*, 1st Ser. III, IV, XIII; *Journals of the Governor and Council of New Jersey*, Vol. I; Sonmans to Dockwra, 10 Feb. 1710/11, 27 Mar. 1711, 30 May 1711, B.M. Add. MS. 14034, ff. 118–19, 135–42; C.O. 5/969–70; Pomfret, *The Province of West New Jersey, 1609–1702*.

[37] Scharf, *History of Maryland*, Vol. I, Ch. XIII; Andrews, *History of Maryland*, pp. 192–220; Charles B. Clark, 'The Career of John Seymour, Governor of Maryland', *Md. Hist. Mag.* XLVII (1953), pp. 134–59; Steiner, ed., 'Unpublished Manuscripts from Fulham Palace', *Md. Hist. Mag.* XII (1917), pp. 115–41; William Hand Browne, ed., 'Proceedings and Acts of the General Assembly of Maryland', and 'Proceedings of the Council of Maryland', *Archives of Maryland*, Vols. XIX, XXII, XXIV, XXVI, XXVII, XXIX (Assembly), XX, XXIII, XXV (Council) (Baltimore, Md., 1899–1909).

In South Carolina many of the governors—with the exception of Johnson, Craven, and Archdale—were residents of the colony or neighbouring colonies. They were local politicians commissioned by the proprietors, but already associated with one faction by the time they assumed the governorship. Significantly, when a majority of voting proprietors were Whig, as they were before 1698 and after 1708, they allowed Colleton County supporters to assume the governorship.

And so the governors served as liaisons between their patrons in England and their allies in the colonies. But their politics served also to bring about the association of their enemies on both sides of the Atlantic. For when the governor's English patron lost office, there was an almost irresistible opportunity for his colonial opponents to send over a complaint against him to the new ministers. A new administration did not replace wholesale the colonial appointees of its predecessors, but with innumerable followers clamouring for office the ministers found it tempting to accept with sympathy complaints against incumbent governors. So a change of ministry in England was often the signal for hostile colonists to begin a transatlantic campaign to unseat the governor. Letters complaining of his corruption, county resolutions opposing particular policies, unofficial protests against favouritism from a group of representatives in the provincial Assembly, petitions signed by prominent town dwellers, would flood Whitehall; ship captains going to London would be given information against the governor and sent to see the 'right people'.[38]

Thus, for example, the greatest danger to Governor Dudley, a Tory, came in 1707 under a Whig ministry (when Dudley's opponents accused him of conspiracy with the French),[39] and in 1714 again under the Whigs. (His colonial opponents refused to recognize his authority as governor when his appointment was slow to be renewed on Queen Anne's death.) Governor Robert Hunter, a Whig, found his colonial opponents indefatigable in their appeals to Whitehall once the Tories came into office in 1710. Lewis Morris, the inveterate enemy of

[38] For one list of complaints against a colonial governor see A. N.'s fifteen charges against Governor Spotswood, *Spotswood Letters*, Vol. II, pp. 190–219.

[39] Luttrell, *A Brief Historical Relation of State Affairs*, Vol. VI, p. 152: 'Colonel Dudley, Governor of New England, is to be recalled and Colonel Hunter will succeed him.' See also pp. 193–260.

Governor Cornbury of New Jersey (a Tory), got Cornbury dismissed on charges of favouritism and corruption, through an effective campaign aimed at the Whig ministry which came into office in 1706.[40]

So the campaigns could be extremely damaging to a governor's prestige in London, even with a Board of Trade that, despite its own partisan representation, usually tried to be fair to colonial appointees. The campaign was particularly destructive when there was in England a former governor of the colony, familiar with provincial politics, naturally sympathetic to the opponents of the man who had displaced him, and grasping any opportunity to carp at his successor. During the Tory administration of 1710–14, for example, Lord Cornbury, a former New York governor and now First Lord of the Admiralty, was in constant communication with the colonial opponents of Governor Hunter, a Whig. Cornbury gave continual encouragement to Hunter's opponents in the colonies, testified against him before the Board of Trade, and worked to keep the Board from presenting to Parliament a Bill, which would appropriate certain New York customs revenues to the governor's salary.[41]

At the same time Governor Spotswood of Virginia, who also owed his appointment to a Whig ministry, accused former Governor Nicholson of keeping one of Spotswood's supporters from taking his place on the Virginia Council. And somewhat earlier former Governor Fletcher of New York was apparently working against Governor Bellomont in London, and also conniving with New York City merchants in a campaign to elect a provincial Assembly hostile to Bellomont.[42]

And so the governors served to link Whig and Tory parties in

[40] When a governor was out of favour with the ministerial party at home it was also tempting for his opponents to weaken him in the colony by spreading rumours of his impending dismissal. Robert Carter, for example, was charged by Governor Nicholson with spreading a rumour that Nicholson was being replaced by Lord Portmore (17 June 1703, *Executive Journals of the Council of Colonial Virginia*, Vol. II, p. 324).

For Morris's attack on Cornbury see Morris to Secretary of State, 9 Feb. 1707/8, Whitehead, ed., *Documents Relating to the Colonial History of the State of New Jersey*, Vol. III, pp. 274–85.

[41] My enemies were 'prompted all along from the other party by a late governor of these Provinces' (Hunter to Lords of Trade, 28 Mar. 1715, *New Jersey Archives*, 1st Ser. IV, p. 207).

[42] Spencer, *Phases of Royal Government in New York*, p. 19.

the colonies. But they were not the only liaisons between English and American parties. In addition there were the colonial agents, ministers of the Church of England, and the colonial merchants. These were, above all, lobbying groups concerned with colonial issues and colonial patronage. Like the governors they identified themselves with particular colonial interests (often they associated directly with colonial factions), and like the governors they worked through the channels of Whig and Tory parties.

Ever since the Bishop of London had been recognized as head of the Anglican Church in the colonies in 1675 he had made the most of his position to influence colonial policy. From 1675 to 1696 the Bishop had been a member of the old Lords of Trade; when the new Board of Trade was created the Bishop was not a member, but he could sit in on meetings *ex officio* and he knew most of the Board members personally. In addition the Bishop was well connected with the dominant figures in both Whig and Tory parties, and though he withdrew from political circles for a few years after William passed him over for Archbishop of Canterbury in 1691, he was slipping back into politics when Queen Anne came to the throne.[43]

Not only did the Bishop have behind him the individual influence of his friends in the government; after 1701 he also had the powerful organization of the Society for the Propagation of the Gospel, which he and Archbishop Tennison had organized for the express purpose of studying the position of the Anglican Church in the colonies. The S.P.G. was composed of prominent prelates and politicians; together they not only encouraged the missionary work of the Church among the Indians, but also kept watch for such things as colonial laws discriminatory to the Church,[44] difficulties between ministers and their congregations, or friction between governors and the Anglican ministers of their provinces.

In addition to the direct influence on colonial administration which the Bishop enjoyed through the S.P.G. and his personal

[43] Edward Carpenter, *The Protestant Bishop* (London, 1956), see esp. Ch. 14, 'The Plantations of America'; Arthur Lyon Cross, *The Anglican Episcopate and the American Colonies* (New York, 1902), *passim*. He had been one of the seven famous signers of the invitation to William.

[44] Some examples of S.P.G. review of colonial laws are in the S.P.G. Minutes, Bodleian MS. Rawl. C. 934, *passim*.

friends he also had an indirect influence through the commissaries he appointed for some colonies. Commissaries were the Bishop's own representatives in America, and wherever they were allowed to be—in Maryland, Virginia, the Carolinas, and New York—they had enough influence over Anglican communities to obstruct local officers or policies that they or the Bishop did not like.

Commissaries did not hesitate to play partisan politics in the colonies, even to the point of using their influence to bring down a royal governor. And, like the commissioners and customs inspectors before them, they were formidable leaders in 'loyal' opposition; it was impossible to label them seditious, and make the label stick, when they were clearly in the colony to represent the Established Church.[45] Through local Anglican congregations the commissaries could work to get letters of protest or praise to Whitehall; through Church councils in the colonies they could get resolutions passed, attacking or supporting a governor, resolutions which the Bishop could discreetly pass in to the Board of Trade or ministers; through political positions, particularly councillorships, which the Bishop got them the commissaries could work for or against a governor. The most notorious of all commissaries was James Blair of Virginia, whose political activity even the Bishop found excessive.[46] Despite the fact that he was several times outvoted by the Virginia Council of Ministers, and was in the majority of the Virginia Council only little more than half his career, Commissary Blair managed to unseat three, possibly four, Virginia governors, and at one time was even acting governor of the colony himself. In Carolina Commissary Johnson came to quarrel with the governor over the governor's assent to a law allowing congregations to turn out their ministers. Governor Hunter of New York accused Commissary Vesey of undermining his influence by spreading rumours that Hunter was out of favour with the home government.

[45] See Alison G. Olson, 'The Commissaries of the Bishop of London in Colonial Politics', in Alison G. Olson and Richard M. Brown, eds., *Anglo-American Politics, 1675–1775* (New Brunswick, N.J., 1970), Ch. VII.

[46] Daniel Esten Motley, *The Life of Commissary James Blair*, Johns Hopkins University Studies in History and Political Science, Ser. XIX, No. 10 (Oct. 1901), *passim*; *Executive Journals of the Council of Colonial Virginia*, ed. McIlwaine, Vol. II, p. 334. (At a Council meeting, 26 Aug. 1703, Governor Nicholson presented evidence that Blair was trying to undermine him with the Bishop of London.)

The widespread influence of the Bishop in London and in the colonies made ministers and the Board of Trade think twice before putting in policies or appointees the Bishop disapproved. Whenever a provincial law concerning the Church came up for review, it would be sent to the S.P.G. and the latter consulted for its opinion. In 1704, for example, the Board of Trade sent the Society the South Carolina law making Anglican ministers responsible to their congregations, and the Society recommended against it. Moreover, the Bishop made his own nominations to political office in the colonies. In 1706 he nominated one Edward Hill to the Virginia Council,[47] and in 1704 he even nominated a colonial Port Collector. In 1698 and 1704, respectively, he worked to turn out Governors Andros and Nicholson from office in Virginia.

Just as the Bishop of London and the Anglican Church lobbied effectively for the Church in the colonies, so also the merchants trading to the colonies, though not organized in a formal group like the S.P.G., found occasion to review laws and suggest policies relating to trade. In the first few years after the Glorious Revolution merchants to the colonies used to meet at the Exchange, the clearing-house for colonial investments, located just a few blocks away from the wharves, where ships from the colonies docked with the latest news, as well as passengers and produce, from the colonies. At first there had been so few colonial merchants that all of them could meet conveniently at the Exchange during a day's work; but as the numbers grew, merchants trading to particular colonies came to meet and exchange news on certain designated walks around the Exchange. By 1690 there was a New England walk, walks for Maryland and Virginia merchants, and quite probably a New York and a Carolina walk. Here merchants received their mail, exchanged the newest information in from the ships and the newest rumours out of Whitehall, and talked over provincial politics with colonists visiting London. A colonial agent like Mather or a visitor like Samuel Sewall, for example, found a daily visit to the Exchange almost indispensable.

Some time during the 1690s people with colonial business began transferring their meetings from the Exchange walks to the more

---

[47] Recommendations for councillors, 1706–11, are in B.M. Add. MS. 15483 (L.C. Transcript).

comfortable nearby coffee houses. At first groups of merchants went to coffee shops at random; the Sunflower Coffee House, for example, or the Elephant, were probably so frequented by individual merchants and their closest associates.

But slowly particular coffee houses came to be frequented by merchants trading to particular colonies. By 1715 the merchants were well on their way to having a separate coffee house for merchants trading to New England, and separate houses for each of the middle and southern colonies.

Here they gradually moved all the activities they formerly carried on at the Exchange—receiving mail, buying up shares in outgoing cargoes, arranging the insurance for their ships (for insurance underwriters did their business in the coffee houses). Here, over cups of strong coffee, they would peruse the newspapers laid out on the tables or read letters just in from business associates in the colonies, or hear the reports of ship captains lately from the colonies, and these could set off discussions of anything from the sailing of the next convoy to the candidates for vacant colonial offices.[48]

Here also a colonial agent could come for the latest information, and for support, if the merchants agreed with him, in lobbying for a colonial project. For it was not long after their establishment that the potential of coffee houses as lobbying organizations began to be realized. Several colonial agents, like Micajah Perry of Virginia and Peter Pagan of Maryland, were themselves London merchants who frequented coffee houses. Some of the wealthier merchants like Perry were already getting some influence of their own on colonial patronage, but they realized, too, that when a colonial issue affecting the merchants came up, there was strength in numbers. A petition left on the front hall table of a coffee house and signed by its patrons would carry some weight with the Board of Trade. For most of the seventeenth century only the wealthier merchants had had any influence on colonial administration; now for the first time the lesser merchants came to have some importance. In 1699 the New York City merchants appealed to the London merchants trading to New York to petition for the removal of

---

[48] Aytoun Ellis, *The Penny Universities: A History of the Coffee Houses* (London, 1956), esp. pp. 115–16, 126–7. For a guide to the coffee houses see Bryant Lillywhite, *London Coffee Houses* (London, 1963).

the Earl of Bellomont, who was governor of the colony. In 1706 Joseph Boone, a Carolina merchant, got the other Carolina merchants to join him in appealing against the approbation of the Carolina law excluding Dissenters from the provincial Assembly.[49] In 1706 the merchants of Virginia and Maryland asked for tobacco convoys twice a year, but when they appeared before the Board of Trade the Virginia merchants disagreed with the Marylanders over just when the convoys should sail.[50] Eventually the Secretary of the Board drew up a proposal to be considered by the Virginia and Maryland merchants separately. In 1714 Governor Spotswood complained that appointments to the Virginia Council were being made in the coffee house.[51] It is dangerous to overestimate the importance of the merchants as colonial lobbyists at this point; undoubtedly they had less influence as a group than the S.P.G. or the colonial agents. What was important was the lesser merchants' growing interest in colonial politics, their growing specialization, and their growing capacity for organization.

Working through the S.P.G. and the coffee houses were the colonial agents. Up to 1689 colonial agents had been appointed to handle a particular issue. Some of them, like John Leverett, had stayed in England for considerable lengths of time, but on the whole the early colonial agents were colonists who came on a special mission and wanted to get back home as soon as possible. After 1689, however, colonists came gradually to see the value of having permanent agents in England; sending only the occasional special agent left the colony unrepresented in emergencies, or at the cases that dragged on for decades—like boundary disputes. Moreover, since the government had been demanding in the case of more and more colonies that they should submit provincial laws for review, and demanding of provincial office-holders that they should have agents in London to pay their fees, there was certain to be the need for an agent's services at least once a year, when laws arrived or commissions had to be taken out, and so more and more colonies took to the appointing of agents on a long-term basis.

[49] McCrady, *South Carolina*, p. 428.
[50] Popple to Blakiston (25 Feb. 1706), and Council of Trade and Plantations to Secretary Hedges, 26 Apr. 1706, *Cal. S.P. Col., 1706–8*, Nos. 137, 295.
[51] Spotswood to Colonel Blakiston, 1 Dec. 1714, 'Spotswood Letters', *Colls. Va. Hist Soc.* N.S. II, p. 79.

The agent might be someone colonial Dissenters knew through their friends in Dissenting Churches in England, as Sir Henry Ashurst was. He might be a merchant that the provincial merchants had met or provincial planters worked with, as were Peter Pagan of Maryland, Nathaniel Blakiston of Virginia and Maryland, and the Perrys of Virginia.[52] He might be a lesser government official like William Blathwayt, Jeremiah Dummer, or Thomas Povey, whom colonists had come across in their dealings with the British government. Occasionally he was a distant relative of one of the colonists. Again, he might simply be the personal friend of a governor, as Ashurst was of Phips, Champante of Bellomont, or Ambrose Philips of Governor Hunter; or the friend of a previous agent, as Jeremiah Dummer was of William Ashurst.[53] He was any Englishman or colonist with business in England who was willing to do some lobbying for a reasonable fee.[54]

Nominally the agent represented the colonial government, or at least one part of it—the governor, Council or Assembly. The British government expected agents to be elected by provincial Assemblies and approved by the governor; and occasionally, of course, such an agent was actually sent; Jeremiah Dummer from Massachusetts, beginning in 1710

[52] Elizabeth Donnan, 'Eighteenth-Century English Merchants: Micajah Perry', *Journal of Economic and Business History*, IV (1932), pp. 70–99; Ella Lonn, *The Colonial Agents of the Southern Colonies* (Chapel Hill, N.C., 1945), p. 30.

[53] Alice Lounsberry, *Sir William Phips, Treasurer, Fisherman and Governor of the Massachusetts Bay Colony* (New York, 1941), pp. 237–47; Cotton Mather, *The Life of Sir William Phips*, ed. Mark Van Doren (New York, 1929), p. 119; Edward P. Lilly, *The Colonial Agents of New York and New Jersey* (Washington, D.C., 1936), p. 45; Bellomont to Champante, 6 Sept. 1699, Bodleian MS. Rawl. A. 272, f. 60. For Addison, Smithers, *Life of Joseph Addison*, p. 149; Sanford, 'Jeremy Dummer', p. 132.

[54] Lists of 'official' agents can be found in Lonn, *The Colonial Agents of the Southern Colonies*, pp. 392–6; James J. Burns, *The Colonial Agents of New England* (Washington, D.C., 1935), pp. 148–9; Lilly, *The Colonial Agents of New York and New Jersey*, pp. 225–6. Mabel Pauline Wolff (in *The Colonial Agency of Pennsylvania, 1712–1757* (Philadelphia, Pa., 1933), p. 305) mentions Joshua Gee, Henry Goldney, Simon Clement, and Thomas Story as forerunners of the Pennsylvania agents, and presumably George Whitehead, William Mead, and Thomas Lower, to whom David Lloyd appealed for assistance in 1704, should also be included in this category (Lokken, *David Lloyd*, p. 149). See also Samuel James Ervin, Jr., *The Provincial Agents of North Carolina*, The James Sprunt Historical Publications, XVI (Chapel Hill, N.C., 1919), pp. 2, 63–77. In 1707 John Porter went to England on behalf of the Dissenters' Party of North Carolina. He dealt only with the proprietors, who had become predominantly Whig by the time Porter returned to the colony.

(though Dummer later lost the support of the Assembly over the land bank issue), Henry Ashurst from Massachusetts, beginning in 1692 (though Ashurst later fell out with Governor Dudley), and John Champante from New York, in 1716, were all agents approved by the governors and both branches of the colonial legislature. But more likely than not, the governor, Council, and Assembly could not agree on a candidate; so each, or two together, would manage to find the money for an agent. By title these agents would represent the branch of the provincial government by whom they were sent, but in fact they usually represented a colonial party and they sought support from the appropriate parties in England.

Sometimes the nature of the issues dividing colonial factions determined what support an agent could get. When there was a real division between Anglicans and Dissenters in a colony, for example, English politicians took sides on the issue itself. When Increase Mather was lobbying for the restoration of the Massachusetts charter of 1629 and the virtual restoration of the old theocracy, his support came from the Whigs in the House of Commons.[55] The amendment was thrown out by the Tory House of Lords, and the next year, when a Tory House of Commons was elected, Mather said flatly that it was hopeless to bring the charter question before them.[56] When Joseph Boone came over on behalf of South Carolina Dissenters who were excluded from the provincial Assembly by a newly-passed law, his support was clearly Whig, and one Whig, Daniel Defoe, even wrote a pamphlet on behalf of these Dissenters.[57]

In general, also, the Whigs seem to have been more sympathetic to those factions involved in the provincial rebellions of

[55] There are no division lists on the Bill, but all Mather's personal advisers in the Lords were listed by the Tory minister Danby as being in opposition to his government in 1691 (Browning, *Danby*, Vol. III, pp. 175–6). They included the Earls of Devon and Bedford and Lord Wharton. All his advisers in the Commons later voted for the 'Sacheverell Clause', a strictly party motion which would have excluded Tories from virtually all local offices in England (Walcott, *English Politics*, pp. 83–4); Robert Walcott, Jr., 'Division Lists of the House of Commons, 1689–1715', *Bull. Institute of Historical Research*, XIV (1936), pp. 26–7; Browning, *Danby*, Vol. III, App. V; Burnet, *History of My Own Time*, Vol. IV, pp. 68–90.

[56] Mather MS. Diary, 1690, Mass. Hist. Soc.

[57] See *The Case of the Protestant Dissenters in Carolina* (London, 1706); McCrady, *History of South Carolina*, pp. 430–5.

1689, and more unsympathetic to the political groups who had supported James's government in the colonies. This would explain their apparent support for the efforts of Jacob Leisler, Jr., towards the restitution of Leislerian estates,[58] and their apparent sympathy with the Maryland rebels led by Coode and Cheseldyne, as well as their support of Mather.[59]

But what usually counted for more than the issues at stake were the personal associations of the agents themselves. Generally the close personal acquaintances of most agents were themselves not very influential men. With the possible exception of William Byrd II, the colonists who came to London on special missions were not acquainted with high-ranking English aristocrats, and few of the regular agents were high in English political circles. What strikes one in trying to trace the background of various agents at this time is their relative obscurity. They and their friends were middle-class merchants, prospering, but still not affluent, Dissenting ministers who were certainly neither rich nor influential, politicians of a distinctly lower rank. What they had to do was to get any of their friends who happened to know someone high in politics to arrange an introduction. A minister with a noble lord in his congregation, a writer who had written pamphlets for a member of the government, a politician who frequented his coffee house: these were the people the agent looked to for help.

Some of the agents, like William Byrd II,[60] Richard and Micajah Perry, Nathaniel Blakiston, and even Jeremiah Dummer and William Ashurst, seem to have had friends in a number of English camps. But other agents had all their connections in one English party, or even with a personal faction within the party. The agent whose friends were mainly other Dissenters would be unlikely to meet many Tories; the agent with business connections dating back to the Restoration era would be likely to find all his supporters from Tory ranks. When the agent did find his support predominantly in one party, it was natural for the colonial faction who employed

---

[58] Reich, *Leisler's Rebellion*, p. 131; Stock, *Proceedings*, Vol. II (1927), pp. 116–31.
[59] See Note 1 at end of chapter.
[60] See William Byrd, *The London Diary, 1717–21*, Ed. Louis B. Wright and Marion Tinling (New York, 1958), pp. 54, 58, 60, 203, 259, 332, 334. Byrd's connections in this period right after the Hanoverian succession were mainly old Tories, but he did know Nathaniel Blakiston and Sir Henry Ashurst.

him to associate their fortunes in some way with that party. From this it followed that they became more and more interested in the party struggles in England, even to the point in some colonies of feeling that it was futile to appeal local disputes if the opposing party was in power.

This was least true, of course, in a colony like Virginia, which had only transitory factions and had agents with connections in both English parties. It seems to have been most true for a colony like New York, where the Leislerian–anti-Leislerian feuds continued throughout the period. Brook, Sloper, and Thrale, the anti-Leislerian agents, all held office in Tory governments; Philips and Champante, the Leislerian agents, had Whig connections; and the reversal of Leisler's attainder was accomplished when the Whigs held a majority in Parliament.[61] To some extent the New York interpretation of English politics spilled over into New Jersey, since the governors were the same and the factional struggle continuous.

Less clear, but still surprisingly evident, is a connection between Massachusetts moderates and the English Tories, and Elisha Cooke's faction and the Whigs. The connections appear intermittently—in the assistance Whig magnates gave Increase Mather and Cooke in their efforts to get back the old charter; in the appointment (1702) of Joseph Dudley, himself a Tory M.P. in the 'government' interest, to the governorship that year; in the 'moderate' faction's choice of the Tories' Constantine Phipps and Jeremiah Dummer as agents; and in the continued services of Sir Henry Ashurst, himself a Whig and inveterate enemy of Dudley, as agent for the popular 'old charter' party, which began with Mather and soon fell under Cooke. In New Hampshire, as in New Jersey, the politics of the large colony with the same governor seem to have rubbed off on the smaller neighbour. In all these colonies politicians spoke directly of their connections with English politics.

In New York Governor Bellomont wrote, 'There are parties here as in England, Whigs and Tories, or rather Jacobites.'[62] The Leislerian Attorney General wrote in 1702 about the

[61] See James S. Leamon, 'Governor Fletcher's Recall', *W.M.Q.* 3rd Ser. XX (1963), pp. 527–42; see also John D. Runcie, 'The Problem of Anglo-American Politics in Bellomont's New York', ibid. XXVI (Apr. 1969), pp. 191–217.

[62] Bellomont to Lord Somers, 12 May 1698, Bodleian MS. Clarendon 102, f. 19 (L.C. Transcript).

accession of Queen Anne, who was inclined to the Tory Party, 'Ye King's death . . . discourages us but we find rejoices our enemies.'[63] Peter Sonmans, of Basse's faction (though a different wing of it) in New Jersey, wrote with satisfaction that the Whig Governor Hunter would have turned Sonmans' friends out of the Jersey Council in 1710, if the Tories had not come to power in England that year.[64] Increase Mather, working on behalf of the 'old charter' party in Massachusetts in 1690, gave up hope of getting the charter restored by Parliament when the Tories were returned with a majority. 'The . . . House of Commons being disaffected to New England . . . was an end of all our endeavors to obtain relief by ye Parliament.'[65] The Carolina proprietors instructed their governor to 'employ no Jacobite' and 'beware of the Goose Creek men'.[66]

In the other colonies one glimpses occasional evidence of identification with English politics: enough to know it existed, not enough to know how strong it was. Sometimes, as with the proprietary colonies, it is easy enough to tell where the proprietors and their provincial supporters looked for help. Penn and Baltimore both had friends among predominantly Tory factions,[67] while the political make-up of the Carolina proprietors shifted recognizably from year to year. This being the

[63] Weaver to Champante, 2 June 1702, Bodleian MS. Rawl. A. 272, f. 159, Champante wrote Governor Nanfan on 10 Apr. 1703, 'The subject matter I am forced to handle is, as our present ministry stands . . . very delicate' (ibid. f. 201).

[64] Sonmans to William Dockwra, 12 Feb. 1710/11, B.M. Add. MS. 14034, ff. 120–1.

[65] Mather MS. Diary, 1690, Mass. Hist. Soc., Boston.

[66] McCrady, History of South Carolina, pp. 236–7.

[67] Olson, 'William Penn', W.M.Q. 3rd Ser. XVIII (1961), pp. 188–93. Joseph E. Illick, William Penn the Politician, disputes this conclusion (pp. 208–9, ns. 71–3) on the basis of Walcott's studies of personal interest groups, arguing that Penn could hope to carry the Harley–Foley group, the Hyde–Granville–Gower–Seymour connection, the Nottingham–Finch connection, and the Junto connection, but would not carry the Court Peers, the Marlborough–Godolphin connections, the Newcastle–Pelham–Townshend connections or the government interest. I would accept much, but not all, of this analysis: it seems to me that Penn's connections, at least by 1700, with the Junto lords were very weak, but that on the other hand he could expect to carry the Marlborough–Godolphin connection and at least some of the government interest. If this breakdown is followed, then all Penn's 'connections' were Tory groups of varying shades, and the question whether Penn's support came from Tories or from various groups of Tory persuasion becomes almost—though not entirely—an academic one. Mr. Illick's book is published under the title William Penn the Politician, his Relations with the English Government (Ithaca, N.Y., 1965).

case, their provincial opponents probably appealed to their
opponents at home, but while there are some clear instances of
just such appeals, in other instances the evidence is simply
lacking. Clearly Ashe and Boone, having failed to get the proprietors to veto the laws excluding Dissenters from the Assembly, turned to the proprietors' political opponents for help in
Parliament; and Coode, leader of the anti-proprietary rebellion in Maryland, had Whig connections in England. But while
the Anglican opponents of Penn had English connections of
some influence (in another segment of Tories), there is no
evidence that David Lloyd and the anti-proprietary Quakers
were particularly aware of English political divisions; and had
the North Carolina agent not secured a proprietary veto of the
provincial Act in 1710, there is no evidence that they considered an appeal to Parliament—indeed, it would have been
futile to have appealed to the Tory-dominated Parliament of
that year.

So, although the various provincial factions were not all
equally able to utilize connections in English politics, and did
not have the same idea of the usefulness of English connections,
there was, nevertheless a growing awareness of the nature of
Whig–Tory rivalry and the way it would be used for colonial
advantage. Through their agents they were developing partisan connections with English politicians.

Thus the settlement of the most important colonial issues and
the gift of some of the choicest patronage depended ultimately
on the colonists' connections with Whig and Tory politicians in
London. Indeed, the colonies bore much the same relationship
to Westminster as did the English counties: their local disputes
were woven into the fabric of partisan politics at the national
level, and factions in the colonial Assemblies began to feel
themselves a part of the fabric of imperial politics. Later on in
the eighteenth century it was argued that colonial representation in Parliament would be meaningless and impractical;
from 1689 to 1715 it was neither of these.

NOTE

1. That colonial issues were consistently settled along party lines is indicated
by the other major pieces of colonial legislation that came before Parliament.
In 1695, too, the Whigs initially supported the Bill creating a parliamentary

Committee of Trade. There are no voting lists on the Bill, and party divisions are somewhat conjectural. But Shrewsbury and Sunderland, two of the Whig Junto lords, were almost certainly behind the Bill in the beginning, and two supporters of John Locke, who was in with the Junto lords, were the tellers for the Bill. Not until well after he had named his own Committee of Trade did William seem to be able to put pressure on the Junto lords not to oppose it. On three other issues—the Post Office Act, parliamentary regulation of colonial coin, and the salary for Governor Hunter, the evidence is still more conjectural, but, again, the Whigs seemed on each occasion to have favoured parliamentary intervention and the Tories to have attacked it. Certainly the Post Office Bill and the Bill regulating coinage were passed by the Whig Parliament of 1706–10, and the salary of Hunter, who was himself a Whig, was neglected by the Tory Parliament of 1710–14. (The draft Bill for Hunter's salary had been approved by the Attorney General in March 1710, just four months before the Whig Ministry of Marlborough and Godolphin was replaced by a Tory ministry.) Moreover, the Tories were the strongest opponents of parliamentary Bills to take away the charters of the proprietary and corporate colonies in 1701, 1702, and 1706. The Tory William Penn himself led the opposition to the Bills, and enlisted in his support Robert Harley, Edward Seymour, Christopher Musgrave, and Sir John Lowther. Seymour, Musgrave, and Lowther represented the 'old Tories', so conservative that they had once even refused to recognize William and Mary. Harley represented the 'new' or younger Tories. Penn was also helped by Sir Heneage Finch and Simon Harcourt, both conservative Tories in the House of Commons, and in the Lords by the Duke of Somerset, the Duke of Devonshire, the Marquis of Normanby, and Lord Godolphin, all of them Tories at the time (Alison G. Olson, 'William Penn, Parliament and the Proprietary Governments', *W.M.Q.* 3rd Ser. XVIII (1961), pp. 188–93).

Moreover, with their belief in parliamentary supremacy in domestic affairs it was the Whigs who encouraged their friends to bring up colonial matters in Parliament, while the Tories seem to have urged their associates to work with the Privy Council instead. The parliamentary issue was particularly evident behind the Whigs' support of a parliamentary Committee of Trade in 1695, and behind the Tory opposition to parliamentary restoration of the Massachusetts charter. As the Secretary of State, Lord Nottingham, put it to William, when writing about the clause restoring Massachusetts' old charter in 1689, 'Here is no dispute in this matter between parties unless it be between them who would support your regal, just authority and those who by little and little would leave you none' (31 July 1691, Finch MS. III, Historical Manuscripts Commission, *Report*, XXLI (London, 1957), p. 188).

There may also have been still another difference between the Whigs' and Tories' policies on the colonies, a difference perhaps more important than either Anglicanism or parliamentary supremacy: on particular questions of policy and procedure the Tories came to support the colonial policies of Charles II and the Whigs came to oppose them.

Thus after the dissolution of the Dominion of New England the Tories made no objection to restoring the charters of Rhode Island and Connecticut, since both charters were confirmed by Charles II and remained effective throughout his reign, but they did object to restoring the charter of Massachusetts, which Charles had abrogated by *quo warranto* proceedings in 1684. The Tory William Blathwayt, in a pamphlet, *Considerations humbly presented to the Parliament*, appealed to the Tories not to let Parliament declare void a decision of Charles II. (A printed copy of this is in C.O. 5/856, ff. 460–7. The draft in Blathwayt's hand is ff. 464–8.) And for all their opposition to restoring the Massachusetts charter the Tories were bitter opponents of the Bills to resume proprietary and corporate colonies to the Crown. Why did they defend the charters of Pennsylvania, the Carolinas, Maryland, Rhode Island, and Connecticut, while they attacked that of Massachusetts? Simply because the Massachusetts charter had been abrogated by Charles II, while the other charters had, all except for Maryland, been given by him, and without exception had been recognized until the end of his reign.

IV 'The face of affairs respecting party is surprisingly altered'

WITH Queen Anne's death the comfortable, informal working relationship that colonial factions had enjoyed with their English allies came to an end. The main reason for this was, surprisingly enough, the demise of the old Tory Party. The end of the French War and the acceptance, however reluctant, by the English people of a Hanoverian monarchy with settled powers, eliminated the most live issues in English politics; Bolingbroke's disastrous flight to the court of James III, coupled with the unfortunate association of some Tories with the abortive rising against George I in 1715, disgraced the Tory Party and left the political field to the Whigs.

The divided Tory leaders, some jailed, some exiled, and some futilely trying to dissociate themselves from their rebellious colleagues, could hold on to a very little following. In the first Parliament of the new reign the Whigs already had a solid majority of about 150; as the reigns of George I and George II went on the Tory Party dropped into virtual oblivion.

So shaken were the Tories that the first effective opposition to the new ministry came not from them but from within the Whig Party itself. Indeed, the first effective opposition to a Hanoverian ministry came from the Whig, Sir Robert Walpole, who was temporarily out of office in 1717. Around himself and his brother-in-law, Lord Townshend, Walpole gathered the nucleus of a Whig opposition. When Walpole and Townshend returned to office without their supporters in 1720 those Whigs who remained in opposition found themselves, like their Tory counterparts, without effective leadership.[1]

[1] For a clear discussion of Walpole's opposition see J. H. Plumb, *Sir Robert*

By the time Walpole took the Lord Treasurership in 1722, then, there were two quite different groups of government opponents, one Whig, one Tory, both dispirited, both without leadership. Then in 1723 Lord Bolingbroke returned from exile and immediately began to infuse spirit into some parts of the badly divided Tory Party, and soon afterwards the brilliant William Pulteney, disgruntled because Walpole had passed him over for Secretary of State, did for the remnant of opposition Whigs what Bolingbroke was doing for the Tories. It was not long before Bolingbroke and Pulteney, meeting together at Bolingbroke House, began combining their exceptional talents, devising opposition attacks which would unite their heterogeneous parliamentary followers, stirring up opposition 'out of doors', particularly in the City of London, and combining talents in editing the famous *Craftsman*.

But this coalition of markedly disparate groups, however brilliantly led, was rarely an effective match for Walpole. Walpole's chief supporters were the monarchs George I and II, the London financial interests, the government contractors, and the Whig magnates, and against these Bolingbroke and Pulteney made very little ground.[2] When the coalition of opposition factions finally defeated Walpole in 1742, it was the Prime Minister alone who fell. The rest of his colleagues remained in office, gradually taking in segments of the coalition as the 1740s went on.

At first glance the collapse of the Tory Party and the development of a heterogeneous opposition might seem to have had little effect on colonial administration. In fact, however, its effect on Anglo-colonial relations was devastating: for Americans the changes in British politics in the generation after 1715 were as ominous as any in the whole period before 1760.

For one thing the disappearance of the old Tory Party meant the end of a useful and informal set of associations between English and American political factions. This was partly because some of the colonies never, or only slowly, developed

Walpole, The King's Minister (Boston, Mass., 1956), *passim*, esp. pp. 122–40. See also C. B. Really, *The Early Opposition to Sir Robert Walpole, 1720–27* (Lawrence, Kans., 1931); Archibald S. Foord, *His Majesty's Opposition, 1714–1830* (Oxford, 1964), esp. pp. 114–21; John B. Owen, *The Rise of the Pelhams* (London, 1957).

[2] See Lucy S. Sutherland, *The East India Company in Eighteenth Century Politics* (Oxford, 1952), Ch. II.

court and country parties which paralleled the Court and Treasury Party and the opposition in England.[3] In Virginia two factions emerged in competition for western lands, but it is awkward to call either a court or country party.[4] The same thing is true for North Carolina, where until the Albemarle–Cape Fear struggle over representation the main political divisions were between the supporters of Henry McCulloch's land purchases and the owners of blank patents to some of the same lands.[5] Similarly, in Rhode Island and Connecticut, where violent factional disputes were developing along eco-

[3] There is a great unevenness in the amount of research that has been done on the politics of various colonies in the second quarter of the eighteenth century. Massachusetts, New York, Pennsylvania, and South Carolina have been covered well in books and theses, Virginia in theses, and New Jersey in Donald Lorenzo Kemmerer's *Path to Freedom, the Struggle for Self-Government in Colonial New Jersey, 1703–1776* (Princeton, N.J., 1940); Richard L. Bushman's *From Puritan to Yankee: Character and the Social Order in Connecticut, 1690–1765* (Cambridge, Mass, 1967) is a sophisticated treatment of that colony. Jere Daniell, *Experiment in Republicanism; New Hampshire Politics and the American Revolution, 1741–1794* (Cambridge, Mass., 1970) covers the last part of the period for New Hampshire, and there are two completed dissertations which touch on mid-century politics; moreover, Belknap's standard history, as far as it goes, is reliable. But a Ph.D. thesis on North Carolina stops at 1730, and, excluding the biographies of particular governors, there is no general, reliable interpretation of this colony for the period 1730–65. Rhode Island is even more difficult: there is no general interpretation of that colony's politics before 1760. Perhaps the reason so little has been done in the early history of Connecticut, Rhode Island, and the Carolinas is that the manuscript materials are so scattered and collections so fragmented that it would be difficult to piece together a reliable interpretation from the material available, and the published official records of the colonies do not offer much of a guide to the way politics actually worked.

[4] In 'Political Alignments in Colonial Virginia Politics, 1698–1750', op. cit. p. 305, Alan Williams argues that factions developed after the early 1730s, when Governor Gooch lost a good deal of patronage, because politicians no longer feared that the governor could play off parties against each other. Drysdale's administration and the last years of Spotswood's administration represented a period of some confusion and new alignments, followed in Gooch's administration by the emergence of factional tendencies. Jack P. Greene, 'Foundations of Political Power in the Virginia House of Burgesses, 1720–1776', *W.M.Q.* 3rd Ser. XVI (1959), p. 486, says 'Organized political parties did not exist in colonial Virginia.' With this I certainly agree; colonial factions had only the most rudimentary organization.

[5] *The Colonial Records of North Carolina*, ed. William L. Saunders, Vols. II–IV (Raleigh, N.C., 1887–8), *passim*; Jack P. Greene, *The Quest for Power: the Lower Houses of Assembly in the Southern Royal Colonies, 1689–1776* (Chapel Hill, N.C., 1963), pp. 42–5. The best general survey from which to piece together the alliances is still Ashe, *History of North Carolina*, Vol. I. Julian P. Boyd, 'The Sheriff in Colonial North Carolina', *N.C. Hist. Rev.* V (1928), pp. 151–80, while arguing against the governor's use of patronage to build up a party, shows how partisan sheriffs were chosen who would in turn mismanage elections to the advantage of their partisan supporters. See Lawrence F. London, 'The Representation Controversy in Colonial

nomic and religious lines, but where there were no royal or proprietary governors, one could not speak of court and country groups. But in the majority of the colonies the terms were applicable.

In the existing proprietary colonies a court party gathered around the proprietors and a country party around the opposition (though the court parties seem to have been much more steady in Pennsylvania[6] and New Jersey[7] than they were in

North Carolina', ibid. XI (1934), pp. 255–70. An interesting description of the way in which one country was dominated by a clique of Justices of the Peace, and how this affected Assembly politics, is in Nannie May Tilley, 'Political Disturbances in Colonial Granville County', ibid. XVII (1941), pp. 339–59. Paschal, *Proprietary North Carolina*, op. cit., covers the period to 1729, but is not concerned with factions in the later years.

[6] The old division between Quaker farmers who opposed the proprietor, Quaker merchants who generally—though not necessarily—supported him, and a third faction of Anglicans also inclining to oppose the proprietors, persisted acrimoniously for a decade after Queen Anne's death. Then for another decade there was peace, after David Lloyd went over to the support of proprietary governor Gordon. But by the end of the 1740s the proprietary strife was reviving, this time with the Quakers as a whole opposed to the proprietor, and the Anglicans coming over to support him. Frederick Barnes Tolles, *Meeting House and Counting House: The Quaker Merchants of Colonial Philadelphia, 1682–1763* (Chapel Hill, N.C., 1948), p. 21.

For the career of the outstanding Quaker politician in New Jersey and Pennsylvania see Edwin B. Bronner, 'The Disgrace of John Kinsey, Quaker Politician, 1739–1750', *Pa. Mag. Hist. & Biog.* LXXV (1951), No. 4, pp. 400–16, esp. p. 402 for Kinsey's Jersey career. See also Penn MSS., Official Correspondence, Vols. I–IV, Private Correspondence, Vols. I–III; Penn Letter Book, Vols. I and II; Henry S. Drinker Papers, Box 1; Quaker Scrap Book I, Am. 12780; Stauffer Coll. IV; Gratz Coll. Case 2, Boxes 12, 24, 33–a; Pemberton Papers, Vols. III and IV; Logan Papers, Vols. I and II; all in the Pennsylvania Historical Society.

[7] In New Jersey, where the contest had earlier been between Lewis Morris's faction on the one hand and the Cox–Sonmans group on the other, both factions having some supporters among the East and West Jersey proprietors, the principal division became one between proprietary and anti-proprietary parties. Morris's faction remained intact, the irascible old Morris leading it himself until his death in 1746; the Cox–Sonmans faction over several decades evolved into the anti-proprietary party, and seems to have been supported by the Quakers as a group in the 1740s. Donald Kemmerer, in *Path to Freedom: The Struggle for Self-Government in Colonial New Jersey, 1703–1776*, says that in the 1740s there were four factions in New Jersey: the Scots, the people of Elizabethtown, the small farmers, and the Quakers (p. 187). But on crucial issues—centred on the proprietary rights over the land—the last three groups joined against the first, the Scots leading the proprietary interests and the other three groups constituting the anti-proprietary faction. Governor Morris was himself a leader of the proprietary faction, Governor Belcher was cornered into supporting their opponents. For detailed descriptions of the New Jersey Council and Assembly and their members from year to year see Edgar Jacob Fisher, *New Jersey as a Royal Province, 1738–1776*, Columbia University Studies in History, Economics and Public Law, XLI (New York, 1911), and

Maryland, where shifting cliques drifted in and out of the proprietors' favour).[8] In Massachusetts the court–country difference was quite clear, though there was a slight shift in the components of the factions at the time of Governor Belcher's retirement.[9] In New Hampshire and New York the court

---

Edwin P. Tanner, *The Province of New Jersey, 1664–1738* (New York, 1908), *passim*.

This period is covered in the *New Jersey Archives*, Vols. V to VII, which include most of the important manuscripts in the New Jersey Historical Society. The New Jersey Historical Society also has transcripts of Jonathan Belcher letters (the originals are in the Massachusetts Historical Society), mostly dealing with New Jersey affairs (the years 1731–48 are on pp. 1–295). See also Gordon B. Turner, 'Governor Lewis Morris and the Colonial Government Conflict', *Procs. N.J. Hist. Soc.* LXVII (1949), pp. 260–304; William T. McClure, Jr., 'The West Jersey Society, 1692–1736', ibid. LXXIV (1956), pp. 1–20; Keith Trace, 'The West Jersey Society, 1736–1819', ibid. LXXX (1962), pp. 266–80.

[8] Scharf, *History of Maryland*, Vol. I, p. 502; Charles Albro Barker, *The Background of the Revolution in Maryland* (New Haven, Conn., 1940), pp. 174–80. *The Archives of Maryland*, Vols. XXXVII, XXXIX, XL, XLII, XLIV, provide voting lists for the Maryland Assembly from 1732, when yea and nay votes were first recorded, to 1747. These indicate that there was the nucleus of a proprietary 'court' party in the eastern shore counties and especially in Annapolis and St. Mary's, while the anti-proprietary strength seems to have come from the tobacco growers, many of them Catholic, on the western shore. In between were the uncommitted cliques, like the Dulaney–Tasker clique and the Carroll–Bordley one; it was quite possible to have a strongly anti-proprietary vote on the question of a particular publication and a proprietary victory on quitrents both in the same session. James High, in 'The origins of Maryland's Middle Class in the Colonial Aristocratic Pattern', *Md. Hist. Mag.* LVII (1962), p. 337, argues that the middle class was the 'country party'.

[9] A succession of governors after Dudley were opposed by Elisha Cooke's 'popular' party; the land banks, the prerogative, and Cooke's interest in Maine lands were the chief points at issue. Cooke's personal leadership of the opposition seems to have collapsed about 1734, but his 'wing' of the opposition became the land bank supporters of 1740. At the end of his administration Belcher was opposed both by the land bankers and by conservative opponents who spread rumours in London that Belcher was not really opposing the land bankers. Belcher's successor, Governor William Shirley, built a court or prerogative party from all the elements opposed to the land bank group.

The materials for Massachusetts history in this period are very full. Metz, 'Politics and Finance in Massachusetts', is so far the most useful analysis of Massachusetts politics in the period. Sanford, 'Jeremy Dummer', pp. 285–413, touches on Massachusetts politics, as does Perry Miller, *New England Mind*, pp. 310 et seq. See also Albert Mathews, *Colonel Elizeus Burgess*, Pubs. Col. Soc. Mass. XIV (1911–1913), p. 366. For Governor Belcher's correspondence, see The Belcher Papers, *Colls. Mass. Hist. Soc.* 6th Ser. VI and VII (Boston, 1893–94). For Shirley see *The Correspondence of William Shirley*, ed. Charles Henry Lincoln (2 vols., New York, 1912), John A. Schutz, *William Shirley, King's Governor of Massachusetts* (Chapel Hill, N.C., 1961); and Schutz's article on 'Succession Politics in Massachusetts, 1730–1741', *W.M.Q.* 3rd Ser. XV (1958), pp. 508–20; G. A. Wood, *The*

parties seem to have been the factions allied with the governors of the moment, though after 1741 the Wentworth faction in New Hampshire[10] was consistently the court, and throughout the period the Morris group in New York thought of themselves as the country party.[11]

So there was in fact a substantial number of colonies where

Public Life of William Shirley (New York, 1920). See also Susan Martha Reed, 'Church and State in Massachusetts, 1691–1740', University of Illinois Studies in the Social Sciences, III, No. 4 (Urbana, Ill., Dec. 1914); Mass. Hist. Soc., 'Papers Relating to Massachusetts, 1720–1724', Add MS. 15486, Jeremiah Dummer's letters in Misc. Bound MSS., and scattered letters in the Belknap, Cushing, Peperell, and Coleman, MSS.

[10] In New Hampshire the old issue of the colony's relationship to Massachusetts was woven in and out of politics. It combined with personal disputes over patronage, personal opposition to the Wentworth group, and some agrarian opposition to the Portsmouth mercantile interests, to form one basis for factional disputes. The lull in factional warfare of the twenties ended with Governor Belcher's quarrel with Benning Wentworth over patronage and Wentworth's salary as lieutenant-governor. Thereafter the Wentworth group gave the governor no peace, though as governor of Massachusetts Belcher did pick up support from the old Massachusetts faction. When Wentworth himself became governor of New Hampshire, independent of Massachusetts, Belcher's friends became the country party, and continued until the early fifties to press for a governor from Massachusetts. The most recent interpretations of the period after 1741 are in Jere Daniell, 'Family Government: The Structure of New Hampshire Politics during the Administration of Governor Benning Wentworth, 1747–1767', Faculty Seminar Paper, Dartmouth College, 1965, published in revised version as 'Politics in New Hampshire under Governor Benning Wentworth, 1741–1767', W.M.Q. 3rd Ser. XXIII (1966), pp. 76–105; and John Francis Looney, 'The King's Representative: Benning Wentworth, Colonial Governor, 1741–1767' (Ph.D. thesis, Lehigh University, 1961). See also two old but reliable histories, Jereby Belknap's History of New Hampshire (Boston, Mass., 1791–2) and William Henry Fry's New Hampshire as a Royal Province (n.p., 1908).

[11] In the 1720s the old Leislerian party of New York split in two on the issue of regulating the Albany fur trade, the de Lanceys on one side, the Livingstons and Morris on the other. The division continued into the Cosby–Van Dam dispute, basically a struggle for power between the de Lancey faction and the Morris–Alexander faction. Under Cosby's successor, Lt.-Governor Clarke, who began a de Lancey man but shifted to Morris, the Assembly disputes died down, but Governor Clinton, who also shifted his support from de Lancey to Morris, revived the dispute by trying to take de Lancey's offices away from him. See Beverley McAnear, 'Politics in Provincial New York, 1689–1761' (unpublished Ph.D. thesis, Stanford University, 1935–36), pp. 349–730 passim, for the Morris party as the 'country party'; 'Cadwallader Colden's History of William Cosby's Administration', in The Letters and Papers of Cadwallader Colden . . ., 1711–75, Vol. IX (New York, 1937), p. 351; Milton M. Klein, 'Democracy and Politics in Colonial New York', New York History, XL (1959), pp. 221–46; Carl Becker, 'Nominations in Colonial New York', A.H.R. VI (1901), pp. 260–75; Donald Rhodes Alter, 'Mid-Century Political Alignments in the Middle Provinces, 1740–1760' (Ph.D. thesis, University of Illinois, 1934); Docs. re Col. Hist. N.Y., Vols. V, VI, esp. pp. 20–4,

court and country affiliations suggested themselves. Moreover, despite the transitory nature of some of the issues before the colonial Assemblies, there was enough continuity in a number of colonial factions to make it possible for them to develop long-range connections with English factions, whether or not they could be identified as court or country parties themselves. Admittedly, the new factions continued to represent personal connections, groups of assemblymen clustered around one or two leading individuals. Factional disputes flared up one year and lay dormant the next: the Morris–Alexander faction mobilized tremendous opposition to Governor Cosby and the de Lancey faction in 1734, and two years later Lieutenant-Governor Clarke could write that party 'heats' were remarkably abated in the colony.[12] The dispute between John Kinsey, the Quaker anti-proprietary leader in Pennsylvania, and the proprietary governor of the colony flared up with great heat in 1741, but had quieted down by 1743.[13] Governor Wentworths's admission of representatives from new areas to the New Hampshire Assembly became such a bitter issue in 1748 that no legislation was passed for three years; then the conflict evaporated.[14]

Such was the sporadic development of colonial parties. But for all that, there does seem to have been a continuity in the factional divisions which kept Assembly politics from being purely kaleidoscopic. In colonies like Massachusetts and Connecticut there was already a noticeable difference between 'conservatives' and 'radicals', the main issues being the land

---

34–5, 36, 42–4, 53–4, 73, 84, 112, 152–3, 163, 248–9, 260–2, 270–1, 277–8, 312–14, 353–7, 407, 410, 428–32; Stanley Nider Katz, ed., *A Brief Narrative of the Case and Trial of John Peter Zenger* . . . (Cambridge, Mass., 1963), esp. pp. 6–7. See also Katz's book on *Newcastle's New York; Anglo-American Politics, 1732–1753* (Cambridge, Mass., 1968), and Patricia Bonomi, *A Factious People: Politics and Society in Colonial New York* (New York, 1971).

[12] Clarke to Board of Trade, 26 July 1736, *N.Y. Col. Docs.* VI, p. 73.

[13] Pa. Hist. Soc., William Allen to John Penn, 27 Mar. 1741, Governor Thomas to John Penn, 27 Oct. 1741, Allen to Thomas Penn, 24 Oct. 1741, Richard Hockey to Thomas Penn, 27 May 1742, Governor Thomas to John Penn, 4 June 1742, in Penn MSS., Official Correspondence, Vol. III (1736–43), ff. 143, 197, 201, 217, 219. Richard Hockley wrote, 5 May 1745, 'Mr. Kinsey is called E——l of B—th so that I find still theres Malecontents on both sides, but on the whole the face of Affairs respecting Party is surprisingly altered and a good Harmony subsists in general . . .' (to Thomas Penn, ibid. f. 257).

[14] Daniell, 'Politics in New Hampshire', *W.M.Q.* 3rd Ser. XXIII (1966), pp. 98–105.

bank in Massachusetts, and the Great Awakening and the claims of the Susquehannah land company in Connecticut. Kinsey's overt opposition to the Pennsylvania proprietors may have been sporadic, but a group of the same Quaker assembly-men always opposed the proprietor and his officials when they found opportunity to do so. The efforts of Governor Went-worth's New Hampshire opponents to replace him with a governor from Massachusetts may have brought trouble for only a few years, but Wentworth's opponents were the same men who had opposed him and supported Governor Belcher of Massachusetts nearly twenty years before. It would have been possible, therefore, for a number of colonial factions to develop long-range connections with English factions, despite the fact that not every colony had a 'court' and a 'country' party.

But this did not happen. After the rout of the Tory Party in 1715 there was only one time when it seemed possible to develop any workable alliance between American factions and the English opposition. This was between 1726 and 1732, the early years of the Bolingbroke–Pulteney collaboration on the *Craftsman*. For most of the years the opposition was simply too weak to be of any use to the colonists; only during the brief Bolingbroke–Pulteney alliance did it seem strong and syste-matic enough to offer a real alternative to the Walpole minis-try, and hence strong enough to be worth cultivating by colonial politicians. For a brief while the alliance created the promise of a new alignment of transatlantic political factions which might have changed the nature of Anglo-colonial poli-tics. The promise ended abruptly with the Excise scheme, one of the significant turning-points in Anglo-colonial history.

It was inevitable that Bolingbroke and Pulteney should get around to colonial politics sooner or later, because both men had a particular personal interest in colonial administration, Pulteney's coming from his brother Daniel, who had briefly, but quite actively, been on George I's Board of Trade, and Boling-broke's coming from his experience as Secretary of State under Queen Anne.

More immediately, they shared with a small but growing group of contemporaries a particular interest in the relationship between colonial parties and imperial politics. They were familiar, for example, with the debate about whether partisan

divisions spread from the mother country to the colonies or
vice versa. 'Cato's' explanation was that corrupt ministers in
England '. . . will create Parties in the Commonwealth, or keep
them up where they already are; and by playing them by
turns upon each other, will rule both'.[15] The Earl of Shaftesbury had offered a contradictory explanation: "Tis in such
bodies as these [the colonies] that strong factions are aptest to
engender. The associating Spirits, for want of Exercise, form
new Movements, and seek a narrower Sphere of Activity, when
they want Action in a greater. . . .'[16] At the same time a scathing
attack on Governor Belcher appearing in the *Political State of
Great Britain* had reflected pointedly:

> In all nations Oppression and arbitrary Sway has generally taken
> its rise in the most remote Parts, like dead Palsy, it generally seizes
> the Hands and Feet, but from thence it soon reaches the Heart, and
> makes an end to the Body Politick. For this Reason I have been and
> always will be Particularly interested in the Affair of that Colony,
> because I am afraid it should one time or another serve as a
> Precedent at Home.[17]

As English writers of the 1720s and 1730s theorized about the
politics of the preceding generation, and as ageing politicians
in the opposition looked back over their own earlier experience
with colonial politics, they began to agree on the same thing:
the contagion of faction, whatever its source, might spread

---

[15] *The Second Collection of Cato's Political Letters in the London Journal*, No. 22 (London, 1721).

[16] Anthony, Earl of Shaftesbury, *Characteristics of Men, Manners, Opinions, Times*,
6th edn. (3 vols., London, 1732), Vol. I, p. 114.
Defoe had contributed to the debate as early as 1705, by explaining the nature
of colonial parties in terms of the infancy of provincial Assemblies ('Party Tyranny',
in *Narratives of Early Carolina*, ed. Salley, p. 225). Walter Moyle had indirectly
offered another interpretation: colonies were useful to the mother country by
draining off seditious characters ('An Essay upon the Roman Government', in *The
Works of Walter Moyle*, Esq., 2 vols., Vol. I (London, 1726), p. 127); hence it was
easier to foment partisan strife there. The argument over the relationship of domestic political parties to provincial ones continued through the reign of George II.
In John Brown's *An Estimate of the Manners and Principles of the Times*, 7th edn.,
reprinted in Boston from an English edition of 1758, Brown argued that English
factions were unhealthy, because they differed only on questions of selfish interest,
while provincial factions could be healthy, since some of them differed on public
issues (Evans 8094).

[17] *Extract from the Political State of Great Britain for the Month of December, 1730*
(Boston, 1731; Evans Microprint, No. 3467).

quickly throughout an empire. Connections between American and English country parties, moreover, might prove a very useful weapon against the ministry.

Bolingbroke and Pulteney began their attack on Walpole's colonial government quite soon after the *Craftsman* was started: two essays in the winter and spring of 1726 compared the colonial governors to the stewards of country estates—'indigent and ignorant Persons' who oppressed the tenants—and compared Walpole to the absentee landlord who paid no attention to his tenants' grievances.[18] Throughout these and later essays there was an emphasis on the economic importance of the colonies to Britain and the stupidity of leaving them ill-governed and ill-defended. Then on 14 October 1732 came the most vitriolic attack of all. The entire issue of the *Craftsman* was devoted to a criticism of the current colonial governors, in a manner appealing to opposition parties in the colonies and to the hatred that English country gentlemen felt for courtiers and placemen:

These hopeful deputy kings incite the meaner sort of the People, extreamly apt to copy the examples of their superiors, to all manner of rapine and injustice while the more reasonable and substantial part of the colony, looking upon these temporary governors only as so many court Spunges, sent by some favourite minister to suck up the treasure of the land and to devour the fruit of their honest Labours instead of obedience and affection pay them nothing but hatred and contempt.[19]

Exactly how much Bolingbroke and Pulteney intended to appeal to the colonists, and how much they were simply looking for a good issue at home, is hard to say. Clearly, most of the essays were written to appeal to the English merchants, while the remainder had the country gentry in mind; on the other hand, there is evidence that Pulteney carried the opposition beyond the *Craftsman* and into the colonies themselves, where he corresponded with colonial political leaders, urging them to make the governors' positions untenable by creating disturbances. In New York Governor Cosby complained that his opponents were inspired by 'the Boston people [who] . . .

---

[18] *The Craftsman* (London, 1726–36), 3 Jan. 1726 (No. 25), 20 Mar. 1726 (No. 30). See also 28 Dec. 1828 (No. 130) and 10 Jan. 1728/9 (No. 133).
[19] *The Craftsman*, No. 328, pp. 264–70.

are sparked up by that faction at home',[20] and added that Pulteney was corresponding with the malcontents of Connecticut and Rhode Island. In Massachusetts Governor Belcher complained of the same thing.[21] In South Carolina Governor Johnson called Benjamin Whitaker, who had just engineered the passage of a quitrent Act which the governor did not like, 'the Craftsman among us'.[22] One might dismiss these as contrived excuses of hard-pressed governors, were it not for the fact that at least one colonial faction (the Morris–Alexander group in New York) did adopt Pulteney's slogan of 'King George, Liberty, and Law',[23] and the fact that the complaints were quite uncommon in colonial history after 1715, the only years in which they were mentioned being 1732 and 1733.[24]

The attack on colonial governors was carried on in the press and in the colonies; the following year opposition leaders attacked in Parliament. In 1733 the opposition joined the merchants trading to the Northern Colonies in fighting the government's proposal for a nearly prohibitive tax on molasses imported by the mainland colonies from the French West Indies. The Act set a precedent both for parliamentary taxation of the colonies for revenue, in addition to regulation, and for governments' favouring the West India interest over that of the mainland. In the mainland colonies it drew violent opposition, and in Parliament Pulteney and Wyndham (one of Bolingbroke's followers) took the side of the mainland.[25]

---

[20] George Chalmers, *An Introduction to the History of the Revolt of the American Colonies*, Vol II (Boston, 1845), p. 137.

[21] *Cal. S.P. Col., 1733*, p. xv.   [22] Sirmans, *Bull Family*, p. 346.

[23] Katz, ed., *Brief Narrative of the Trial of John Peter Zenger*, pp. 6–7.

[24] Just how the *Craftsman* got to colonial readers is still a mystery. Clearly people were reading the *Craftsman*, but how did they get copies? Occasionally colonial newspapers printed brief extracts from it: the *South Carolina Gazette, Pennsylvania Gazette*, and *New York Weekly Journal* all have occasional references to the *Craftsman*. But the printer who depended heavily on contracts to do government printing would have been foolish to print whole issues of, or long sections from, the leading opposition journal in England. There is no evidence I know of about numbers of the *Craftsman* being shipped to the colonies, or of private correspondents enclosing copies in personal letters. Yet the *Craftsman* was so widely known that Massachusetts merchants opposing Governor Shirley's proposal for an excise tax in Massachusetts in 1752 copied both the tactics of Bolingbroke and Pulteney against Walpole's excise scheme and the style of the *Craftsman*. Paul S. Boyer, 'Borrowed Rhetoric: The Massachusetts Excise Controversy of 1754', *W.M.Q.* 3rd Ser. XXI (1964), pp. 328–51.

[25] This can be inferred from the fact that Pulteney and Sir William Wyndham

Looking at the activities of Bolingbroke and Pulteney in 1732 and 1733 it appears that what they and their American interpreters were dreaming of was a remarkable kind of transatlantic co-operation—a co-operation between country parties on both sides of the Atlantic.[26] There were, indeed, profound possibilities here. But they came to nothing, on account of Walpole's Excise scheme of 1733.

Ostensibly the scheme was based on a plan voted by the Virginia Assembly in 1732 and brought to the British government by Peyton Randolph, agent of the Assembly.[27] For this reason Bolingbroke and Pulteney should have supported it. But on the other hand the group who would be most seriously hurt by the scheme were the lesser London merchants, an increasingly effective force that the opposition were eager to develop. Potential English allies were more crucial than American ones, and so Bolingbroke and Pulteney, reluctant to throw away the first occasion they had ever really had of bringing Walpole down, opposed the Excise Bill. They struggled hard to convince colonial readers that they were not opposing the true wishes of the Virginia planters: in two issues the *Craftsman* argued that the original proposal was passed by the Virginia Assembly only under secret pressure from the British ministers, and that once the Burgesses read the Excise Bill as the government presented it they opposed it as strongly as the London merchants did.[28]

Nevertheless the Excise crisis made two things clear: the lesser London merchants most likely to be in the forefront of English urban radicalism, and most likely to support Bolingbroke and Pulteney, were also inclined on crucial issues to be

---

were tellers for the 'yea' side of a motion to allow the Rhode Island petition against the Molasses Act to be read (Chalmers, *Introduction to the Revolt*, Vol. II, pp. 122–3).

[26] On 6 Dec. 1734 Governor Cosby wrote the Lords of Trade that his leading opponents had acted 'Upon the weak hopes they had entertain'd and which they have often spoken out, that a New Parliament would introduce a New Ministry, and that something more would follow which I shall unwillingly name to your Lordship . . .' (O'Callaghan, ed., *Docs. re Col. Hist. N.Y.*, Vol. VI, p. 22).

[27] St. George Leaken Sioussat, *Virginia and the English Commercial System, 1730–1733* (Washington, 1906), pp. 81–3, is now outdated. See John Mickle Hemphill II, 'Virginia and the English Commercial System, 1689–1733; Studies in the Development and Fluctuations of a Colonial Economy under Imperial Control' (Ph.D. thesis, Princeton University, 1964).

[28] *The Craftsman*, Vol. X, No. 360, pp. 36–43, and No. 369, pp. 100–7.

hostile to their colonial counterparts, and when they were, Walpole's parliamentary opponents were prepared to support the merchants at the Americans' expense. It was the lesser English merchant as much as anyone who made impossible the development of any kind of transatlantic co-operation among Walpole's enemies.

It is not too much to suggest that the Excise scheme and the dilemma into which it put the English opposition was a turning-point in Anglo-colonial history, for two reasons. First, it seems to have completely changed the approach of the opposition leaders towards the colonies for the next thirty years—until the decade just before the Revolution, in fact. Second, it destroyed the promising transatlantic partisan connections of Queen Anne's reign, and left many of the American country parties to shift the focus of their attention from Whitehall to the provincial electorate.

(i) THE ENGLISH OPPOSITION

Over the ten years after the defeat of the Excise scheme English opposition leaders reversed themselves on questions of colonial policy, and began to play with the idea of supporting measures so strict that they would prove unworkable in the colonies, thus bringing colonial governments to a slowdown and providing material for an embarrassing parliamentary debate.[29] Such a measure was a Bill of 1740 regulating paper money in the colonies, and making instructions to the governors effective as parliamentary law. The measure was vastly unpopular with all sections of the colonial population, but the opposition appears to have supported it anyway, with the idea that it would almost certainly provoke disturbances against the government in the colonies. As Richard Partridge wrote of the proposals,

. . . it is observable that they were proposed and carried through at the Instance of three of the members principally who are on the side of the Minority of the House being Anti-Courtiers viz Sir Jno Barnard, Sam. Sandys and Allr Hume Campbell Esquires and it is

[29] In 1734 the government forced postponement of a resolution in the House of Lords that the laws of all colonies, corporate as well as proprietary and royal, must be submitted to the government for review within six months of passage.

believed that the chief aim of some of them in it was more with a view to puzle and perplex the Ministry and Spirit up the Plantations against them with anything else.[30]

On other measures the evidence of a changing opposition stance is circumstantial but still strong. In 1734 the House of Lords considered a resolution requiring all colonies to submit their laws for English review within six months of passage. In 1741 Parliament voted the Massachusetts Land Bank illegal; in 1744, 1749, and 1751 it considered Bills limiting issues of colonial paper currency, and also giving governors' instructions the force of parliamentary law. Of all these only one seems to have had even lukewarm support from the government: Carteret, temporarily prime minister early in 1744, seems to have had some personal enthusiasm for the paper-currency Bill of that year.

The rest of the measures had been, in fact, tailor-made for uniting the scattered elements of English opposition ever since 1715. For colonial administration, like foreign negotiations, was a question of 'management'; an M.P. did not necessarily have to have a 'position' on it, as he might, for example, on a recurring domestic issue like the powers of the House of Lords or the privileges of Noncomformist Churches. On matters involving the colonies an M.P. could vote issue by issue, incident by incident, without necessarily having to develop any consistent principles. This might not have been entirely true right after the Glorious Revolution, when Whigs and Tories did make the colonies a party question, and when colonial factions consistently appealed for English support. But by the 1720s any moderate ministerial proposal mentioning the colonies could either bring accusations that the colonists were being oppressed, or could inspire the opposition to propose even stricter—even unworkable—changes in order to embarrass the government in carrying them out. To propose that Parliament should pay for the salaries of colonial officials, give certain executive orders the force of parliamentary law, or sanction any administrative reorganization, was to give the opposition an issue where it could unite on a genuine point of difference with the ministry, arouse

[30] Partridge to Wanton, 2 May 1740 (Kimball, *Corr. R.I. Govs.*, Vol. I, pp. 152–4). Barnard was a leading London merchant, Sandys was in the Carteret–Bath faction, and Hume Campbell one of the Prince of Wales's group.

some measure of public opinion, and possibly take the opportunity to urge unworkable changes far beyond anything the
ministers desired.[31]

As long as the leaders of the parliamentary opposition were
in sympathy with the country parties in the colonies, however,
they were reluctant to bring up legislation which those country
parties opposed. And so for ten years after Walpole became the
leading minister he succeeded in keeping colonial affairs out of
Parliament altogether. In 1729 he had to ask Parliament for
money to buy out the rights to the government and land of
South Carolina from the proprietors, and after Georgia was
settled he agreed, though with a reluctance which increased
over the years, to support proposals for parliamentary grants for
the infant colony's expenses.[32] But these were the exceptions,
for Walpole was otherwise able to keep controversial questions
out of Parliament. In 1721, for example, the Board of Trade
brought up its traditional proposal for buying out the remaining
proprietorships, resuming charter colonies to the Crown, and
sending a commander-in-chief over the united colonies.[33] The
Board wanted its plan submitted to Parliament, but neither
Walpole or Lord Townshend approved the submission. Three
years later the governor of Massachusetts got into a quarrel
with his Assembly over the right of a governor to veto the
Assembly's election of a Speaker. The Privy Council not only

[31] This interpretation helps to explain the discrepancy between two well-
known analyses of Parliament's refusal to legislate on colonial government.
Chalmers (*History of the Revolt*, Vol. II, p. 315) says that the ministers consistently
refused to apply to Parliament for help, while Andrews (*Colonial Period*, Vol. IV,
p. 407) comments that Parliament was unwilling to back the ministers up. If one
assumes that the ministers were reluctant to take matters to Parliament for fear
that the opposition might take such an occasion to put them on the spot, then
Andrews and Chalmers seem to make more sense taken together than taken
separately.

Archibald S. Foord (*His Majesty's Opposition*, pp. 173–5) says of the Bolingbroke–
Pulteney opposition: 'The Government knew their weaknesses as well as they, but
ncessant criticism and the potential threat of a vigorous offensive imposed caution
and vigilance upon the ministry. In sum, the coalition with all its infirmities served
as a restraining and inhibiting force upon the Government with all the attendant
possibilities of good and evil.'

[32] Richard S. Dunn, 'The Trustees of Georgia and the House of Commons,
1732–1752', *W.M.Q.* 3rd Ser. XI (1954), pp. 551–65 *passim*.

[33] Not everyone would agree that the proposal of 1721 was simply traditional.
Stanley M. Pargellis, *Lord Loudon in America* (New Haven, Conn., 1933), p. 9,
thought the Plan of 1721 marked a fundamental change in the policies of the Board
of Trade.

decided in favour of the governor, but also demanded that the principle of the governor's right to veto the Speaker should be recognized by the colony. But how should the colony be forced to grant such recognition? Should Parliament legislate to that effect, or should the matter be handled entirely by the administration? Under the ministry's direction the Council decided to issue a supplementary royal charter, and not to seek parliamentary legislation unless the charter was flagrantly disobeyed.

The controversy over the Massachusetts Speakership occurred during the administration of Governor Shute; Shute's successor, Governor William Burnet, also had trouble with the Massachusetts Assembly, this time over the Assembly's refusal to vote him a salary for more than a year at a time, though his instructions required him to get five-year grants. Burnet wanted Parliament to vote him a salary, but the ministry decided to let him accept the annual grants instead.[34]

These were just three of the problems that might have been handled by Parliament, but were not. There were a good many others: New York land grants contested by rival factions within the colony, the demand for parliamentary legislation recognizing the Georgia charter, the demands of New Hampshire political leaders to be independent of Massachusetts, and of New Jersey leaders to be independent of New York. Significantly, between the rise of Robert Walpole in 1721 and the height of his power in 1730 there were fewer colonial issues before Parliament than in any other comparable period in the eighteenth century.[35]

[34] Governor Burnet himself wanted parliamentary legislation (*Cal. S.P. Col.*, *1728-29*, pp. 227, 430). His correspondence with the Secretary of State and the Board of Trade is in C.O. 5/867, 868. B.M. Add. MS. 15486 contains 'Papers relating to Massachusetts, 1720-1724', including the Report of the Attorney and Solicitor General and the Report of the Board of Trade. Reports of the Massachusetts agent's hearing before the Privy Council are in the Belknap Papers (30 Apr. 1725, 1725 MSS., f. 116) and the Cushing MSS. See also extract of a letter written by the agent, Elisha Cooke, 5-7 July 1725, MS. 12, Mass. Hist. Soc.; Burnet to De La Faye, 26 Oct. 1728, Bancroft Transcripts, Vol. 2, ff. 61-2, New York Public Library. Not long after this Governor Belcher was in a similar predicament, and explained to Richard Partridge, 'As you observe I must walk very circumspectly lest the House of Commons should think I bear to hard upon the privileges of the people' (1 Nov. 1731, Belcher Papers, *Colls. Mass. Hist. Soc.* 6th Ser. VI, p. 38).

[35] On Walpole's later efforts to keep colonial issues out of parliament note Lewis Morris's comment: 'It is not the injustice of the thing [Cosby's Acts] that affects

After 1733, however, the opposition leaders were no longer reluctant to affront the colonists, and now, in the 1730s, they saw, as they had not seen before, a chance to bring into that opposition two new groups—the merchants and the members of the Board of Trade. The American merchants, long accustomed to dealing with the Board of Trade, now organized for appealing to Parliament; the Board of Trade members, used to working with Parliament, but in support of the government, now joined the parliamentary opposition. The opposition had given up a chance to combine with the American radicals in favour of a coalition against them.

A. *The Merchants*

Customarily the merchants relied on the Privy Council and the Board of Trade to obtain copies of colonial laws and review them for possible disallowance within the time required. In 1734 they pressed Parliament for an Act requiring Connecticut and Rhode Island, hitherto exempt from sending their laws for review, henceforth to do so, and requiring all colonies to send their laws within a shorter time than previously allowed. In the 1720s merchants had constantly appealed to the Board to disallow colonial laws providing for extravagant issues of paper money; in the 1740s merchants began urging Parliament to prohibit all such laws.[36] Since governors were often forced to assent to paper-currency laws in spite of their instructions, the merchants began pressing also for an Act giving gubernatorial instructions the force of law.

Why did the merchants begin to seek parliamentary legisla-

those concerned in recommending him provided it can be kept a secret and the people not clamor' (Morris to Alexander, 30 Mar. 1734/5, *The Papers of Lewis Morris, Governor of the Province of New Jersey from 1738–1746*, N.J. Hist. Soc. Memoirs, IV (Newark, 1852), p. 24.

Some time later Cadwallader Colden, adviser to Governor Clinton of New York, wrote that the scheme of the de Lancey party in opposition to the governor was to raise up so much popular disturbance that the ministry would remove Clinton in order to keep the colony quiet. 'The whole artifice of the party consists in raising clamours among the people by base and false calumnies in hopes that the ministry will think it prudent to comply with the humours of the people at this time as the easiest method to quiet matters and make themselves easy from more trouble' (Colden to Catherwood, 29 Nov. 1749; *Colden Papers*, Vol. IV, p. 160).

[36] Complaints of the English merchants that the colonists disobeyed royal orders limiting currency issues were responsible for the paper-money Bills of 1744 and 1749 (Root, *Pa. and British Government*, pp. 196–7).

tion on issues they had formerly entrusted to executive action? There are several answers. For one thing, as merchants in many different colonies became aware of their common problems they began to think that general legislation would be more useful than *ad hoc* decisions by the Board of Trade on five or ten basically similar questions, each affecting a different colony. For example, when only one or two colonies had made post-war issues of paper money, there was no point in parliamentary action on the general question of currency issues; when nine or ten had, there was a point to such action. When only the merchants of Virginia had difficulty in collecting their debts, parliamentary action against every colony would have seemed punitive; when merchants of several colonies had the same problem, it was not.

For another reason, as the 1720s went on the ministry's reluctance to undertake any drastic colonial reforms became apparent. Even if the ministers had been willing to begin reforms it was doubtful if they would have gone out of their way to help the merchants, for by 1730, and certainly by 1733, the American merchants were in open opposition to Walpole.

Walpole's financial support came from London's commercial magnates—in particular the directors of the Bank of England, the East India Company, and the South Seas Company. These companies held the National Debt; it was absolutely necessary to the government's financial credit that Walpole should cultivate good relations with them,[37] and accordingly he favoured not only their requests for financial privileges but also their nominations to a good many local and colonial places, especially in customs offices. The proprietor of Pennsylvania, for example, found that the ministers handled with great dispatch the formalities for approving a provincial governor, once the proprietor had secured a favourable introduction to Walpole from a Director of the East India Company.[38]

Most of the merchants trading to the American colonies, however, were not in this circle of London financial magnates. They seem instead to have been middling or lesser merchants, men who had no financial connections with the government,

[37] Sutherland, *East India Company*, pp. 5-7.
[38] John to Thomas Penn, 3 Aug. 1733, Penn Letter Book I, ff. 88-9, Pa. Hist. Soc.

and men who, as members of the London livery companies that elected the City's aldermen and members of Parliament, deeply resented Walpole's attempts to interfere in the City's government. Over the years, urged on by Bolingbroke and Pulteney, the middling merchants became more and more hostile to Walpole.[39] In 1733 when Walpole proposed an excise tax on the tobacco which many of them handled, and coupled his proposal with the galling, if wholly justified, explanation that the Excise Scheme was intended as an administrative reform to keep these very merchants from continuing to defraud the government of customs duties, London merchants looked on the proposal as the last straw. Their coffee houses became centres where copies of the opposition paper, *The Craftsman*, were distributed, where the Lord Mayor and Alderman hostile to the government could circulate petitions, and where orators could berate Walpole's government.

A few of the American merchants had wealth or influence sufficient to put them above the middling group, but most of these, for all their wealth and position, considered themselves as associates of the middle-class merchants rather than of London's financial directorate. In this group were colonists like the Wraggs of South Carolina and Theodore Atkinson of New Hampshire. Atkinson—by virtue of his trade with the West Indies—and his associates the Wentworths—through their trade with Spain—had immense wealth, and consequently they were able to influence English appointments in New Hampshire. From 1741 on, a Wentworth was always governor of colonial New Hampshire. The Wraggs of South Carolina nominated several councillors in that colony and had enough influence with the Board of Trade to affect their acceptance or rejection of currency laws passed by the colonial Assembly.[40]

[39] Plumb, *Walpole*, p. 200; Lucy S. Sutherland, *The City of London and the Opposition to Government, 1768–74, a Study in the Rise of Metropolitan Radicalism*, The Creighton Lecture in History, 1958 (London, 1959), *passim*.

[40] John and Capel Hanbury, English merchants whose business was mostly with the Chesapeake colonies, seem to have had a similar influence on appointments to Virginia and Maryland, though this influence tended to be exerted as much on the proprietor of Maryland and the absentee governor of Virginia as on the ministers themselves. See, for example, Albemarle to Newcastle, 29 Nov. 1743, B.M. Add. MS. 32701 f. 265. For Wragg see M. Eugene Sirmans, 'The South Carolina Royal Council, 1720–1763', *W.M.Q.* XVIII (1961), p. 383. For the Hanburys see A. Audrey Locke, *The Hanbury Family* (2 vols., London, 1916), Vol. II, pp. 249–50, 289–90.

But the Wraggs and the Wentworths and others like them never seem to have identified themselves with the merchants who gathered around Walpole.

If the lesser American merchants and the wealthier ones as well were occasionally or consistently hostile to Walpole, the richest merchant of them all, Micajah Perry, became his inveterate enemy. Perry was a Virginia tobacco merchant, who boasted in 1733 that he imported as much tobacco as all the other Virginia merchants combined. Unlike most of the other American merchants, he was in the inner circle of London politics: he was M.P. for London and in 1738 Lord Mayor.[41] Moreover, he was agent for various colonies, including Virginia, and had frequently nominated Virginia councillors (through the Board of Trade), customs officials (through the Treasury Board), and even the all-powerful secretary of Virginia. But in 1732 Perry turned against Walpole because of Walpole's proposed excise tax on tobacco;[42] shortly after that he was writing to a friend in New York that he would like to help him get a proposal before the ministers, but he no longer had any influence with them.

Aware of the need for general legislation to handle their common problems in working with the colonies, and conscious of the fact that they and the Board of Trade, who were sympathetic to them, both lacked the influence to get the ministry to issue general directives, the merchants would have been inclined to encourage Walpole's parliamentary opponents to bring up colonial reform. But added to these was a further reason: the merchants themselves in the 1730s were organized to 'lobby' with members of Parliament as they could not before.

Some time around 1730 the wealthier merchants associated with each coffee house seem to have begun separating off from the crowds on the main floor and meeting together informally upstairs or in a back room.[43] There is no way of knowing exactly

[41] Sir William Purdee Treloar, *A Lord Mayor's Diary, 1906–1907, to which is added the Official Diary of Micajah Perry, 1738–1739* (London, 1920).

[42] Alfred James Henderson, *London and the National Government, 1721–1742* (Durham, N.C., 1945), Ch. VI.

[43] Cf. William Thomas La Prade, *Public Opinion and Politics in Eighteenth-Century England, to the Fall of Walpole* (New York, 1936), pp. 270–80, and 'Weekly Essays' in the *Gentleman's Magazine*, IV (Aug. 1734), pp. 431–2 (proposals for a Merchants' Club).

when these merchant clubs began. Indeed, Governor Spots-wood's complaints as far back as 1712 that Virginia councillor-ships were settled in the Virginia coffee house may have indicated that an 'inner group' of Virginia merchants was meeting even then, though there is no evidence on this point. Virginia and Maryland, having more English merchants than other colonies, were no doubt the first to organize clubs. James Knight mentioned the existence of a Virginia club in 1725,[44] and in the same year there was also in existence (possibly it was the same as the Virginia and Maryland clubs) an associa-tion of all merchants trading to Virginia and Maryland presided over by Micajah Perry.

By 1734 the merchants of other American colonies had set up clubs,[45] usually meeting once or twice a month. There is no way of knowing exactly how long these clubs had been in existence, but the fact that in 1731 the merchants of New York, Virginia, and Maryland petitioned Parliament for legislation to help them recover their debts may indicate that the mer-chants of other colonies did not have clubs yet, and that they were formed, therefore, some time between 1731 and 1734.[46]

Only with the development of clubs did merchants seem able to bring pressure on Parliament. A group of merchants in a coffee house might discuss colonial legislation, decide to appeal to the Board against some of the laws, draft a petition to the

[44] Lillian M. Penson, 'The London West India Interest in the Eighteenth Century', *E.H.R.* XXXVI (1931), p. 377.

[45] 'Proposals for a Merchants' Club', *Gentleman's Magazine*, IV (Aug. 1734), pp. 431–2. See Penson, *Colonial Agents of the British West Indies*, pp. 181–96.

[46] At about the same time (1732) the General Meeting of the Dissenting Deputies, an organization of the London Dissenters, was established as a pressure group quite similar to the merchants' clubs. See Carl Bridenbaugh, *Mitre and Sceptre, Trans-atlantic Faiths, Ideals, Personalities, and Powers, 1689–1775* (New York, 1962), p. 42. For a discussion of the Deputies and also of the Quaker political lobby which functioned at the same time, and was the model for the Deputies, see N. C. Hunt, *Two Early Political Associations: The Quakers and the Dissenting Deputies in the Age of Sir Robert Walpole* (Oxford, 1961), esp. p. xiv, describing the means by which the associations could influence Parliament. For the Deputies' particular interest in the colonies see Maurice W. Armstrong, 'The Dissenting Deputies and the Ameri-can Colonies', *Church History*, XXIX (1960), pp. 298–320, esp. 298–315. In 1741 the Deputies' president, Dr. Avery, apparently applied to the ministers for a continuation of Jonathan Belcher as governor of Massachusetts (Belcher to Belcher, Jr., 27 Jan. 1740/1. Belcher Papers, *Colls, Mass. Hist. Soc.* 6th Ser. VII, pp. 366–7). Photostat copies of the Minutes of the Dissenting Deputies are in the Library of the Presbyterian Historical Society, Philadelphia.

Board, to be left in the coffee shop as patrons drifted in, post a notice on the wall of the shop urging patrons to attend a particular meeting of the Board, and thus impress the Board with their unanimity of opinion. But it was impossible to deal effectively with 435 members of Parliament this way. A club, unlike a coffee house, could collect dues and use them to publish pamphlets to be circulated among M.P.s, could with system and regularity review colonial conditions, could divide the House of Commons up among its members and see that each member was encouraged to support the merchants' demands, and could pool the influence club members had with leading debaters in Parliament.

Doubtless the merchant clubs evolved very gradually from the coffee house atmosphere. The difference in the effectiveness of the group of friends who met regularly around a coffee table to talk about the latest colonial news and the merchants organized into a club was one of slight degree; the merchants continued to seek help from the Board of Trade as they always had, and because of the overwhelming opposition to most of their proposals by the Court Party the merchants at first were not notably successful in their parliamentary appeals. But when all this is said, it still remains true that after 1730 the English merchants did begin to turn more and more to Parliament for legislation affecting the colonies, and though they could rarely buck the government's majority they found more than nominal support. In 1732 a Bill to facilitate the merchants' recovery of their American debts was introduced. In 1741 Parliament abolished the Massachusetts Land Bank. In 1744 a parliamentary Bill preventing colonies from issuing paper bills of credit was introduced by a leading merchant, Sir John Barnard.[47] And in 1751 Parliament limited the paper currency issues of four New England colonies, a measure long pressed by merchants.[48]

The development of merchants' clubs did not mean the dying out of colonial coffee houses or the decline of interest in the colonies in other coffee houses. These continued to flourish as

[47] Stock, *Proceedings*, Vol. V, p. 187 (H.C., 4 May 1744).

[48] The 1751 Bill came after the London merchants trading to Rhode Island had petitioned against the emission of further bills of credit by that colony. Stock, *Proceedings*, Vol. V. p. 464 (H.C., 12 Mar. 1750/1); Burns, *New England Agents*, p. 61.

centres of what eighteenth-century writers called 'democratic discussion'. Every major colonial controversy soon excited coffee-house arguments. In the 1750s the argument between the proprietor of Pennsylvania and the Quakers of the Pennsylvania Assembly was carried to the coffee houses.[49] Secretary Calvert of Maryland wrote that having a colonial dispute discussed there gave the argument a 'popular' character,[50] and Governor Dinwiddie, on learning that his controversy with the Virginia Burgesses over the 'pistole fee' was widely argued in the coffee houses, remarked defensively that it did not take much to start a controversy there.[51] As late as 1765 an agent like Charles Garth of South Carolina could attract merchants at a Board of Trade hearing of charges against Governor Boone by posting a notice on the wall of the Carolina Coffee House.

There are some points worth noting in these examples. Each remark referred to a quarrel between a governor and his Assembly. None of the quarrels was taken up by Parliament: there were issues in several which might have warranted parliamentary legislation, but the coffee-house merchants were not equipped for an appeal to Parliament, and the controversies went instead to the Board of Trade. There is no evidence on all the issues as to which way coffee-house opinion leaned, but the general sentiments seem to have been against at least two of the governors, Dinwiddie and Boone, and the Board reflected these sentiments by deciding against both of them.

B. *The Board of Trade*

In appealing to Parliament the merchants could either work directly with M.P.s who were in opposition to the government, or they could work through the Board of Trade. On first thought one might expect the Board to have opposed the

[49] John J. Zimmerman, 'Benjamin Franklin: A study of Pennsylvania Politics and the Colonial Agency, 1755-75' (Ph.D. thesis, University of Michigan, 1956), p. 27.

[50] Calvert to Governor Sharpe, 12 Jan. 1758 (The Correspondence of Governor Horatio Sharpe, *Archives of Maryland*, ed. William Hand Browne (Baltimore, Md., 1890), Vol. IX, p. 129).

[51] Dinwiddie to Abercrombie, 26 Apr. 1754 ('The Official Records of Robert Dinwiddie, Lieutenant Governor of the Colony of Virginia, 1751-58 . . . '. ed. R. A. Brock, *Colls. Va. Hist. Soc.* N.S. III and IV (Richmond, Va., 1883-4), Vol. III, pp. 139-40).

merchants instead of supporting them, since the Board members were appointed by the ministers and were supposedly responsible to them. But the Board had their own reasons for wanting some colonial issues to come before Parliament; they had long been pressing for legislation to back up their decisions. More than this, the relations between the Board and the ministers—especially the Duke of Newcastle—deteriorated rapidly between 1730 and 1735, so the Board no longer felt particularly constrained to go along with the ministers' policy of keeping colonial matters out of Parliament.

In this period the overwhelmingly pre-eminent member of the Board of Trade was Martin Bladen. In 1730 Bladen had already had fifteen years' experience on the Board; he wrote the vast majority of reports, attended far more meetings than any other member, and at some meetings was the only member who attended at all. He was also a member of innumerable parliamentary committees set up to investigate colonial problems. Only two other members approached Bladen's influence at the Board—Paul Dominique (who was also a West Jersey proprietor, and hence personally interested in the colonies) and the Earl of Westmorland, President of the Board. Dominique and Westmorland were both fairly regular in their attendance at the Board and contributed to the writing of reports, but the other Board members did considerably less work. Men like Brudenell, Herbert, and Plumer were not lacking in opinions of their own, but with their irregular attendance at the Board and their lack of background information on many issues they must often have found preliminary reports drafted and lines of procedure drawn up by Bladen without them.[52]

In 1730 Bladen was already known as a wealthy merchant, high-ranking diplomat, and distinguished soldier, but, more important, as a dogged worker, an astute politician, and a man who was not interested in colonial government for nothing.

[52] For example, on 5 Jan. 1739/40 Bladen wrote Newcastle that he had finished drawing up instructions for several governors of North America and had used his own discretion on many of the clauses (C.O. 5/5 ff. 147–8). Bladen also drew up a plan for colonial union which he himself sent to Walpole (Jack P. Greene, 'Martin Bladen's Blueprint for a Colonial Union', *W.M.Q.* 3rd Ser. XVII (1960), pp. 516–30). When Britain faced a war with Spain in 1739 Bladen resurrected once more the old plan for a Captain General of the colonies (Bladen to Walpole, 27 Dec. 1739, Walpole MSS., Cambridge University Library).

In considering problems of colonial government Bladen always had at heart two questions: what would Walpole wish (not the other ministers, only Walpole himself), and what would help Bladen's own interest most. As to the first, there was no doubt of Bladen's complete loyalty to Sir Robert. Although he had sufficient fortune to buy his own seat in the Commons, he was immensely unpopular there for his work in negotiating a generous treaty with Spain in 1729; without Walpole's backing he would have had little prestige in the Commons, few opportunities to speak, and few committee assignments. Moreover, although he was appointed to the Board of Trade long before Walpole became prime minister he considered that he owed his continuation in that office to Sir Robert alone. He was, in fact, the very epitome of the 'man of business', the minor servant whose dutiful loyalty to Walpole was the strength of the Court and Treasury Party.

For the second point, Bladen's interest in the American colonies, like his constant support of Walpole, was by no means altogether altruistic or detached. By marrying a West Indian heiress he had acquired extensive estates on Barbados, a fact which always inclined him to favour West Indian trading interests over those of the mainland. He also had, like his earlier parallel William Blathwayt, a finger in several colonial companies, like the Company organized to develop the 'Equivalent Lands' in New York,[53] and his support or opposition to provincial governors might well rest on their attitude towards Bladen's investments. His support for governors might also depend on whether or not they got on with Bladen's friends in particular colonies[54] (he did not like Governor Belcher of Massachusetts and New Hampshire, because Belcher opposed

[53] C. H. Collins Baker and Muriel I. Baker, *The Life and Circumstances of James Brydges*, First Duke of Chandos (Oxford, 1949), pp. 349–51.
[54] Among various things, Bladen nominated councillors in North Carolina, Virginia, New Jersey, New York, and New Hampshire (C.O. 324/49 *passim*). The only other Board member who came close to having Bladen's influence was Francis Fane, who began as the Board's legal adviser and was appointed a Board member in the 1740s. In 1729 Bladen wrote Governor Montgomerie of New York on behalf of some of Bladen's friends who were setting up a copper mine in the colony (31 Jan. 1729, C.O. 5/1093, f. 56). A letter from a Mr. Couraud to Mr. Keene enclosed two letters on logwood-cutting, written by Bladen 'to whose opinion, in the points of Business to which they relate a good deal of deference is paid here' (8 May 1739, B.M. Add. MS. 32800, f. 421).

Bladen's very good friends the Atkinsons and the Wentworths of New Hampshire, nor did he like Governor Burrington of North Carolina, who did not get along with Bladen's brother-in-law, the secretary of the province). He also took note of the amount of support the governors gave officials whom Bladen sent out to their colony (Bladen had engrossed virtually all the Board's remaining patronage in his own hands), and it was even important that Bladen should like the governors personally (he could not stand the irascible Burrington).

The issue between Bladen, the other Board members, and the ministry centred on whether certain colonial governors who were having trouble with their legislature should be supported or dismissed. With personal criteria in mind Bladen and some of the other Board members took a strong dislike to some of the governors. It would probably be going too far to say that the Board consciously tried to harry the governors out of office but they certainly made it clear which governors they disapproved.

Bladen and the Board in general were annoyed at the low calibre of the governors appointed to the colonies after the accession of George II in 1727. Although, strictly speaking, all the colonial governors had to be approved by the Secretary of State, they had in fact been appointed by a variety of people in the cabinet. Walpole and Lord Wilmington were responsible for getting Governor Gordon confirmed for Pennsylvania, Walpole himself seems to have moved Governor Burnett from New York to Massachusetts, and he certainly was responsible for appointing his friend and Norfolk neighbour William Gooch to the governorship of Virginia. Lord Townshend, then Secretary of State for the North, obtained Jonathan Belcher's appointment to Massachusetts when Burnet died in 1729.[55] Only in 1730 did Newcastle seem to have got his own nominees in as colonial governors, and his choices then, Burrington for North Carolina and Cosby for New York, were certainly the worst he ever made.

It was clear from the start which of these governors Bladen and the Board would approve and which they would disapprove. Ever since the seventeenth century it had been true that to be safe a governor had to keep his opposition from

[55] Wood, *Public Life of William Shirley*, p. 22.

appealing vociferously to England. But now he had in addition
to cultivate the support of leading ministers and get along with
Martin Bladen's friends and associates. By these criteria the
safest governor of all was William Gooch, chief executive of
Virginia from 1727 until he retired for reasons of health in 1749.
Gooch's family were Walpole's neighbours in Norfolk, and
Gooch always had the prime minister's friendly support. Moreover he had the faithful services at court of his brother, the
Bishop of Norwich,[56] he was liked by Bladen,[57] managed to
avoid overt factional disputes in the colony which might bring
politics to an impasse, acquiesced gracefully in the steady
growth of the Burgesses' power, and usually submitted when
the absentee governors made appointments to various offices
in Virginia. Gooch occasionally had troubles over patronage
with Lord Albemarle, the absentee governor,[58] but generally
British officials left him alone to enjoy two decades of peaceful
administration.

By the same criteria the governors who were in greatest
trouble in the years immediately after 1720 were Cosby,
Belcher, and Burrington. All had aroused popular opposition
(Belcher governed both Massachusetts and New Hampshire,
and his opposition at this time was stronger in New Hampshire).
None was appointed by Walpole and none had his personal
support, and Belcher and Burrington did not get along with
Bladen's friends in their colonies. Only Cosby had a claim to
Bladen's favour: he was using all his powers as governor of New
York to further the claims of Bladen and some of his friends to
lands in the colony. The brunt of the Board's harassment,
therefore, was directed against these three governors, though
Bladen held back from the attack on Cosby.

[56] Norwich's solicitations on Gooch's behalf are found throughout the Newcastle
papers. For example, Norwich to Newcastle, 3 July 1746, B.M. Add. MS. 32707,
f. 392, and 15 Sept. 1746, Add. MS. 32708, f. 292.

[57] Gooch to the Bishop of Norwich, 4 Apr. 1728 (Gooch MSS., Williamsburg,
Virginia).

[58] Albemarle was annoyed that Gooch appointed an adjutant without telling
Albemarle in 1739. Gooch defended himself in a letter explaining to Albemarle his
desperate need for every one of the few patronage positions left to him (3 Sept.
1739, C.O. 5/1337, pp. 114–17).

Gooch himself had to put up with the Board's occasional rejection of some of his
nominees for councillorships. See, for example, C.O. 5/1322, pp. 303–5, 319, where
the Board appointed David Bray to a councillorship to which Gooch had recommended Mr. Harrison.

The Board could not dismiss a governor; that was up to the Secretary of State. But by refusing to approve their nominees for councillorships, publicly encouraging their opponents, not allowing them to make salary concessions, and even, in New Hampshire, securing the appointment of a lieutenant-governor openly hostile to the governor, and encouraging him to obstruct the governor in every attempt to get favourable legislation from the local Assembly, the Board made it perfectly clear to the provincial politicians that the governor did not have its support. To some extent this had happened to governors in the past: hostile appointments from home or unfavourable review of important provincial legislation had undermined their authority. Indeed, ministers had misguidedly thought that variety brought strength to colonial governments. But the Board of Trade was most certainly trying to do a good deal more than broaden the base of colonial governments; they were making it quite clear which governors they did not like. Newcastle, for his part, while recognizing that the governors in question were not exactly the best he could have picked, nevertheless resented the actions of the Board.

For several years the situation deteriorated. Burrington had to be recalled. Belcher found himself saddled with an openly hostile lieutenant-governor, and in desperation wrote his agent to bribe Bladen, and, if that did not work, to see that future controversies went to the Privy Council and not to the Board. Finally, when Governor Cosby was attacked by Lewis Morris a majority of the Board supported Morris.

Morris brought before the Board his charge that Cosby had acted improperly in dismissing him from the New York Council. The Board was divided: Bladen, aware of Cosby's faithful support of the Equivalent Lands claimed by his friends in New York, backed the governor, but a slight majority of the Board, including Dominique and Westmorland, supported Morris. When Cosby sent over counter charges against Morris, Westmorland blocked the hearing on them, so that Morris's charges could be heard first. Meanwhile, Newcastle got Morris's charges referred to him, and tried to keep them holed up indefinitely on his desk so that the Board could not vote on them. Morris waited, and nothing was done.

Finally Morris's friend Dominique died, and Newcastle, now

one vote short of a majority for Cosby, dismissed Westmorland from the Board and replaced him with Lord Monson, who was willing to clear Cosby of the charges. Once more the matter was brought up before the Board and this time Cosby was acquitted. But the matter had generated a good deal of controversy, so a secret meeting of ministers was held to discuss what to do about Cosby. Here again Newcastle stuck by the governor and persuaded Walpole and Henry Pelham to do the same.[59]

Newcastle's work in the Cosby case ended the most extreme of the Board's attempts to undermine certain colonial governors. But it also created a good deal of friction and hate between the Board and the Secretary of State, and left the remaining members of the Board personally disgruntled, inclined to be unco-operative with the minister, and more bitter than ever at their lack of power. All along they had been advocating stricter colonial administration; now, once again, they began looking for devious ways of getting their ideas before Parliament.

Theoretically the Board could not present reports unsolicited to Parliament: the procedure was for Parliament to address the King for papers bearing on a particular aspect of colonial government, and the ministers or Board members would then make the presentation. Thus the Board could get its recommendations before Parliament only by responding as subordinates to the ministers, who were in turn requested to present information to the Commons or the Lords. But there were ways of getting around this seemingly passive position. The members of the Board were themselves usually members of Parliament, and while some never spoke at all on colonial or any other questions, and rarely sat on committees, others, like Bladen and Westmorland, were regular debaters in the House and served on nearly every committee concerned with the colonies. They or one of their parliamentary associates might move for papers, or they might get merchants outside Parliament to petition for

[59] For Morris's case see, for example, Beverly McAnear, 'An American in London, 1735–1736', *Pa. Mag. Hist. & Biog.* LXIV (1940), pp. 164–217, 356–406; *N.Y. Col. Docs.* VI, pp. 35–7; Lewis Morris Papers, Rutgers University Library; Alice Mapelsden Keys, *Cadwallader Colden* (New York, 1906), pp. 42–53; Letters and Papers of Cadwallader Colden, 1730–42, *Colls. N.Y. Hist. Soc.*, Vol. III, *passim,* and Vol. IX, pp. 283–355; McAnear, 'Politics in Provincial New York', pp. 395–451; Katz, 'Newcastle's New York', and Katz's edition of additional Morris letters in *W.M.Q.* XXVIII (July 1971), pp. 439–84.

redress of grievances against the colonies, making a request for the appropriate information inevitable.[60]

Vastly different objectives and a very unholy alliance, but the colonial significance of the *ad hoc* coalitions between merchants, Board of Trade members, and Walpole's parliamentary opponents was far greater than their ineffectiveness in England would suggest. Before the period of the Excise Scheme and the failure of the *Craftsman* circle to create an Anglo-colonial 'country' association, the merchants, the parliamentary opposition, and the Board of Trade would not have thought of working together to bring up colonial questions in Parliament, though it could well have been to their advantage to do so. But in those years a peculiar combination of events threw the three groups together. The merchants developed effective pressure groups, and they were thrown into the arms of the opposition by Walpole's Excise Scheme; the opposition, defeated in the attempt to create new transatlantic political alliances, began to advocate legislation for the stricter governance of the colonies, legislation which the Board of Trade had wanted all along. The Board had refrained from using its own means to appeal to Parliament before; now it was willing to abandon this restraint, because, among other things, many of its members were particularly annoyed with the Duke of Newcastle. The alliance of merchants, Board members, and opposition was never a formal or constant one, nor was it ever openly acknowledged. But it was there, and its effect on the colonial image of Parliament was devastating.

(ii) THE SEVERING OF RELATIONS

The Excise crisis and the reconstitution of the English opposition had strongly suggested to colonial politicians that there were few parliamentary factions to whom they could turn, no London connections who might be useful to partisan colonial interests; the suggestion was reinforced by changes affecting two other groups of individuals who had served as informal

[60] On a paper-currency Bill before Parliament in 1740 Richard Partridge wrote, 'We can give no reason how or for what reason they were stirred up to do it unless it proceeded originally from the Lds of Trade who are also members of Parliament' (Partridge to Wanton, 2 Jan. 1739/40; Gertrude Selwyn Kimball, ed., *The Correspondence of the Colonial Governors of Rhode Island, 1723–1775* (2 vols., Boston, 1902), Vol. I, pp. 125–7).

transatlantic liaisons—the colonial agents and the commissaries of the Bishop of London.

One change was in the work of agents, official and unofficial. The personal agency declined altogether: Lewis Morris's trip to England to unseat Governor Cosby and secure his own appointment as Chief Justice of New York in 1734 marked the virtual end of personal trips by Anglo-colonial politicians on personal business. (Significantly, Morris, 'the Craftsman' of New York in 1732, was snubbed by the Bolingbroke circle on his trip to England three years later.[61])

Morris was serving as his own agent; the official agents, men whose primary usefulness had been as partisan links between Whigs and Tories under William and Anne, now found that they, too, had nothing to gain from associating with the English opposition, and they were forced into an increasingly formal relationship with English ministers. Agents out of favour with the ministers were useless to their constituents. Micajah Perry told a New York friend in 1733 that he could be of no help, since he was out of favour at court.[62] Richard Partridge went out of favour with the ministers and the Board of Trade in 1740 for simultaneously defending two different positions on paper currency; he could get no hearing before the Board or any of the ministers for a year or two.[63] Peter Leheup was dismissed as Virginia agent in 1754; admittedly he had been convicted of fraud, but might it not have been significant also that Henry Pelham, who had kept him on because Leheup was a relative of Walpole's and a member of the Court and Treasury Party, had died and there was about to be a ministerial turnover?[64]

At the same time the tasks as well as the connections of the agents began to change: the agents became less responsible for initiating measures of parliamentary relief and more responsible

[61] Morris's visit is chronicled in Beverly McAnear's 'American in London', *Pa. Mag. Hist. & Biog.* LXIV, No. 3 (July 1940), pp. 164–217. Robert Morris's letters (Morris Papers A, Rutgers University Library) indicate that he saw the Duke of Newcastle several times, and Sir Robert Walpole probably more than once, but never socially.

[62] Perry to Colden, 19 Mar. 1733/4, *Colden Papers, 1730–42*, pp. 105–6.

[63] Marguerite Appleton, 'Richard Partridge, Colonial Agent', *New England Quarterly*, V (1932), p. 307.

[64] Dinwiddie to Jas. Abercromby, 26 Apr. [1754] and 18 June 1754, Dinwiddie Papers, *Colls. Va. Hist. Soc.*, Vol. III, 139, 211; Lonn, *Colonial Agents of the Southern Colonies*, p. 295, n. 51.

for heading off measures the colonists would find unpalatable. Occasionally agents nipped the Bills before they were presented; at other times they had the 'sting' removed from the Bills after they were first brought in, but before the final reading. The Molasses Act as finally passed levied a steep duty on molasses imported into the northern colonies, but even this was an improvement over two previous Bills which completely prohibited such importation.[65] In 1729 the agents got a clause requiring the destruction of colonial forges struck from a Bill dealing with the preservation of mast-pines.[66] In 1740 a friend of the Penns got fish excluded from a Bill prohibiting exports from the northern plantations.[67] In 1744, 1749, and 1751 Bills were presented in Parliament restricting colonial issues of paper money and giving governors' instructions the force of law. Each time the agents objected to the first clause, but were far more averse to the second; each time the second clause was struck out before the final reading.[68]

This shift in the agents' work suggests that Americans had begun to think of Parliament as an English institution rather than an imperial one. (It was no coincidence that the 1730s were the decade of the first restrictive Bills and virtually the last colonial appeals to Parliament.)

All this in turn pointed to the end of the agent's role as an informal link between parties on either side of the Atlantic. Moreover, by the end of the same period the commissaries of the Bishop of London, men who were also serving as partisan

[65] Albert B. Southwick, 'The Molasses Act, Source of Precedents', *W.M.Q.* 3rd Ser. VIII (1951), p. 398.

[66] Arthur Bining, *British Regulation of the Colonial Iron Industry* (Philadelphia, Pa., 1933), pp. 51–2.

[67] John Penn to Thomas Penn, 21 Dec. 1740, Pa. Hist. Soc., Penn Letter Book I, f. 352. The exclusion was agreed to in the House of Commons, but the friend who requested it was also a friend of Walpole's.

[68] For 1749 see Root, *Pennsylvania and the British Government*, p. 197, quoting Thomas Penn to Governor Hamilton, 6 June 1749 (Pa. Hist. Soc., Penn Letter Book II, ff. 268–70). Richard Partridge wrote of 'the sting' being taken out of the Bill of 1751 (Kimball, *Corr. R.I. Govs.*, Vol. II, pp. 130–4). Partridge had earlier written of a Bill presented in 1748: 'I make no doubt but we shall get alterations in it if we don't succeed so as to get it entirely dropt . . .' (Partridge to Kinsey, 4 Mar. 1748, Pa. Hist. Soc., Pemberton Papers). 'We had a strong party in the House of our side and a great deal of debate there was about the paper currency bill. Wherein as I think I may already have advised thee that the 2 last clauses was agreed to be entirely dropt . . .' (Partridge to John Kinsey, 30 May, 1749, Pa. Hist. Soc., Pemberton Papers, f. 105).

liaisons, virtually disappeared. For two or three decades after 1714 most commissaries used their local influence and English connections to help the opponents of various provincial governors. Commissary Henderson actively opposed Governors Hart and Calvert of Maryland, writing pamphlets and even travelling to England to use his influence against legislation that Governor Calvert approved.[69] Commissary Price had misgivings about some of the 'ambitious men' who opposed Governor Belcher, but he joined in their attempts to bring Belcher down. Belcher protested that the clergy 'seem to incline to ride over' the government, and Price later lamented that Governor Shirley was just as bad as Belcher.[70] Commissaries Cummings and Jenney attacked proprietary government in Pennsylvania (Jenney advised a congregation that their minister 'must not be under any prepossession or Attachment which may lead him into such an Obligation to any great Man as may lay him under a Necessity of abetting his political Designs, which may run counter to the Interest of your church').[71] Even Governor Gooch was on the defensive against Commissary Blair less than two years after Gooch's arrival in Virginia.[72] At the same time the change in the nature of the agency, the decline of the commissaryship, and the growth of a merchant interest sympathetic mainly to conservative interests in the colonies, contributed to the decline of other informal transatlantic associations which had paralleled and reinforced the party ties.

Before this colonists had appealed to Whitehall, Lambeth, Westminster, or to merchant acquaintances for help against an unco-operative governor; now they looked more to the local

[69] Nelson Waite Rightmyer, *Maryland's Established Church* (Baltimore, Md., 1956), pp. 64–83; A. W. Werline, *Problems of Church and State in Maryland During the Seventeenth and Eighteenth Centuries* (South Lancaster, Mass., 1948), pp. 30–1; Jacob Henderson, *The Case of the Clergy of Maryland* (see Lambeth–Fulham MSS., Vol. II). A copy of Henderson's *Fifth Letter to Daniel Dulany, Esq. in Relation to the Case and Petition of the Clergy of Maryland* is in the New York Historical Society.

[70] Price to Bishop of London, 5 Nov. 1733; Price to Secretary, S.P.G., 5 May 1744; William Stevens Perry, *Historical Collections relating to the American Colonial Church*, Vol. III (n.p., 1878), pp. 293–5, 380–2; Belcher to the Bishop of London, 5 Oct. 1733 (Lambeth–Fulham MS. Reel II, Vol. 5).

[71] Jenney to the Vestry of Christ Church, Philadelphia [1747], William Stevens Perry, *Historical Collections relating to the American Colonial Church*, Vol. II (n.p., 1871), pp. 246–9; Richard Peters to Bishop of London, 29 Nov. 1737, and Cummings to Bishop, 20 Mar. 1738 (Lambeth–Fulham MS. Reel III, Vol. 7).

[72] Gooch to Bishop, 9 Oct. 1729 (Lambeth–Fulham MS. XII, pp. 146–7).

electorate for support in limiting the governor's powers and making his position untenable. Benning Wentworth's opponents in New Hampshire, for example, combined a not too hopeful appeal to Whitehall against the governor in 1749 with a massive local campaign against him.[73] As the provincial constituency began to replace the imperial one, ironically, colonial politicians began to take up once again, as they had in the 1680s, English country-party ideas passed from the first Earl of Shaftesbury to the eighteenth-century Tories, and to apply them to local politics. In particular, they developed in the local context Bolingbroke's attack on 'court spunges' who robbed the community from positions of legislative and administrative power. The poor were taxed to provide money for their fees, their contracts, and their private benefits which cemented the court parties. They were parties in the worst sense, as the pamphleteers suggested—a small part of the community benefiting itself at the expense of the whole. And it followed, by implication, that since the money of the poor was voted and allocated by court-controlled legislatures, they were taxed without being represented.

What was to be done to get rid of such corruption? The author of *Vincit Amor Patriae*, who wrote for the Zenger Press and was therefore probably associated with the Morris–Alexander faction in New York, attacked politicians who blindly followed the colonial governors and advocated annual elections to keep the public from becoming disenchanted with their representatives.[74] *O Liberty, Thou Goddess Heavenly Bright* also advocated frequent elections and peace Bills to destroy court parties within the Assemblies.[75] *A Letter to a Gentleman* pleaded for a regulation of offices, and an Act assuring the independence of judges.[76] All the authors attacked with passion factions which opposed 'the general interest of the country'; all of them (they were published in New York in 1732 at the height of the *Craftsman*'s influence) advocated annual elections, limits on fees or places, and independence of judges, measures designed to prevent the governors' sustaining such factions.

One might have expected the radical ideas of the 1730s to cast an odium on all parties in the colonial Assemblies, as indeed

---

[73] Daniell, 'Politics in New Hampshire', *W.M.Q.* 3rd Ser. XXIII (1966), p. 104.   [74] Andrew Fletcher (pseud.; New York, 1732).
[75] New York, 1732 (Evans 3595).   [76] Robert Dissolution (pseud.; Evans 3530).

their counterparts attempted to do for parties in Parliament. But they did not necessarily have this effect. There was, of course, a great deal of criticism of faction itself in the colonial press, but along with this, occasional leaders of the old colonial factions, having lost much of their *raison d'être* at Whitehall, now felt the need to justify themselves before the local electorate.

The first step was the publication of platforms—rudimentary in the extreme, but still recognizable as appeals to the public on not one but a number of related issues. Along with this went the occasional printed appeal to elect—or defeat—slates of candidates whose voting record on a variety of issues was—or was not—satisfactory. I. Q. Cincinnatus, in *A Letter to the Freeholders and other Inhabitants of the Massachusetts Bay* (1749),[77] made a direct plea for the defeat of the assemblymen who refused to consider the plight of the Cape Breton soldiers. The same year another *Letter to the Freeholders and Qualified Voters* attacked the management of the Canada expedition, the currency measures, and the expulsion of James Allen, and urged the defeat of the men—their names were given—who had voted against Allen's expulsion.[78] The following year a spate of pamphlets appeared against the silver interest, with proposals for a variety of legislation. *Many of the Electors of the Two to the Electors of the Four*[79] in New York (1739) put forth a series of questions about possible legislation which candidates would be required to answer before the election. In the 1745 New Jersey election two distinct platforms were published, pro- and anti-proprietary to be sure, but also embodying a variety of issues: paper money, Indian and Mulatto slaves, the militia Bill, tenure of sheriff, and support of Governor Belcher. The Pennsylvania election of 1742 produced a pamphlet conflict which focused on military service in particular, but covered all the legislation of the last session.

[77] The pamphlet includes a typical exhortation to elect men who cannot be bought, etc.

[78] *A Letter to the Freeholders and Qualified Voters relating to the Ensuing Election* (Boston, Mass., 1749).

[79] The questions had mainly to do with supporting the ballot, refusing to take office, refusing to vote the governor support for more than one year or money without specific appropriation, and supporting the printing of minutes of the Assembly. The pamphlet was answered by *An Unanswerable Answer to the Cavils and Objections (Printed, or not Printed, or not worth Printing) Against a Paper lately Published called 'Many of the Electors of the Two to the Electors of the Four'* (New York, 1939).

Political pamphlets of the 1740s are still sparse, and pamphlet activity was episodic (1742–6 in Pennsylvania, 1739 in New York, 1744–55 in New Jersey, 1749–51 in Massachusetts were crucial periods), but what stands out clearly is their attention to the issues. Running through them is the theme that political factions are justified in appealing for popular support.

Occasionally, also, they exalted party activity itself. A proprietary opponent in Pennsylvania wrote in 1742: '. . . and since even the Religion of Peace exhorts us to contend earnestly for the Faith, tis to be hoped a moderate contention, for the Blessing next in value, will not be blameable. . . .'[80] 'Americanus', a Massachusetts writer of 1739, launched a biting attack on Governor Belcher, with an indirect justification of a very partisan appeal: 'What is done here in imitation of those valuable letters [Cato's] cannot be judged to be factious, or against the interest of the public.'[81]

What was beginning to occur in some of the colonies, therefore, was a shift in orientation from the imperial centre to the local electorate. The decline in the number of local places in the governor's disposal, the decline of the need for a governor's partisan services in English politics, undermined the governor's informal leverage over the provincial assemblymen; the informal leverage threatened to be replaced by formal authority embodied in Acts of Parliament.

Moreover, the object of the governor's provincial opponents was to produce an Assembly so balky that the governor's position was untenable; the object of the measures concerning the governor's instructions, which were proposed by the English opposition, was the same. Thus as early as the 1730s there were more than a few politicians in England and America who thought their local interests best served by making the imperial machinery fail to work.[82]

[80] *A Letter from a Gentleman in Philadelphia to his Friend in the Country* (Philadelphia, Pa., 18 Sept. 1742).

[81] *A Letter to the Freeholders and other Inhabitants* (Newport, R.I., 1739). In 1750 a New York pamphleteer advised: 'Chuse, therefore, Persons that will quit the calm Retreats of private Life, and intermix with Faction, and the Embroilments of the Province, only because their Country needs their Service' (*A Letter to the Freemen and Freeholders of the City of New York; relating to the Approaching Election of their Representatives*; Evans 6865).

[82] Bernhard Bailyn, *The Origins of American Politics* (New York, 1968).

V 'No violence, no oppression, no particular complaint ... yet ... sinking by degrees'

THE ominous signs of strain in imperial ties which began in the 1730s intensified depressingly in the last decade of George II. Coupled with the glorious mutual successes in the Seven Years' War went the growing alienation of British and American political factions. In England colonial affairs began to assume an importance which would soon make them the major issues distinguishing one faction from another; in the colonies attacks on the corrupt use of provincial revenues to sustain court factions broadened into charges of taxation without representation. Well before 1759, the '*annus mirabilis*' of the Seven Years' War, British and American politicians had developed a set of attitudes towards factional politics which would be crucial in the coming of the Revolution.

In many ways the ministry that Henry Pelham created in 1745, and kept in power until his death in 1754, was much like the earlier ministry of Sir Robert Walpole. Its backbone was Walpole's Court and Treasury Party; its single un-questioned leader was Pelham himself, who took over both Walpole's jobs as Chancellor of the Exchequer and Lord Treasurer and his role as prime minister in the House of Commons, and showed many of Walpole's own talents in work-ing with the King and Parliament. In these respects Pelham simply continued Walpole's government under a new name.

In another important respect, however, the make-up of Pelham's government was different from that of Walpole's: whereas Walpole's ministry was drawn entirely from the Court and Treasury Party, Pelham's was a balance of several political factions. Almost from the beginning of the Hanoverian era

English Whigs had been divided between those in the ministry and those in opposition, but by Walpole's last years in office the Whigs had divided still further into various bands or factions grouped around individual leaders. Some of Walpole's supporters, sensing that the 'Great Man' was in trouble after the Spanish War began, left his sinking ship then, but instead of joining Pulteney they kept as their leader the Duke of Bedford. Meanwhile the Prince of Wales had quarrelled with his father George II, and around him at Leicester House gathered still another band of politicians opposed to the government.[1] Still another group of opponents—perhaps Walpole's sharpest critics of all—were the new group of political youngsters who had just entered politics in the 1730s and were appalled by Walpole's corruption. This faction, called the 'Cobham group', included William Pitt. By the time of Walpole's fall English politicians were beginning to 'travel in bands', and the complicated politics of the Bolingbroke–Pulteney alliance had begun to seem simple.

It was Henry Pelham's great talent that he could create a government in which ministers from the dwindling ranks of the Court and Treasury Party could work in relative harmony with ministers from factions that had attacked that party. For most of his administration Pelham worked with a combination of Walpole's old ministers, the Duke of Bedford and his followers, and a few members of the Cobham group, including Pitt. Under his tactful leadership this diverse group of individuals worked together, if not always in accord, at least successfully enough: by Pelham's last years the ministry had virtually no effective opposition in Parliament.[2]

So much did the ministry rely on Pelham's unifying influence that his unexpected death in 1754 threw the government into tremendous confusion. For over three years there was one cabinet reshuffle after another, until finally, in 1757, the Duke of Newcastle and the remnants of the old Cobham group got

[1] See A. N. Newman, 'Leicester House Politics, 1748–1751', *E.H.R.* CCCI (1961), pp. 577–89.
[2] For a discussion of this talent see John William Wilkes, *A Whig in Power: The Political Career of Henry Pelham* (Evanston, Ill., 1964), *passim*. By cabinet here is meant the inner cabinet. On this see Trevor Williams, 'Historical Revision: LXXXII—The Cabinet in the Eighteenth Century', *History*, XXII (1937), pp. 240–52.

together to form their remarkably successful ministry, the ministry famous for making Britain the greatest imperial power in the world, as a result of her victory over the French in the Seven Years' War.

And so, with the exception of one fairly brief period, the fifteen years before George II's death in 1760 saw ministries in which the old Walpolean party shared cabinet positions with one or a number of other factions. Thus cabinets inevitably represented a considerable diversity of opinions, and one of the issues on which cabinet members came to have sharply conflicting views was the administration of the colonies, for in the last years of George II's reign cabinets were far more interested in, and better informed on, colonial affairs than they had ever been before.

During Walpole's ministry cabinet members had watched with some interest the particular fates of their own appointees in the colonies; they had also kept an eye open for colonies in which other ministers' appointees might be in trouble, and hence where vacancies might be opening up. Walpole, Newcastle, Townshend, and perhaps Wilmington had been greatly interested in certain colonial problems and occasionally issues were discussed at the cabinet level.

What was different about the ministries of Pelham and Pitt was the degree of interest shown by all the cabinet ministers in a variety of colonial problems. The growing number of colonial officials returning to England and colonial visitors coming to England, the increasing importance of colonial trade, the renewed pressures from the Anglican Church for an American bishop, the Rebellion of 1745 and the charge that some colonial leaders were in sympathy with it, all contributed to the new interest in colonial affairs. But, above all, the tremendously enhanced need for colonial defence in the two major wars between 1740 and 1763 meant that scarcely a cabinet member was unfamiliar with the major colonial issues. The era opened just at the end of a war, but the uneasy peace was more of a truce, for the problems that were the causes of the war were left unsettled. It was clear that in the coming war the colonies would be a major theatre of conflict; the buffer zone of Indian tribes and unsettled lands which had long separated the English coastal settlements from French colonies inland was now vanishing, and in any war French troops with their new Indian allies were bound to attack the English frontiers.

The prospects of colonial war were particularly disturbing at a time when a great number of governors had reached an impasse with their Councils or Assemblies over a local issue. For four years there was no legislation in New Hampshire because Governor Wentworth clashed with a majority of the Assembly over representation of new areas. Governor Johnson of North Carolina got legislation from an unrepresentative Assembly, but much of the colony—and most of the wealthier parts—would not recognize it and would pay no taxes. Governor Belcher could get no support from the proprietary-dominated Council of New Jersey, because he had not been sufficiently forceful in urging the Assembly to punish anti-proprietary rioters in the colony. Governor Clinton found his few supporters in the New York Assembly overwhelmed by a majority dominated by James de Lancey, and could not get acceptable legislation. Just a few years later Governor Dinwiddie was in trouble with the Virginia House of Burgesses over his decision to charge a pistole to register new land grants and certain old ones. These controversies made it unlikely that governors could extract generous grants from their colonies in time of war. In these circumstances it is not surprising that, beginning some time in the late 1740s, colonial issues seem to have been discussed far more often by the cabinet than they had been earlier in the century.

Moreover, while the varying opinions of a few individuals in Walpole's ministry could generally be reconciled by some timely negotiations of Newcastle's, the differences of opinion among cabinet members in the Pelham and Pitt coalitions were so great that it taxed all Newcastle's ability to make what compromises he could. There were two major issues on which they divided. First, how strictly should British authority over the colonies be maintained? Second, should the wars be fought mainly in the colonies or on the continent of Europe, and, to the extent they were fought in the colonies, should the fighting be handled by the colonists, British regulars, or a combination of both? As the fifties went on, these became the main issues distinguishing one English faction from another. Domestic constitutional issues had slowly ceased to count for much.

In a general way Bedford's group came to advocate the strict assertion of British authority over the colonies, and fighting in the colonies with British regulars. Similarly, Pitt tended to support a colonial, as opposed to a continental war, dependence on colonial troops, and as little force as possible to assert British authority in colonial areas. In between were the Walpolean Whigs, who tended, when they had to make a decision, to favour both continental and colonial war, fighting with a combination of colonial troops and British regulars, and a minimum of force in asserting British authority over the colonies.[3] Both Pitt and Newcastle agreed that 'measures of Power and Force' should not be used 'in the settlement of our colonies on a proper foot',[4] a statement in which Bedford would not have concurred. There was a substantial difference here on how strictly the colonies should be governed.

Moreover, since all the Whig factions except the Court and Treasury Party had been in opposition to Walpole at the very time when opposition leaders had begun to use proposals for reform in the colonial administration as a means of attacking Walpole in Parliament, they did not seem to share the same antipathy to parliamentary legislation on colonial issues as Walpole's old associates showed. Pitt himself did not care to have Parliament take up colonial issues, but his associates in the old Cobham group had no objection. Nor did Bedford. As it turned out, ministers who were willing to consider parliamentary legislation on colonial affairs never dominated the cabinets before 1760: Newcastle and his supporters were able to perpetuate Walpole's *laissez-faire* approach to the colonies, and ministries did not bring colonial issues before Parliament. It was, however, an ominous sign for the future colonial administration that by no means all his cabinet colleagues agreed with Newcastle on this point.

Although the politicians favouring stricter colonial government never dominated George II's ministries as a whole, they

[3] On the general subject see A. H. Buffington, 'The Canada Expedition of 1746; its Relation to British Politics', *A.H.R.* XLV (1939–40), pp. 552–80; Richard Pares, 'American versus Continental Warfare, 1739–63', *E.H.R.* LI (1936), pp. 429–65.

[4] Bernhard Knollenberg, *Origin of the American Revolution, 1759–1766* (New York, 1960), p. 14. Pitt did, however, think that colonial contraband should be stopped during the war.

did come to hold two of the positions most directly concerned with the day-to-day handling of colonial affairs: the presidency of the Privy Council and the presidency of the Board of Trade; and the factions within the cabinet were not sufficiently structured to absorb and modify all or even the most important of their views. Moreover, the cabinet itself was not structured enough to discipline them for every indiscretion. At the Council Granville's open insistence that the governors' instructions were to be interpreted as legally binding profoundly disturbed colonial leaders, but was let pass by his cabinet colleagues, though most of them wished he had never said it.

Far more broadly concerned with colonial problems, and hence far more difficult to handle, was the Earl of Halifax. For Halifax, influenced by the papers Martin Bladen left at the Board of Trade and by the recommendations of the Bedfordite 'hard-line' governors, produced in the period 1750–4 a series of proposals which, had they been accepted, would have revolutionized colonial administration. It was testimony to the changing nature of cabinet politics that the ministers were able to smother some but not all of them; consequently Halifax became a terror to colonial politicians. He backed down on his support for the 1749 currency Bill, his initial support for a parliamentary law making governors' instructions law, and his initial report recommending that troops should be sent to New Jersey in the wake of riots there; the cabinet would not accept his plan to tax the colonies or his plan of 1754 for uniting the colonies; they denied him the Secretaryship of State, and despite an Order in Council of 1752 giving the Board sole appointment of many colonial officials and the sole correspondence with colonial governors, other ministers continued to nominate colonial governors as usual and correspond with them. By 1754 Newcastle and his friends had managed to stifle enough of Halifax's proposals to leave him disinclined to further efforts at reform. Still, some of his proposals, like that of sending a commander-in-chief and a commissioner for Indian affairs to the colonies, actually were implemented; others, like the authorizing of governors to determine on their own the representation of new areas in the colonies, were allowed to go into effect, and still others, like taxing the colonies, were widely enough known to alarm the colonists though the actual measures were smothered. And although Halifax was never Secretary of State while George II lived, Newcastle was never able to get rid of him altogether. The very ambiguity of Halifax's position illustrates the evolution of the cabinet in the 1750s. Halifax remained in the ministry simply because his divergent views could be more easily controlled within it than outside it. In opposition he would certainly bring up colonial issues in Parliament; in office he might be restrained.[5]

Thus for the first time there was a major difference within the British ministry over colonial administration. There was, in fact, already one significant faction inclined to stricter government of the colonies. This was, indeed, ominously far from the day when opposition factions brought up colonial administration as a temporary expedient to embarrass the government.

Offsetting this development, there was, for a brief time, the prospect that the various groups within the British ministry might, largely because of a chance series of personal acquaintances, develop once again a set of transatlantic connections with American political parties. The connections began indirectly, with rival sets of governors and other provincial politicians lobbying for personal influence at Whitehall. One set of governors closely associated with each other consisted of William Shirley, governor of Massachusetts, George Clinton, governor of New York, Robert Hunter Morris of Pennsylvania (and also proprietary leader in New Jersey), Governor Horatio Sharpe of Maryland, Governor Dinwiddie of Virginia, and Governor Dobbs of North Carolina. In opposition to them was another set of colonial politicians and officials, who worked together almost as closely—Thomas Pownall, Benjamin Franklin and Israel Pemberton of Pennsylvania, William S. Johnson, and, on the periphery of the group, James de Lancey of New York.

In general each group of governors and other political leaders was made up of personal friends, who corresponded with each other while they were in office and sent each other advice on their local problems. Shirley, for example, was a close friend of

---

[5] As Hardwicke's son put it, 'A great deal was done at different times to gain and soothe my Lord Halifax, but I never remember him at a pinch of the least use to my father or D. of N.' (*The Life and Correspondence of Philip Yorke, Earl of Hardwicke, Lord High Chancellor of Great Britain*, ed. Philip C. Yorke, Vol. II (Cambridge, England, 1913), pp. 407–9).

Robert Hunter Morris,[6] and wrote advice to Clinton on how to manage his government.[7] Morris, besides being a friend of Shirley's was also a friend of Governor Sharpe and helped out Clinton in New York.[8] Sharpe in turn was a friend of Governor Dinwiddie,[9] so close a friend, in fact, that Sharpe's brother William helped Dinwiddie in England against the attempts to remove him during the 'pistole fee' crisis.[10] Dinwiddie and Dobbs were friendly correspondents: they had known each other through connections with the Hanbury family and also through the Ohio Company, of which both were members just at the beginning of the 1750s.[11] On the other side, Pownall, Johnson, and Franklin seem to have known each other just as well as the men in the Shirley group.

But the associations of the two sets of political leaders went far beyond personal friendships, business connections, and letters of advice; the governors and their associates did all they could to help their colleagues in other colonies defeat their local rivals. Shirley, Morris, Dobbs, Dinwiddie, and the rest of their circle were in a general way supported by the Duke of Bedford's group; the others had connections with Newcastle's wing of the ministry.

Through working with problems in New Jersey and North Carolina Bedford had become acquainted with Robert Hunter Morris, leading opponent of the New Jersey governor, and Arthur Dobbs, a Carolina property owner who joined several London merchants in protests against the governor of North Carolina. Governor Shirley he met after Shirley had led the colonial expedition against Louisberg in the War of the

[6] *Shirley Correspondence*, I, p. 481, n. 1.

[7] But Clinton was afraid Shirley was trying to get his job in 1750 (Clinton to R. H. Morris, 1 Oct. 1750, R. H. Morris Papers, I, No. 10, N.J. Hist. Soc.).

[8] McAnear, 'Politics in New York', op. cit. p. 679. The Livingston party, which coalesced with the Morris party in the 1750s, was pro-Shirley (ibid. pp. 765–79; Clinton to Colden, Mar. 1749, *Colden Papers*, Vol. IV, p. 202).

[9] Lady Matilda Rideout Edgar, *A Colonial Governor in Maryland: Horatio Sharpe and his Times, 1753–73* (London, 1912), p. 179.

[10] Dinwiddie also offered to join Sharpe's brother William to help get him an army commission in England, 13 July 1759 (Sharpe to William Sharpe, *Correspondence of Governor Horatio Sharpe, 1757–61*, ed. William Hand Browne, Vol. II; *Archives of Maryland*, ix (Baltimore, 1890), pp. 350–1). See also Dinwiddie to Abercromby, 26 Apr. [1754], Dinwiddie Papers, *Colls. Va. Hist. Soc.*, Vol. III, p. 138.

[11] Clarke, *Arthur Dobbs*, p. 92.

Austrian Succession. Bedford and his followers had constituted the most enthusiastic supporters of the expedition among the ministry, and Shirley's energy and initiative as a military commander had impressed them favourably.

Shirley, Morris, and Dobbs were all in England in 1749 shortly after Halifax took over the Board. It was through Bedford and Penn that Halifax became acquainted with them, and with what in fact turned out to be a clique of conservative colonial governors, including also future Governor Dinwiddie of Virginia, Governor Clinton of New York, and Governor Sharpe of Maryland. These men were personal friends who co-operated mutually as leaders of their respective colonial parties; to strengthen their own positions in their colonies, and enhance their reputations for enthusiastic interest in colonial administration, they put forth their own proposals for colonial reorganization or regulation, which were not unlike some of the traditional recommendations of the Board of Trade.

In 1749, for example, Shirley was behind the Board's presentation of a Bill in Parliament to regulate the currency of New England, and, as a rider, to make royal instructions to colonial governors law. Shirley claims to have prepared the Bill; in any event, he was in London and seeing Halifax at the time the Bill was introduced, with most of the members of the Board of Trade sitting on the committee to which it was referred.[12]

Again, the plan for colonial union that the Board drew up in 1754 was at least partly the result of Shirley's suggestion. During the War of the Austrian Succession Shirley had proposed a colonial congress to arrange for mutual defence, and when the next war broke out he continued to think along the same lines. In January 1754 Shirley had written the ministers urging them to set quotas of men and money for each colony in anticipation of possible trouble with the French or the Indians: '. . . the want of such a Settlement, and a method to

---

[12] William Bollan, Shirley's friend and agent for Massachusetts, had prepared a long report on paper money which he presented to the Board. The Board read the report—which Shirley may have had a hand in drafting—with approval, and on 27 Jan. 1749 the Board, with Horatio Walpole in attendance, met with six commissioners to consider the draft of a Bill to regulate the issue of paper money in the colonies. Leave to bring in such a Bill was given in mid February, 5/8 of the committee to present the Bill being on the Board. It received summary treatment in the Commons. See Shirley to Josiah Willard, 13 Feb. 1749, *Correspondence of William Shirley*, I (New York, 1912), p. 498.

enforce its taking effect, will be an obstacle to the carrying into Execution any general plan for cementing an Union among His Majesty's Subjects upon the continent for the Defense of His Majesty's Territories committed to their trust.'[13] Three months later, in a speech to the Massachusetts Assembly, copies of which he sent to London, Shirley urged them to look upon the coming Indian congress at Albany as a chance to prepare and present a plan for permanent political union among the colonies. Shirley sent copies of his speech to the Board of Trade, where Halifax, who had already drawn up a preliminary plan of his own, must have read them with considerable interest. And he must also have read the proposals of Governors Dinwiddie, Morris, and Sharpe[14] for parliamentary taxation of the colonies before he sent the ministers a similar proposal of his own.

For the first half of the 1750s the Shirley group held the field, using to the utmost their connections with Halifax. But in the mid fifties Pownall and Johnson and their associates began working effectively to displace them. Pownall and Johnson allied to undermine the reputation of Governor Shirley with the British authorities in 1756: Johnson quarrelled with Shirley over Indian affairs and the prosecution of the war, and Pownall, then in London, took Johnson's side,[15] while the Livingston–Morris group sided with Shirley. Meanwhile Pownall was offered the governorship of Pennsylvania to appease the opponents of Morris, whom he was to succeed, and Franklin and Pemberton offered him enthusiastic support, while Morris's friends naturally tried to block him.[16] When Shirley was dismissed from the government of Massachusetts, Pownall was

---

[13] *Shirley Correspondence*, II, p. 44.

[14] Edgar, *A Colonial Governor in Maryland*, p. 31; Dinwiddie to Sir Thomas Robinson, 12 Feb. 1775, Dinwiddie Papers, *Colls. Va. Hist. Soc.*, III, pp. 493–4. Morris Paper in Robert Hunter Morris Papers, I, No. 2, N.J. Hist. Soc.

[15] John A. Schutz, *Thomas Pownall, British Defender of American Liberty* (Glendale, Calif., 1951), p. 66.

[16] Ibid. pp. 66–71. The anti-proprietary party of Maryland tried to negotiate an alliance of sorts with Benjamin Franklin when Franklin was leading the opposition to Morris and the proprietary government in Pennsylvania. Aubrey C. Land, *The Dulanys of Maryland; a Biographical Study of Daniel Dulany, the Elder (1685–1753) and Daniel Dulany, the Younger (1722–1797)*, Studies in Maryland History, No. 3 (Baltimore, Md., 1955), p. 242. See also William Alexander to R. H. Morris, 11 July 1756, R. H. Morris Papers II, No. 76, N.J. Hist. Soc.

invited to succeed him, and took that office instead of the governorship of Pennsylvania. Shirley, meanwhile, undertook a pamphlet campaign against Pownall, Johnson, and the de Lanceys together.[17] De Lancey never quite trusted Pownall, who, he feared, was ambitious for the government of New York, which de Lancey also wanted; but he and Pownall and Johnson did co-operate to ruin Shirley's military expedition to Niagara in 1755,[18] and de Lancey always worked well, especially in Albany politics, with Johnson in New York.[19] Franklin joined them out of opposition to the Morris–Livingston party there.[20]

In particular, the Pownall–Johnson group was able to capitalize on the difficulties some of their opponents faced in mobilizing their colonies for war. Dinwiddie, Morris, and Shirley were all unsuccessful in raising the supplies the British government expected; Morris met an absolute refusal from the Pennsylvania Assembly. So one of the earliest military expeditions, the Niagara expedition of 1755, was entrusted by the government to de Lancey, Johnson, and their associates. Then Johnson and Pownall began their successful campaign against Shirley, and by 1756 most of the ministers, and Halifax, too, were convinced that Shirley was not only guilty of mismanaging Indian affairs but, far more seriously, was also guilty of withholding from the government vital information on the movement of French troops in North America. Added to this, the direction of military affairs in North America went in 1756 to

[17] Schutz, *Pownall*, p. 77.

[18] James Thomas Flexner, *Mohawk Baronet, Sir William Johnson of New York* (New York, 1959), p. 127.

[19] McAnear, 'New York Politics', op. cit. p. 875.

[20] Ibid. p. 877. Though Belcher was only on the edge of the circle, he certainly did not suffer for lack of support from the Pownall group. (He had been turned out of his government in Massachusetts by Shirley some years before.) Belcher was a Quaker who supported the Quaker party in New Jersey; it was no coincidence that Franklin and Pemberton led the Quaker party in Pennsylvania, and de Lancey, though not a Quaker himself, used his influence at Whitehall to get a later governorship of New York for Josiah Hardy, a Quaker.
In 1757 Pownall, then serving as an interim governor of New Jersey after Belcher's death, urged the British government to appoint a full-time governor of the colony soon, lest R. H. Morris, as second senior councillor, should get the job by default. Pownall considered that it would be highly unfair to have a proprietary supporter—an 'interested party', as he put it—to govern the colony. Fisher, *New Jersey as a Royal Province*, Columbia University Studies in History, Economics, and Public Law, XLI, pp. 37–8.

the Duke of Cumberland, whose sympathies were with Pownall, and the following year to Pitt, who was also more sympathetic to Pownall and his friends. Halifax went along with the change partly because he had no choice, partly because he was disillusioned with Shirley, and partly because his own daughter married a de Lancey.

At first glance the association of particular sections of the British cabinet with particular colonial politicians, and the shift in the fortunes of certain colonial leaders as the balance of the ministry changed, might appear to have heralded a new set of transatlantic associations: on the one hand, an alliance of sorts between the court, Anglican, and proprietary factions and the Bedfordites; on the other hand, an alliance between anti-proprietary, Quaker, or country parties and the Newcastle, Pelham, or Pitt connections.

But the hopeful associations did not materialize. For one thing, they were simply groups of personal friends manœuvring for preferment in Whitehall; for another, they were not always consistent in their manœuvres. Robert Hunter Morris, just to take one example, went to London partly to help Governor Clinton but also to serve his own interests, in getting the lieutenant-governorship of New York or the administration of another colony. Morris had connections in both the warring circles of Bedford and Newcastle, but Bedford disliked Clinton as a protégé of Pelham and Newcastle,[21] and Morris had no intention of sacrificing his own influence with Bedford by urging him to support a relation of his hated enemy. So Morris helped Clinton—a little, but not as much as he might have done. Similarly Shirley gave Clinton very friendly advice on governing New York, but manœuvred in London to get Clinton's job away from him—a fact Clinton knew.[22] De Lancey and Pownall worked together with Johnson to ruin Shirley's military expedition to Niagara in 1755, but de Lancey never quite trusted Pownall's influence in London, for he feared that Pownall was angling for the government of New York, which de Lancey also wanted.

[21] Clinton to Morris, 14–17 Sept. 1751, R. H. Morris Papers, I, No. 25, N.J. Hist. Soc.
[22] Shirley to Newcastle, 1 Sept. 1750, B.M. Add. MS. 32722, f. 1; Clinton to R. H. Morris, 1 Oct. 1750, R. H. Morris Papers, I, No. 10, N.J. Hist. Soc.

The instability of the transatlantic alliances was in striking contrast to the stability of provincial politics in the 1750s. The encroachments on the governors' patronage from Whitehall and the provincial Assemblies undermined the ability of governors to manipulate factions in creating their own support; the failure of new interest groups to penetrate colonial politics meant little opportunity for new alignments among colonial factions.[23] These were reasons, combined with the failure of political leaders to achieve any new English alliances with far-reaching effects on the balance of political power in the colonies, for a notable stability among colonial factions of the 1750s. From New Hampshire at least as far south as Maryland the factional divisions of the 1760s were still those that existed in the forties.

This is not to say that British influence on local politics was only nominal; it was not. Support from Whitehall could still be decisive in determining the prospects for a governor's friends in local elections. In the opening years of the decade a number of governors were in serious trouble with their Assemblies or Councils—Wentworth of New Hampshire over representation of western lands, Dinwiddie of Virginia over the pistole fee, Belcher of New Jersey over his handling of the land riots, Clinton of New York over personal issues, and Johnson of North Carolina over his sanctioning of the Acts of an unrepresentative Assembly. The British government's response, varying from total support of Wentworth, a friend of Newcastle, to the dismissal of Governor Johnson (an enemy of Bedford and no close ally of Newcastle), and something in between with Belcher and Clinton (both disliked by Bedford but connected with the Newcastle–Pelham faction), showed that the attitude of the home government could still be important in determining the momentary strength of colonial factions. Wentworth's enemies could mount no effective campaign against him after it was discovered there was no effective rival for the governor's position in England, whereas Governor Clinton repeatedly complained that Newcastle's failure to send him a letter of commendation cost him electoral support in New York.

But while traditional support from the home country continued to be essential for the incumbent governor seeking electoral strength for provincial court parties, and hence

[23] See Note 1 at end of chapter.

ministerial factions were still decisively linked with colonial factions, country parties were beginning to develop new lines of appeal to the provincial electorate. One charge of particular importance began to be suggested in pamphlet literature of the 1750s: more and more the governors and court parties were accused of unjust uses of taxation, in language which strikingly anticipated the imperial protestations against taxation without representation in the following decade.

William Livingston argued against the Anglicizing of King's College by the de Lancey faction in New York:

> When the community is taxed, it ought to be for the Defence, or Emolument of the whole: can it, therefore, be supposed, that all shall contribute for the uses, the ignominious uses, of a few? Shall the Government of the College be delivered out of the Hands of the Public to a Party? . . . no particular set of men can claim a Right to dispose of the provincial Taxes but those empowered by the community.[24]

Livingston continued with slight modification the arguments used in the 1730s and 1740s against corrupt court parties. But the Reverend William Stith, opposing Governor Dinwiddie's charge of a pistole fee on new and pending land grants, went considerably further. He explained to the Bishop of London that the fee constituted taxation without legislation,[25] 'and at his table he made it a toast to drink Liberty, Property, & No Pistole . . . also proclaimed the same exasperating words publicly at a Cou[rt] up in the country'.[26] To the Bishop, Stith wrote: 'If this contest between the Governor & the People goes on, Ill venture to affirm, that his Majesty will lose 20 Pistoles for one the govnr gets.'[27]

Stith's arguments on local taxation anticipate the tone of debate in the sixties on imperial taxation. So did the Pennsylvanian who wrote *A Serious address to the Freeholders and other Inhabitants of the Province of Pennsylvania* in 1758, attacking proprietary interference in the formulation of Pennsylvania money Bills,[28] and the author of *A Letter from a Gentleman in New York*

---

[24] *The Independent Reflector*, by William Livingston and others, ed. Milton M. Klein (Cambridge, Mass., 1963), pp. 178–83, 193.
[25] Apr. 1753, Lambeth–Fulham MSS. Vol. XIII.
[26] Blair to Bishop of London, 15 Aug. 1752, ibid.
[27] Stith to Bishop, Apr. 1753, ibid.
[28] 10 Sept. 1758 (New York, 1758), Evans 8237.

to his Friend in Brunswick, attacking the use of tax money for running the New York–New Jersey boundary (a line which concerned only property-holders along it) as the 'unjust use of taxes' which 'Englishmen have always resented'.[29] Several times in the decade William Bollan's salary as agent for Massachusetts was attacked along more traditional but still similar lines in the Massachusetts press, because Bollan represented only the court party and not the popular interest.[30]

In the 1750s, therefore, country parties in a number of provinces were beginning to anticipate arguments against taxation without representation. But usually their appeals 'out-of-doors' were carefully addressed 'to the Freeholders' or 'to the Electors' of the colonies, and a common theme of pamphlets of the fifties is the danger of civil disturbances developing when political factions appeal to the mob. Even Jonathan Mayhews's well-known justification of revolution was a reasoned philosophical treatise, not an emotional incitement to action. Only the occasional pamphleteer went further, like Vincent Centinel, who attacked the governor's party in Massachusetts: 'Oppressors, Oppressors! Who are they? Where do they live? Satisfaction, Satisfaction—'[31] or the proprietary opponent in Pennsylvania, who wrote of some pamphlets by Robert Hunter Morris: 'But lest a more full Portrait of those wicked Libels hinted at above . . . may provoke a much injured and loyal People to revenge themselves upon such accursed but dignified Parricides . . .'[32] Rather, most pamphleteers of the fifties expressed open disdain for mob appeals, a disdain which was to disappear from writings of the following decade.

Thus by the end of the 1750s colonists were becoming familiar with arguments against taxation without representation as they applied to provincial issues, and as they were interpreted to apply not to the actual voting of tax moneys but to their appropriation. From colony to colony, however, the adaptability of

[29] New York, 1750, Evans 6526.

[30] See, for example, *A Letter to the Inhabitants of the Province of the Massachusetts Bay* (Boston, 1751), and *To the Freeholders of the Town of Boston* (Boston, 1760). See also Bushman, *From Puritan to Yankee,* pp. 248–9.

[31] Vincent Centinel (pseud.), *Massachusetts in Agony* (Boston, 1750), Evans 6475.

[32] *A Serious Address to the Freeholders and other Inhabitants of the Province of Pennsylvania.* Phileleutheros, in *An Address to the Freeholders and Inhabitants of the Province of the Massachusetts Bay* (Boston, 1751), warned voters that their lives and liberties depended on the next election.

the issues to the court–country alignment varied considerably. In Virginia, for example, where there was no court party as such, the whole weight of the Burgesses was naturally applied against an unpopular administrative decision like the pistole fee; in Massachusetts an increasingly well-organized country party found it natural to attack the combination of Anglican and silver interests that constituted the court. But while the King's College issue in New York momentarily lent itself to an issue of taxation and representation, the same William Livingston who so ardently opposed the 'court' of the moment later found himself writing in support of another administration: 'The smallest oversights in government were then represented as premeditated encroachments on the rights of the subject; and errors, to the best of men unavoidably incident, agravated into crimes, inexpiable, and enormous.'[33]

From colony to colony the public appeals of various factions began to make clear great differences in the position of the parties themselves in regard to popular pressures on the one hand, and gubernatorial patronage on the other. In the 1760s, when the sanctions against appealing to the mob disappeared, the difference in the position of Assembly factions from colony to colony would become so great as to make a difference between those colonies that took the lead in revolutionary activity and those that held back.

For the moment, the importance of the fifties was in the estrangement between English and American parties. The failure of the gubernatorial circles to develop long-run connections at Whitehall, following as it did upon the failure of the *Craftsman* circle to obtain useful colonial support twenty years earlier, pointed up the futility of attempting to revive the kind of informal (and therefore workable) transatlantic partisan connections that had flourished between 1689 and 1714. The gulf between English and American parties was uncrossable.

[33] *An Address to His Excellency Sir Charles Hardy, Knt.*, by the Author of the *Watchtower* (New York, 1755).

NOTE

1. In every colony factions divided over the same basic issues. To some extent the Anglican Church was an issue in local politics, especially after the Great Awakening had divided both Dissenters and Anglicans in every colony. Thus the

denomination of the newly established King's College in New York, or the payment of clergy salaries in Virginia, or the appointment of a president for William and Mary College there, could all become political issues, as could the establishment of an Anglican mission church in Cambridge, Mass. In the two proprietary colonies of Maryland and Pennsylvania the issue of religion was a vital one in nearly every session of the Assembly. In Maryland it came up in connection with such issues as the establishment of schools; in Pennsylvania Quaker pacifism was at the heart of colonial disputes over measures for the colony's defence. Probably even more important than religious issues, however, were three other issues which recurred almost without exception in every colony—the amount of paper money to be issued, the procedure and charges for issuing land patents, and the extension of courts and legislative representation to the western areas. Thus, for example, Assembly representation of newly settled areas was at the heart of Governor Wentworth's dispute with the New Hampshire Assembly in 1749, of Governor Johnson's dispute with the North Carolina Assembly from 1746 to 1754, and of chronic disputes within the Pennsylvania, New York, and New Jersey Assemblies. In several colonies, most notably North Carolina, Virginia, and New Jersey (and perhaps even New Hampshire, where there was some pressure on the Wentworths to move the capital out of merchant-dominated Portsmouth), the location of the capital, in settled urban coastal centres or farther to the west, was a political issue. Similarly, while Governor Dinwiddie's dispute with the Virginia Assembly over the pistole fee for new land patents was the best known controversy over such patents, favouritism, blank patents, 'black patents', or charges for patents were major issues in both Carolinas, New Hampshire, and New York. Proprietary claims to low-tax land were issues in New Jersey (where the old West Jersey Society was the nucleus of the proprietary party), North Carolina (where Lord Granville's proprietary agents were in constant feuds with Governor Dobbs), Maryland, and Pennsylvania (where the rate of taxes paid on proprietary lands was the main issue in the governor's attempts to get revenue for military support). Finally, in the 1750s there was scarcely a colony that escaped a dispute over the extent or the means of issuing paper money. None of these issues was really new. All had been riding for years in Whitehall and the Assemblies.

VI 'The Tennis Ball of Faction'

ANGLO-AMERICAN POLITICS AND
THE COMING OF THE REVOLUTION

In August 1760 George III succeeded his grandfather on the
English throne. Shortly afterwards Benedict Calvert, secretary
to the proprietor of Maryland, had an interview with him.

His Majesty was pleased to admit me alone with him about an
hour. *Inter al* he spoke of Maryland, asked if the province was
quiet. I replied yes. Says he, 'Quite quiet?' I answered, 'So please
you, Sir, save such persons as are in all governments of Discontented
minds and mischievous too often thro self interest and ambition.'
He smiled and said, 'Of that I know.'[1]

Anyone familiar with the development of British colonial administration will see in George III's concern about keeping the
colonies quiet the typical attitude of British kings and their
ministers in the early and mid eighteenth century. The fact that
the young monarch voiced the concern at all seems to show how
quickly he had picked up the attitudes of George II's ministers,
and how completely he had accepted them. Certainly George
III did not sound like a king bent on making any changes in
the government of the colonies.

And, indeed, in the first few years of his reign there was very
little indication that anyone in the government contemplated a
major alteration in the way colonial problems were handled.
Ministers continued to keep Parliament from passing legislation
unpalatable to the colonists, and to bypass the Board of Trade
when important administrative decisions were to be made. The
main function of ministers, as always, was to see that neither

[1] Lady Matilda Edgar, *A Colonial Governor in Maryland: Horatio Sharpe and His
Times, 1753–1773* (London, 1912).

Parliament nor the Board of Trade got a chance to put across measures which would be totally unacceptable to moderate colonial leaders.

On at least two important occasions—one concerning the controversy over paper money, the other concerning the quartering of British soldiers—the ministers, acting on the advice of the colonial agents, watered down colonial measures then before Parliament to make them less offensive to the colonists. In giving such advice the agents were continuing the same kind of work as they had done in the time of George II.[2]

The first five years of George III's reign, then, were not particularly eventful ones in colonial administration. Problems affecting the colonies were handled much the same as they had been in the reign of George II; ministers continued to work out day-to-day compromises acceptable to political leaders on both sides of the Atlantic; governors and agents continued to advise them on these compromises.

All this changed with George III's efforts to replace the Pitt–Newcastle coalition with a government more acceptable to himself. In looking about he quite naturally turned to the leaders of the factions whose outlines had been but just barely distinguishable in the ministries of the fifties. Most of the men

[2] Some of the old faces, like Paris and Partridge, disappeared in the late fifties, and some of the remaining agents, like Robert Charles and William Bollan, were no longer personally as active as they had been, Bollan being reduced to agent of the Massachusetts Council alone after 1762, when the Assembly dropped him, and Charles simply losing some momentum in his last years. But in general the agents continued to be thought of more and more as popular representatives; it was in 1761, after all, well after George III's accession, that Governor Dobbs of North Carolina was rebuked by the Board of Trade for holding up a revenue Bill because the nomination of the Assembly's agent was attached as a rider.

Besides advising the ministers on colonial Bills, the agents' other duties continued to be much the same. Appeals and legislative review were still handled by reference from the Privy Council, and the deliberate stall was still a technique that interested parties used to drag proceedings out. When the South Carolina Assembly protested against Governor Boone in 1762, for example, Boone, with the support of some representatives in England, was able to postpone the hearing several years—in fact until he had convinced himself that no good would come of his remaining in the colony, since the legislature refused to work with him. When Boone did return to England he was tried by the Board of Trade; the Assembly's case was handled by Charles Garth, agent of the colony, and characteristically Garth had not only assembled all the relevant papers and acquired legal assistance, but he had also arranged to have merchants from the coffee house appear in the chambers when the trial was held (Namier, 'Garth and his Connections', *E.H.R.* LIV (1939, pp. 465–72).

who had led the factions of the fifties either died or retired from public life in the next decade, and their places were taken by younger politicians like Rockingham and Shelburne. But the old politicians stayed active long enough to transmit some oɪ their ideas to the new generation of followers. In the first decades of George III's reign the embryonic packs of politicians of George II's era became full-born political factions, as George III turned to one leader after another to take office: within ten years Bute had been followed in office by Grenville, Bedford (with the old Bedfordites), Rockingham (at the head of the old Walpolean Whigs) and Pitt and the old Cobham group, with Grafton (leading Pitt's old supporters when Pitt retired from office) and Lord North (the only minister in the group leading a party that was in any way new, though many of North's ministers were former Bedfordites). Essentially, each minister took one of the groups of the fifties, composed of his personal followers, some allies, and their political dependents, created a ministry out of them, and left office taking the bulk of these supporters with him. Each former ministry thus became a political faction, united in support of the principles behind the legislation passed during their ministry.

Since the various ministries of the 1760s evolved from the embryonic political factions of the decades before, and since those factions had disagreed sharply about the way colonial problems had been handled, it was inevitable that sooner or later the King would find a leading minister who did not object to tightening up colonial administration and did not object to having Parliament do it. The first such minister George III appointed was George Grenville, working with the Bedford faction; the first such measure was Grenville's Stamp Tax.

The Stamp Act heralded in Parliament the development of political factions operating in a new context, but nevertheless quite recognizably descendents of political groupings of the previous decade. And it was projected into the local politics of well-established provincial factions also finding themselves in a new context.

There were, it is true, some modifications in the colonial factions of the early sixties. The latent western interest gradually crystallized into the Henry faction in Virginia, for example; the old land-bank, anti-Hutchinson faction in Massachusetts revived,[3] as did the opposition of the 'Massachusetts' faction to the Wentworths in New Hampshire; and both the proprietary and Quaker factions in Pennsylvania took up new stances as the proprietary issue lost its significance.[4] But these did not represent any new alignments, and most colonial factions in the years after 1760 were recognizable descendants of factions of the fifties.

What the Stamp Act did was to change the relationship of the Assembly factions to popular pressures. Coming as it did to electorates made familiar by pamphleteers of the fifties with arguments against the appropriation of tax moneys for anything other than the use of the whole colonial community as determined by the provincial legislature (taxation without representation), it was one measure uniquely suited to raising popular pressures on imperial issues. Coming as it did, too, just at a time when the colonies were developing organizations, outside the Assemblies, capable of educating public opinion, it was uniquely timed to create a popular outburst.

Behind the campaigns to educate the public were, on the one hand, the merchants' clubs, and, on the other, the Sons of Liberty in the various provinces. Neither the merchants' clubs nor the mechanics' organizations from which the Sons of Liberty sprang were new. Merchants had been gathering at coffee houses like the British Coffee House in Boston and the London Coffee House in New York since the beginning of the century, and there had been clubs of merchants in the big cities for fifty years. Many of the groups of Sons sprang from almost equally long established workingmen's organizations. Baltimore's descended from the Ancient and Honorable Mechanical Company, Charleston's from the Firemen's

[3] John C. Miller, *Sam Adams, Pioneer in Propaganda* (Boston, 1936), p. 36. In Maryland the protests against the proprietor were rechannelled after 1767. Charles A. Barker, 'The Revolutionary Impulse in Maryland', *Md. Hist. Mag.* XXXVI (1941), p. 137. For early opposition to the Robinson group in Virginia see Ernst, 'Currency Act', *W.M.Q.* XXII (1965), p. 53.

[4] For Pennsylvania see John J. Zimmerman, 'Charles Thomson, the Sam Adams of Philadelphia', *M.V.H.R.* XXXV (1958), p. 471; William S. Hanna, *Benjamin Franklin and Pennsylvania Politics* (Stanford, Calif., 1964), p. 170; John J. Zimmerman, 'Benjamin Franklin: A study of Pennsylvania Politics and the Colonial Agency, 1755–1775' (unpublished Ph.D. thesis, Michigan University, 1956), p. 257; Theodore Thayer, *Pennsylvania Politics and the Growth of Democracy, 1740–1776* (Harrisburg, Pa., 1953), pp. 100–72, *passim*. For New Hampshire see Richard Francis Upton, *Revolutionary New Hampshire* (Hanover, N.H., 1935), p. 2.

Association, Philadelphia's from the Heart and Hand Fire Company, Boston's from the Caucus Club,[5] Connecticut's from holdovers of an earlier paper-money faction joined by 'New Lights'. Grafted on to the organizations in each province were four or five prominent merchants or lawyers, who might be anything from the leading organizers (as was Gadsden from South Carolina) to well-known public benefactors who gave the organization respectability (as John Hancock did in Massachusetts). A radical Assembly member like Gadsden, William Allen, Jr., of Pennsylvania, or Charles Carroll of Maryland might find his prestige in the Assembly enhanced by leadership 'out-of-doors'; he might find that a mass meeting could be used to force an Assembly to take action on issues they might otherwise stay away from.

In all colonies the Sons of Liberty were able to organize riots and mass meetings, draw up resolutions against British Acts, instruct members, and even organize non-importation agreements in 1769.[6] But just how much influence the Sons exerted on the Assemblies, and independently of them, varied from colony to colony, depending on a number of things—how large the urban working class was, how widely the franchise was extended (and used), how experienced and skilled their leaders were. In the cities of the northern colonies, and perhaps also in Charleston, they had the strongest membership; in colonies like Massachusetts and Connecticut, where the franchise was extensive, they had the best chance to influence Assembly elections; in Sam Adams they had their most gifted leader.

[5] Miller, *Sam Adams*. See also Hutchinson to Thomas Pownall, 8 Mar. 1766, Mass. Archives, Vol. XXVI, pp. 207–14, quoted in Edmund S. Morgan, ed., *Prologue to Revolution: Sources and Documents on the Stamp Act Crisis, 1764–1766* (Chapel Hill, N.C., 1959), p. 125. Benjamin Gale wrote Jared Ingersoll in 1765 that Connecticut's Sons were the offspring of 'several factions which have subsisted in this colony, originating with the New London Society, thence metamorphized into the Faction for paper Emissions on Loan, thence into the N. Light, into the Susquehannah and Delaware Factions,—into Orthodoxy,—now into Stamp Duty Opponents'. Quoted in Lawrence Henry Gipson, *Jared Ingersoll, a Study of American Loyalism in Relation to British Colonial Government* (New York, 1920). See also Pauline Maier, 'Popular Uprisings and Civil Authority in Eighteenth-Century America', *W.M.Q.* 3rd Ser. XXVII (Jan 1970), pp. 3–35; Herbert M. Morais, 'The Sons of Liberty in New York', in Richard B. Morris, ed., *The Era of the American Revolution* (New York, 1959); and Richard Walsh, *Charleston's Sons of Liberty, a Study of the Artisans, 1763–1789* (Columbia, S.C., 1959).

[6] For the best description of their work see Philip Davidson, *Propaganda and the American Revolution, 1763–1783* (Chapel Hill, N.C., 1941), esp. pp. 65–82.

From colony to colony, then, the effectiveness of the Sons of Liberty and the mercantile organizations varied, from colony to colony the nature of the factional divisions in the Assembly varied, too. Neither the Assembly factions nor the mercantile and mechanical organizations outside the Assembly were new, but the Stamp Act brought them into contact with one another, as they had not been before. The relationship between them determined in good part which colonies took the lead in resisting parliamentary taxation and which did not.

In Massachusetts, for example, the factional rivalry was between a popular party that was increasingly pressed by well-organized town meetings to resist parliamentary taxation, and a conservative faction dominated by an oligarchy too small to survive without British backing. In Virginia, by contrast, the so-called 'popular faction' of Patrick Henry and the Lees that took shape in the early sixties became within a few years a part of the political oligarchy,[7] and the oligarchy itself was too well entrenched to be in any danger from extra-legal organization. Very different conditions, yet it was Virginia and Massachusetts that took the lead in colonial resistance.

In Massachusetts there were, as 'Massachusettenses' described them, 'two parties . . . of pretty long standing, known by the name of Whig and Tory, which at this time were not a little embittered against each other'.[8] The Tories (John Adams and Sam Adams also used the same terms)[9] consisted of a court clique dominated by the Hutchinson–Oliver families; their opponents in the Assembly shared with the radical leaders 'out-of-doors' a hatred of the clique that was almost as strong and certainly as personal as their hatred of parliamentary legislation. (John Adams, for example, was almost as acid in his comments on Thomas Hutchinson as he was when talking about the Stamp Act.)[10]

---

[7] See Carl Bridenbaugh, *Seat of Empire: The Political Role of Eighteenth-Century Williamsburg* (Williamsburg, Va., 1950), pp. 51–71.

[8] *Massachusettenses: Or a Series of Letters, containing a faithful State of many important and striking facts, which laid the Foundation of the Present Troubles in the Province of the Massachusetts Bay* (London, reprinted for J. Matthews, 1776), pp. 12–13.

[9] e.g., John Adams, 'Novenglus', in *The Works of John Adams*, ed. Charles Francis Adams, Vol. IV (Boston, 1851), p. 18. Sam Adams to James Warren, 9 Dec. 1772, *Warren–Adams Letters, Being Chiefly a Correspondence among John Adams, Samuel Adams, and James Warren*, Vol. I (Boston, 1917), pp. 14–15.

[10] John Adams' Diary 15 Aug. 1765 and 13 June 1771 (Comments on Hutchinson)

Here, Massachusettenses went on, 'If the Tories were suspected of pursuing their private interest through the medium of
court favor, there was equal reason to suspect the Whigs of
pursuing their private interest by the means of popularity.'[11]
Outside the Assembly Sam Adams, and his small group of partisans effectively mobilizing the town meetings, went to the
extent of managing a colony-wide convention as early as 1766,
and had an extraordinarily strong pressure group to influence
the assembly and the provincial elections. Governor Bernard's
letters showed their effectiveness: 'When I came here I found
the province divided into parties so nearly equal, that it would
have been Madness for me to have put myself at the head of
either of them. I had therefore nothing to do but to keep myself
to myself and maintain my own dignity.[12] ... [now] I am
obliged ... to maintain a political warfare with the Popular
party.'[13]

The Whigs or popular party were not always at ease with
Adams's tactics, but their position in the colony, and their
ability to oppose the Hutchinson clique effectively within the
Assembly, clearly depended upon their supporting in retrospect
Adams's provocations once the issues were drawn, and getting
along with the local meetings that Adams's caucus was usually
able to dominate.

Local meetings in Virginia, on the other hand, could be
dominated by the oligarchy itself, and within the oligarchy
there were no fundamental differences of opinion on whether
imperial authority should be maintained. It is true that within
the Burgesses there were marked differences between the
northern and western elements (Henry's group) on the one
hand and Peyton Randolph's group on the other. But Henry's
sceptical attitude towards Randolph was nothing compared
with John Adams's passionate hatred of Thomas Hutchinson,
and after 1765 Henry's partisans were assimilated gracefully
into the committees of the Burgesses so long dominated by

and 18 Dec. 1765 (Comment on Stamp Act), *Works of John Adams*, ed. C. F. Adams,
Vol. II, pp. 151, 154, 278.

[11] *Massachusettenses*, pp. 12–13.

[12] Bernard to Barrington, 1 May 1762, *The Barrington–Bernard Correspondence and
Illustrative Matter, 1760–1770*, ed. Edward Channing and Cary Coolidge
(Cambridge, Mass., 1912), p. 53.

[13] Same to Same, 5 July 1766, ibid. p. 110.

Speaker Robinson's friends. Outside the Burgesses there were no alternative organizations—no caucuses, no town meetings—that could possibly be dominated by anyone but the Burgesses themselves. What pressure groups there were were auxiliary to the Burgesses, not really an alternative to them.

In such circumstances it was natural for the Burgesses to take the lead in opposing parliamentary legislation, but for reasons quite different from those of their Massachusetts counterparts. To the Virginians the Stamp Act and its successors threatened the power of the Assembly itself. There was no opposition to a Crown-supported oligarchy; rather, the oligarchy itself felt its power at stake against the Crown. There was no need to appeal to constituents well organized from 'out-of-doors': the Burgesses themselves were leaders of the mobs. So different were provincial politics in Virginia from provincial politics in Massachusetts that one could almost say the colonies went into the Revolution for different reasons. At the very least they illustrate how local politics more than imperial theories determined the kind of opposition that the various colonies made.

In the rest of the colonies the pattern was equally varied. The colony that hung furthest back from the revolutionary movement was Georgia: whereas almost all the Virginia Burgesses were active in county associations, only 6 of 45 Georgia assemblymen were in the provincial Congress.[14] The reasons were many—a popular governor, the absence of a Henry or an Adams, political inexperience. But the most important factors seem to have been that the extra-legal associations were neither strong enough to dominate the Assembly or weak enough to be controlled by it, and factional rivalries in the Assembly were not sufficiently developed to make any faction as such appeal for the support of the radical associations.

In other Assemblies members of provincial factions seem to have looked at the opposition to imperial legislation largely as a tactical question. The New York Assembly in 1768, for example, divided over the question at what point in the session they should consider the Townshend Duties, because consideration

[14] See Marjorie Louise Daniel, 'The Revolutionary Movement in Georgia, 1763–1777', *Chicago University Dissertations, Partial and Complete* (Chicago, 1935); Asheley Ellefson, 'James Habersham and Georgia Loyalism, 1764–1775', *Ga. Hist. Q.* XLIV (1960), pp. 359–80.

would bring on a dissolution and the Livingston and de Lancey factions differed over the time when they wanted to fight an election.[15] Charles Carroll wrote of Maryland politics at the height of the Stamp Act crisis: 'We have political parties amongst us . . . they seem to me to spring from the same source in which your factions have theirs: the want of a sufficient number of lucrative offices to gratify the avarice or the ambition of the "outs".'[16] And in the public exchange between 'First Citizen' (Carroll) and 'Antilon' (Daniel Dulany, Jr.) Carroll argued tellingly: 'I am sorry that party attachments and connexions have induced you to abandon old principles.'[17] Even Benjamin Gale, who spoke of New Lights and Sons of Liberty in Connecticut as synonymous, had earlier succeeded in labelling the political 'New Lights' simply as 'men ambitious for office'.[18] In the Assemblies of other colonies—in Pennsylvania, Rhode Island, and New Jersey in particular—the strategic opposition to the parliamentary legislation in terms of local advantage was common.[19]

The attitudes of members to extra-legal meetings outside the Assemblies varied from colony to colony, depending on the strength of the Sons of Liberty, the relation of their leaders to the leaders of the Assembly, and the threat they posed to the Assembly itself.[20] The North Carolina assemblymen, possibly

[15] Don Ralph Gerlach, *Philip Schuyler and the American Revolution in New York, 1733–1777* (Lincoln, Nebr. 1964), p. 164. See also Carl Lotus Becker, 'The History of Political Parties in the Province of New York', *Bulletin of the University of Wisconsin* No. 286, History Ser. 11 (Madison, 1909), p. 8.

[16] Charles Carroll of Carrollton to Mr Jennings, 23 Nov. 1765, *Unpublished Letters of Charles Carroll of Carrollton and of his Father Charles Carroll of Doughoregan*, ed. Thomas Meagher Field (New York, 1902), p. 98.

[17] Elihu S. Riley, ed., *Correspondence of 'First Citizen'—Charles Carroll of Carrollton—and 'Antelon'— Daniel Dulany, Jr., 1773* (Baltimore, Md., 1902), p. 46. See also James H. High, 'Reluctant Loyalist: Governor Horatio Sharpe of Maryland, 1753–1769' (Ph.D. thesis, U.C.L.A., 1951), pp. 163–240, *passim*.

[18] Benjamin Gale, *A Reply to a Pamphlet, Entitled 'The Answer of the Friend in the West'* (New London, 1755), Evans 7424.

[19] Connecticut's New Light party used the Stamp Act crisis to defeat their opponents on local issues (Oscar Zeichner, *Connecticut's Years of Controversy, 1750–1776* (Chapel Hill, N.C., 1949), p. 71). See Hanna, *Franklin*, p. 170; David Sherman Lovejoy, *Rhode Island Politics and the American Revolution, 1760–1776* (Providence, R.I., 1958), Chs. III–VIII, *passim*; Mack Thompson, *Moses Brown* (Chapel Hill, N.C., 1962), pp. 31–3.

[20] This subject needs a great deal of study. In general, while assemblymen deplored violence they were not above joining in some of the riots themselves and did not regard the mobs as threats. But they did worry about the colony-wide meetings

because they were confident of controlling any extra-legal organization through their courthouse cliques, were themselves the organizers of back-country meetings and local riots.[21] The Connecticut Assembly, by contrast, declared ineffectually that the local meetings were illegal and ordered the governor to stop them.[22]

In most of the other colonies the assemblymen tried to play it safe: they wanted to preserve the Assemblies as long as possible; they also wanted to control any associations which might provide an alternative to the Assembly in time of crisis. Just how closely the Assembly leaders were associated with groups like the various mechanics' organizations is hard to say. Some people, like Christopher Gadsden of South Carolina, William Allen of the proprietary faction in Pennsylvania, the country party in Maryland, the pro-Massachusetts faction in New Hampshire, the anti-proprietary leaders in New Jersey, and the Livingstons in New York were notably more successful than their opponents in commanding the support of organizations out of doors, but generally all factions tried to dominate the local Congresses.

For example, though the pro-Massachusetts party of New Hampshire, largely in fact because of their Massachusetts associations, was more radical than the Portsmouth merchants who dominated the old proprietary party, it was the proprietary, or seaboard party, who generally got themselves elected to committees of correspondence. Both the Goose Creek and Cape Fear parties of North Carolina were represented in the Continental Congress. And in Rhode Island, though the Hopkins party were early known as radical opponents of the Stamp Tax, it was Samuel Ward who was the colony's most radical representative at the Continental Congress.

How aggressive a colony was in its resistance depended on the relationship of the popular pressure groups to the Assembly, the

organized by a few assemblymen and constituting far more than extra-legal meetings of the Assemblies. On the mobs see Lloyd I. Rudolph, 'The Eighteenth-Century Mob in America and Europe', *American Quarterly*, XI (1959), pp. 447–69; Maier, 'Popular Uprisings', *W.M.Q.* 3rd Ser. XXVII (Jan. 1970), pp. 3–35, *passim*.

[21] Charles Grier Sellers, 'Making a Revolution: The North Carolina Whigs, 1765–1775', in *Studies in Southern History*, ed. J. Carlyle Sitterson, The James Sprunt Studies in History and Political Science, XXXIX (Chapel Hill, N.C., 1957), pp. 21–32.

[22] Zeichner, *Connecticut's Years of Controversy, 1750–1776*, p. 62.

relationships of Assembly factions to one another, and the relationship of factions to the popular groups. If the organizers of pressure groups could use existing local institutions, like town meetings, which members of the Assemblies could not control, the colony was likely to be pushed into an aggressive course. If on the other hand all the local institutions were sufficiently dominated by the assemblymen, or men who did not differ very much from them, they were likely to create a pressure group themselves to influence the governor, the British government, and lagging compatriots.

If the factional divisions within the Assembly had been in a rough sense along radical/conservative lines before the issue of parliamentary taxation came up, the new imperial issues were simply grafted on to a system already established. Most divisions between radical and conservative factions had originated some time back in local issues, but decisions at Whitehall and Westminster had helped the conservative factions in local politics. With this background most of the adherents of the 'popular' factions, who were not really sure what to do, were willing to follow the lead of three or four of their most violent members, men like Adams and Trumbull, who were themselves organizers of the pressure groups outside the Assembly.

If, however, it was doubtful whether the pressure groups could or could not dominate the provincial government, and if there was not one clearly radical and one conservative faction in a colony, then factional rivalry became important out of doors, as assemblymen struggled to win control of the popular movements not only for the Assembly in general but for their faction in particular.

And so, in some sense, it was the relationship of the old Assembly factions to the new popular pressure groups that determined which colonies took the lead in opposing Parliament. But the Assembly member had, after all, won a measure of local success just by being in the Assembly, and he was not sure he wanted to gamble on a new situation.[23] To each provocation—

[23] When the first Continental Congress met '. . . the fundamental importance of the power struggle *within* New York became quite evident as the men who enjoyed the greatest influence in the establishment tended to support those institutions on which their power was based (royal government, Parliamentary sovereignty) while the men who enjoyed less power, the old Livingston interests led now by Philip Schuyler, tended to embrace the extra legal-movement . . .,' Gerlach, *Schuyler*, p. 242.

from his own province or from London—he reacted with genuine feeling, but he was not eager to force the issue. He reacted in terms of local factional rivalry, and once his protest had been drawn up or the delegate to a Congress elected, he wanted to get back to local issues as fast as possible. With local issues he was at home and, like his counterpart in Parliament, he did not like to contemplate what would happen if the quarrel between the colonies and the mother country persisted.

What is striking here is the absence of any effective imperial pressures on the assemblyman, the inability of the British government to build up any important nucleus of imperial sentiment within the colonial factions. Ministers gave no significant help to existing Tory or 'Conservative' parties; they made no attempt to build and bolster new ones.

This was particularly curious in view of the government's inclination to look at colonial radicals very much as Charles II had looked at the provincial oligarchies a hundred years before—as unscrupulous political manipulators stifling legitimate opposition. There is something remarkably reminiscent of Edward Randolph's comments in the House of Commons address lamenting that Americans 'had been made the Instruments of the ambition and traitorous designs of those dangerous men who have led them step by step to the standard of rebellion, and who have now assumed the powers of sovereign authority which they exercise in the most despotic & arbitrary manner';[24] or the English writer who warned the Americans, 'Your crafty leaders may buoy up the people with such presumption . . . a few of them [may] feather their nests with the spoils of the deluded people.'[25]

But despite this tendency to hark back to the past, British ministers did nothing to encourage moderate leadership in the colonies and nothing to build up groups of imperial supporters. For one thing, the colonial merchant associations and the Anglican parishes which earlier had served as liaisons between English ministers and sympathetic colonists, were badly divided now. Anglican ministers, for example, who might earlier have

---

[24] Quoted in Ira D. Gruber, 'The American Revolution as a Conspiracy: the British View', *W.M.Q.* 3rd Ser. XXVI (July 1969), p. 370.

[25] *Common Sense: in Nine Conferences between a British Merchant and a Candid Merchant of America, in their Private Capacities as Friends* (London, 1775), p. 17.

served as the leaders of 'loyal opposition' to the radical leaders pressing forward in the Assemblies, were now divided in their own minds.[26] And so, for that matter, were many of the royal officials in the colonies, men whose own hesitation was increased by the failure of the British ministers to back them up in their efforts to keep open the imperial channels. 'Aiding innocent people . . . is a spirit, however, that our Superiors on both sides of the Atlantic seem to want else they would not suffer government and the friends of government to be insulted as they daily are' wrote James Murray.[27] In 1766 Governor Bernard wrote equally pointedly:

> It is high time for every Crown Officer in America, who has distinguished himself by his fidelity to the King, to get away before his retreat is cut off. If the administration of Great Britain is not able to take necessary Measures, to support its Authority over the Colonies, it cannot be expected that they should be able to protect the King's officers against the popular power of the colonists.[28]

Thomas Hutchinson said the same thing:

> Without a proper support afforded to the King's officers, the respect due to government will of course fail. . . .[29]

The pleas of Hutchinson, Bernard, and Murray are typical of royal officials or Americans in any way inclined to encourage imperial sentiments within the existing factions. They saw themselves alone, powerless without support or protection from the mother country, unable to rally local support against John Dickinson's acid charges: 'Men, who either hold, or expect to hold certain advantages, by setting examples of servility to their country men . . . from them we shall learn how pleasant and profitable a thing it is, to be for our submissive behavior well spoken of at St. James, or St. Stephens; at Guildhall, or the Royal exchange.'[30] The weakness of the governors, the mobbing

[26] See Ezra Stiles's notes, 19 Dec. 1766, quoted in Gipson, *Ingersoll*, n., p. 193–4.

[27] Murray to Charles Stewart, 3 Sept. 1770, *Letters of James Murray, Loyalist*, ed. Nina Moore Tiffany (Boston, Mass., 1901), p. 173.

[28] Bernard to Barrington, 1 Sept. 1766, *Barrington–Bernard Correspondence*, p. 113.

[29] Hutchinson—[Auchmuty], 1 May. 1768, *The Letters of Governor Hutchinson and Lt. Governor Oliver, etc.* [ed. Israel Mauduit] (London, 1774), p. 26. See also Cadwallader Colden to the Board of Trade, 23 Nov. 1767, The Colden Letter Books II, *New York Historical Society Collections*, X (New York, 1877), p. 140.

[30] John Dickinson, *Letters from a Farmer in Pennsylvania* (Dublin, 1768), p. 70. Jared Ingersoll spoke of the ' "Ship-wreck" of my Reputation among the People, for

of Stamp distributors, the popular hostility to the Customs Collectors (Thomas Hutchinson lamented that 'there is no office under greater discouragements than that of the Commissioners'[31])—all testify to the end of the traditional role of English officials in encouraging loyal dissent against the local authority of provincial oligarchies. What is important is not only their uselessness in the particular imperial crisis but also their general ineffectiveness in using their imperial position to protect local dissenters from the power of their provincial adversaries.

The crises over the Stamp Act and the Townshend Duties thus demonstrated the weakness of the ministry in legitimizing opposition factions in the colonies. What was equally disturbing was the disappearance—as contemporaries viewed it—of a constructive opposition to ministers within the English Parliament. It was British reaction to the crisis which ultimately undermined the last connections between English and American factional politics.

The initial effect of American resistance was to make the emerging British factions take even more distinct public stands on American policy. Grenville's opposition to Repeal, Chatham's opposition to the Declaratory Act, and Rockingham's support of both, put each group on record with a stand that it was at least embarrassing to give up in public.

In private, of course, the differences were not so clear-cut. In the decade before 1775 American issues passed on and off the parliamentary stage, and when they were not foremost in the public eye politicians had little reluctance to abandon their public stands. In 1767, when Bedford was negotiating for a coalition with Rockingham, he let it be known that, although he himself favoured the strict maintenance of Parliament's authority over the colonies, he would not take any action against the colonies that Rockingham objected to, provided the coalition could be arranged.[32] On the other side, even Pitt urged that the issue of New York's non-compliance with the Mutiny Act should be taken up by Parliament.[33] And as late as

accepting this very obnoxious office' (Ingersoll to Commissioner of Stamps, 4 June 1766, in Jared Ingersoll, *Letters Relating to the Stamp Act* (New Haven, Conn., 1766), p. 58).

[31] Hutchinson to [?], Aug. 1768. *Hutchinson Letters*, ed Mauduit, p. 6.

[32] Newcastle to Lord Mansfield, 8 Apr. 1767, B.M. Add. MS. 32981, f. 65.

[33] John Norris, *Shelburne and Reform* (New York, 1963), p. 39; Chatham to

1769 the Marquis of Rockingham wrote Burke that the Marquis's best bet was an alliance with—of all people—George Grenville, because Grenville's bad relations with George III would make it impossible for him to come between Rockingham and the King.[34] Privately, in fact, most of the political leaders agreed with the Duke of Newcastle that 'it is easier to know what not to do than what to do' with regard to America.[35]

Publicly, however, the factions were on record with varying and inflexible approaches to the colonial problems, and this meant that after 1770, when colonial measures were increasingly before Parliament, Rockingham and Chatham in opposition could almost never agree on concerted debate against ministerial proposals. Chatham would rarely give advance warning to Rockingham when he intended to present a motion, nor would he alter motions to make them acceptable to Rockingham, nor did he feel obliged to come to town to support a protest motion Rockingham might make. The Rockinghams' astonishment gave way to disgust with Chatham's methods and for Chatham personally, and while Chatham respected a few of Rockingham's friends, like Richmond, he had little more than contempt for most of them. This in itself was a decisive change, which meant, among other things, the removal of one factor inhibiting the ministry from bringing up punitive colonial legislation in Parliament.

And so the position of colonial issues in parliamentary politics had been exactly reversed after 1765. Before that time ministers had feared to bring up the colonies in Parliament, because they constituted one of the few types of issue on which all groups of government opponents could co-operate; after 1765 colonial issues were one thing on which the factions out of office could not unite.

Even more unfortunate was it that, in their competing attempts to justify their various American stands and put themselves forward as the only factions capable of solving the

Shelburne, 3 and 7 Feb. 1767, *Correspondence of William Pitt, Earl of Chatham* (4 vols., London, 1838–40), Vol. III, pp. 189, 194.

[34] 15 Oct. 1769, *The Correspondence of Edmund Burke*, ed. Lucy S. Sutherland, Vol. II (Cambridge, England, 1960), p. 93.

[35] Newcastle to White, May 1767, B.M. Add. MS. 32981, f. 326. Newcastle was discussing the Quartering Act in this letter but his comments could be interpreted to apply to the general situation.

American problem, the Rockingham and Chatham parties reverted to traditional, and by now quite outmoded, ways of looking at colonial factions. Most notably, both Chatham and Burke took up the imperial approach that Bolingbroke and the *Craftsman* circle had used in the early 1730s.

There is in Chatham's speeches a reiteration of the ideas in the *Craftsman* which makes him clearly the last British link in the tradition of agrarian populism stretching from the country gentlemen of the 1630s through Shaftesbury, the Tory writers of Queen Anne's time, and Bolingbroke, to Jefferson. But there is also in Chatham's methods and aspirations a harking back to Bolingbroke's techniques. American affairs he made his chief domestic issue;[36] indirectly he suggested that the British Empire would be best administered when the leading minister was someone the people—and this included the Americans—could trust.[37] Exactly in the manner of the *Craftsman* circle Pitt was looking to American disturbances to embarrass the ministry and project him into office.

Burke was less direct in his approach and more explicit in his disclaimers of Bolingbroke's influence. But he, too, was well aware of the *Craftsman*'s approach. *The Present Discontents*, though not written with American opinion immediately in his mind, was in part a superb restatement of Bolingbroke's attack on parliamentary corruption; moreover, an earlier speech of Burke's, in which he noted that men left out of government will appeal to the public for redress, even to the point of beginning revolution, was hardly lost upon the Americans.[38] Nor did he intend it to be. As he wrote the Marquis of Rockingham: 'It is unnatural to suppose that in making an accommodation the Americans should not choose rather to give credit to those who all along have opposed the measure of ministers, than to throw themselves wholly on the mercy of their bitter, uniform, and systematic enemies.'[39] But on another occasion Burke lamented that the Americans did not know who their real friends were: they did not, in short, make it clear who they did and did not

---

[36] Burke to Rockingham, [24] Nov. 1769, *Burke Corr.* II, p. 112.

[37] Burke to Rockingham, loc. cit.

[38] William Burke to William Dennis, [3–6] Apr. 1770, *Burke Corr.*, II. p. 128.

[39] 6 Jan. 1777; H. D. Mahoney, ed., *Edmund Burke, Selected Writings and Speeches on America* (Indianapolis, Ind., 1964), pp. 208–9.

want in office.[40] And he was quite right. Burke's and Chatham's imitation of Bolingbroke's methods brought them no more American support than Bolingbroke himself had won. Early in the 1760s Israel Mauduit, agent for Massachusetts and presumably in a position to understand British politics, said that he did not know a thing about the various English parties. In 1767 William S. Johnson, a considerably more astute and well-connected observer than Mauduit, said that the colonies had few friends 'on principle' in British politics; he could see no common objective of the government's opponents other than a desire of the 'outs' to return to office on any issue they could find.[41] Johnson was, it is true, writing when both Rockingham and Bedford were opposing a divided Chatham ministry; but in 1769, when Chatham and Rockingham were in opposition to a ministry already notably immoderate, Thomas Pownall complained that no party in England was really interested in the colonies themselves; all they cared for was using colonial issues for their immediate advantage.[42] Similarly Henry Laurens wrote, after the repeal of the Stamp Act: 'Glad am I upon the whole that the Act is repealed tho I know not yet what cause to ascribe it to.'[43] Not only did Rockingham and Chatham fail in their efforts to capitalize upon disturbances in the colonies, but their efforts backfired in England, where they were tarred with charges of inciting the Americans to resistance. George Grenville was representative of a substantial segment of opinion in England when he wrote in defence of the Stamp Act:

I thought we had the clearest right imaginable, and that we were bound, by every tie of justice and wisdom, to do this; and I am

[40] Ross J. S. Hoffman, ed., *Edmund Burke, New York Agent, with his letters to the New York Assembly and Intimate Correspondence with Charles O'Hara, 1761–1776* (Philadelphia, Pa., 1956), p. 187.

[41] Johnson to Pitkin, 11 Apr. 1767, 'The Trumbull Papers,' *Colls. Mass. Hist. Soc.* 5th Ser. IX (Boston, 1888), p. 226. Also Johnson to Pitkin, 3 Jan. 1769, ibid. p. 310. 'It is surprising how few friends we have there [the House of Commons] who are so upon real principle . . . ,' Johnson to Pitkin, 26 Apr. 1769, ibid. p. 338.

[42] Pownall to Cooper, 5 Dec. 1769, and speech of Pownall's, 12 Apr. 1769. B.M. King's MS. 202, ff. 26, 39–47. In *The Administration of the Colonies*, 4th edn. (London, 1768), Pownall wrote similarly: 'The colonies will for some time belong to some faction here, and be the tool of it, until they become powerful enough to hold a party for themselves and make some faction their tool' (p. 29).

[43] Henry Laurens to John Lewis Gervais, 12 May 1766, Laurens Letterbook, 1762–6, Pa. Hist. Soc., ff. 417–19.

convinced it would have been accomplished, without any considerable difficulty, if America had not received such encouragement to oppose it from *hence* as no other people would have resisted. To this the present confusion is entirely owing.[44]

Somewhat later Commodore Hood wrote in a similar vein:

The leading men [in America] boast letters from very respectable characters in England, advising them to go on in the plan they have adopted, and that the end would answer their wishes. How then, my Lord, can any conciliating measures take effect here till harmony is restored at home?[45]

Henry Cruger wrote an American correspondent:

The opposition in the House of Commons flatter themselves that the confusion in your country will overthrow the ministry in this. But, my Peter! you and my countrymen may believe me let them come in when they will, they must adopt, and they know it, nearly the same measures with America that have been pursued by the present administration or they cannot hold their places a single session. To get in is what we all want, and patriots in one station are great tyrants in another.[46]

Joseph Galloway later saw a 'settled design' among some British politicians to 'encourage and support' the 'republican colonists'.[47] So widely held, in fact, was the idea that British opposition factions were encouraging American rebellion that Lord Hillsborough referred publicly in his circular letter of 1769 to 'insinuations . . . from men with factious and seditious views' in England.[48] The role of the opposition in the developing crisis became itself the subject of controversy, and William

[44] Grenville to Pownall, 17 July 1768; *The Grenville Papers: being the Correspondence of Richard Grenville, Earl Temple, K.G., and the Right Hon. George Grenville, their Friends and Contemporaries*, ed. William James Smith, Vol. IV (London, 1853), p. 318.

[45] Hood to E. Temple, 2 Sept. 1768, ibid. p. 440

[46] Cruger to Peter Van Schaak, 3 May 1769; Henry C. Van Schaak, *The Life of Peter Van Schaak, L.L.D., Embracing Selections from His Correspondence and Other Writings during the American Revolution and his Exile in England* (New York, 1842), p. 38.

[47] Joseph Galloway, *Reflections on the Rise and Progress of the American Rebellion* [1780], p. 63.

[48] 18 May 1769. See also *A Complaint against a Pamphlet intitled, A Speech intended to have been Spoken on the Bill for Altering the Charters of the Colony of Massachusetts Bay* (London, 1775), p. 2; and [James MacPherson], *The Rights of Great Britain asserted against the Claims of America: being an Answer to the Declaration of the General Congress* (London, 1776), pp. 25, 54.

Pulteney felt compelled to defend the opposition parties: '. . . the American objections to parliamentary taxation, were not first suggested by factious men here, but were the result of ideas, which naturally occurred, from a consideration of the subject, amongst themselves'.[49]

Included among the 'factious and seditious' men in Hillsborough's eyes were not only the members of opposition factions in Parliament but their allies, some of the better known colonial agents; and the opposition's growing reputation for irresponsible behaviour was in some measure a cause of the eclipse of the colonial agency. Burke was himself agent for New York; Chatham worked fitfully but notoriously with two other agents, Lee and Franklin; the growing sentiment against the English opposition was coupled with resentment of the agents. This was reflected by John Mein when he wrote that 'those who find their emolument in deceiving the colonies will continue to deceive them as long as their emolument continues'.[50] In the same vein Jonathan Boucher complained that 'those entrusted to communicate such intelligence are themselves either too ignorant, or too knavish to give any to be depended upon'.[51]

In 1769, the year that Hillsborough sent out his circular letter, he also ordered that agents must be chosen by Act of the colonial legislature,[52] approved by governor, Council, and Assembly. In explaining the order Hillsborough said that the agent should rightly be considered as a cross between an attorney[53] and an ambassador. Hillsborough never explained precisely what he meant by this; he implied at once that agents were to handle petty legal details and yet that they were able to bind their colonies in unspecified negotiations. By one interpretation Hillsborough was going back to the old Restoration

[49] William Pulteney, *Thoughts of the Present State of Affairs with America, and the Means of Conciliation*, 5th edn. (London, 1778), p. 16. But see also *A Letter to G. G.*, [by L.] (London, 1776), for a partisan attack on Grenville on behalf of his parliamentary opponents.

[50] Mein to James Murray, 11 Jan. 1775, *Letters of James Murray, Loyalist*, p. 171.

[51] Boucher to the Rev. John James, 9 Dec. 1765, Letters of the Reverend Jonathan Boucher, *Md. Hist. Mag.* VII (1912), pp. 295–6.

[52] According to Bollan, 'he said among other things that the appearance of agents for the colonies had been attended with great uncertainty and irregularity so that it sometimes could not be known who had good right to appear . . .' (Bollan to Thomas Hutchinson, 15 Apr. 1771, Bowdoin-Temple. MS., Mass. Hist. Soc.)

[53] Fisher, *New Jersey*, p. 96.

idea of what an agent ought to be: some of his descriptions sound remarkably like what the Lords of Trade expected from the Massachusetts agents under Charles II, namely that they were to represent their entire colony, not a party within it, that they were to be plenipotentiaries with power to commit their governments rather than delegates representing popular opinion, and that they were not to attempt to influence the workings of the British legislature.

But by another interpretation, probably more correct, what Hillsborough meant was that he had no use for colonial agents at all. He recognized that by 1770 very few agents could get the appointment by the Act he demanded, and those who could, like Burke[54] and Franklin,[55] would decline to accept the constraints on their independence that would exist if a royal governor could veto their reappointment. Thus, reasoned Hillsborough, it would be an easy matter eventually to declare all agents acting without authority, and to dispense with them altogether.

Before 1765 agents complained of apathy among officials, delays in getting business taken care of, or of personal run-ins with some of the ministers. But it is only after 1765 that one begins to hear leading agents like Garth complain that the government was against agents altogether. Garth actually wrote this to the Maryland Assembly in 1767; the following year he wrote that the government 'does not fancy the trouble from agents lately'.[56] In 1769 William Bollan's friends on the Massachusetts Council accused Hillsborough of using his influence with some members of the Massachusetts Assembly to keep them from choosing any agent at all.[57] Two years after

54 For Burke see Calvin Stebbens, 'Edmund Burke, His Services as Agent of the Province of New York', *Procs. Amer. Antiq. Soc.* N.S. IX (Oct. 1893–Oct. 1894, Worcester, Mass., 1895), pp. 89–101; Burke's views on the new requirements for the agent's election are in Hoffman, *Burke*, pp. 105–7, and in Burke to de Lancey, 14 Dec. 1771, ibid. pp. 200–3.

55 Franklin to William Franklin, 30 Jan. 1772; *The Writings of Benjamin Franklin*, ed. Albert Henry Smyth, Vol. V (New York, 1907), pp. 380–1.

56 Garth to South Carolina Ctee. of Correspondence, 14 Aug. 1768, Garth MS. (L.C. Transcripts), p. 128. Thomas Pownall wrote a correspondent in Boston (Dr. Samuel Cooper), 22 Mar. 1769, that agents were a needless expense, doing the colonies more harm than good. Pownall Papers, B.M. King's MS. 202 (L.C. Transcripts), f. 10 (see also f. 12).

57 Draft letter from the Massachusetts Council to William Bollan, 26 July 1769, Bowdoin-Temple MS., Mass. Hist. Soc.

that Franklin said that ministers objected to the colonial agents as superfluous:

> Under the present American administration they [agents] are rather looked on with an evil eye, as obstructors of ministerial measures; and the Secretary would, I imagine, be well pleased to get rid of them, being, as he has sometimes intimated of opinion that agents are unnecessary. For that, whatever is to be transacted between the assemblies of colonies and the Government here, may be done through and by the governor's letters, and more properly than by any agent whatever.[58]

Thus the colonial agency was sucked under in the wave of resentment against the English opposition, and one of the last channels of partisan communication was cut off. Beyond this, the reaction to the tactics of the British opposition had even more significance. There is a striking discrepancy between the actual effect of opposition rhetoric on the Americans and the effect English politicians thought it had. Some writers went so far as to assume that the tactics of the English opposition brought into question the effectiveness, or at least the maturity, of English parliamentary politics in general.

Both Englishmen and Americans tended to view the parliamentary opposition to the ministries' American measures as unconstructive: 'factious against government, instead of being watchful to preserve liberty'.[59] But some American and English writers went deeper, and criticized English politicians for not recognizing parties as a fact of political life and adapting parliamentary politics to make them useful. 'In a constitution like that of Great Britain, there ever will be (I wish never to see the day when there shall not be) parties. The bulk of the people will be divided, and espouse one or other side . . . while each party continues formidable to the other, and upon an equal footing, neither will dare to attempt, because neither can oppress', wrote one.[60] 'If the authority of the Crown and

---

[58] Franklin to Thomas Cushing, 5 Feb. 1771; *Franklin Writings*, ed. Smyth, Vol. V, p. 295. For a general explanation of the agents' decline see Michael Kammen, *A Rope of Sand* (Ithaca, N.Y., 1968); Jack M. Sosin, *Agents and Merchants, British Colonial Policy and the Origins of the American Revolution, 1763–1775* (Lincoln, Nebr. 1965), pp. 145–61.

[59] *Common Sense: in nine Conferences . . . in their private Capacities as friends*, p. iv.

[60] Peter Van Schaak to Henry Van Schaak, 27 Jan. 1769, *Life of Peter Van Schaak*, p. 11.

measures of Government are the Sport of faction, there is no help for that . . . ', wrote another.[61] There is among some contemporary writers, aware that the greater strength of local Assemblies *vis-à-vis* the local governors, the greater assurance of colonial factions in appealing 'out of doors', and the longer tradition of legitimate opposition to royal authority, gave the colonists more experience than their British counterparts in working with political factions, at least a suspicion that the instability of parliamentary factions was at the heart of the imperial problem. The British government was 'not to be kept honest without the opposition and cannot be quiet with it'.[62] The instability of British ministries may even have been the cause of turning American thoughts to revolt: 'The greatest evil arising from them is their inuring the minds of the people to revolutionary ideas.'[63]

Thus the break-up of the coalition ministries of the fifties, and the further development of the factions which had composed them, produced on the one hand the ministry that drew up the Stamp Tax, and on the other the factions of Chatham and Rockingham who opposed it. All the English factions saw themselves in the traditional role of cultivating American associates: Grenville (along with Bedford and North) by encouraging colonial conservatives to dissent against the tyranny of local demagogues, the other factions by encouraging some of the 'popular' leaders in their local opposition to particular imperial measures. But Grenville, Bedford, and North were totally in-

[61] James Murray to Dr. John Murray, 21 June 1766; *Letters of James Murray, Loyalist*, p. 56.

Thomas Jefferson reflected the American view years later when he wrote, 'In every free and deliberating society there must from the nature of man, be opposite parties, and violent dissentions and discords . . . . Perhaps this party division is necessary to induce each to watch and relate to the people the proceedings of the other' (James Truslow Adams, *Jeffersonian Principles and Hamiltonian Principles* (Boston, 1932), pp. 89–90).

[62] *Common Sense: in nine Conferences*, p. 73.

[63] Jonathan Boucher, *A View of the Causes and Consequences of the American Revolution in Thirteen Discourses* (New York, 1797), p. xi. On this see Christopher Gadsden to William Samuel Johnson, 6 Apr. 1766; Richard Walsh, ed., *The Writings of Christopher Gadsden, 1746–1805* (Columbia, S.C., 1966), p. 73.

The colonists' concern about the stability of British parties may also have been reflected in the reprinting of Paul de Rapin-Thoyras's *Dissertation on the Rise, Progress, Views, Strength, Interests and Characters of the Two Parties, Whigs and Tories* in Boston in 1773. The book, originally written half a century earlier, was an attack on both Whig and Tory parties of that time.

effective in backing conservative supporters in the colonies; the tactics of Chatham and Rockingham elicited a cynical sneer from some colonial politicians, and profound doubts about the British party system from others. The failure of all these attempts revealed the fact that the informal partisan associations so essential to empire were dead.

For a century and a quarter factional disputes had spilled over to the colonies from the home country, through the transatlantic connections, official and unofficial, of Englishmen in the colonies, through the handling of Anglo-colonial patronage, through English divisions over colonial appeals, through English political journalism read in the colonies; the more marked the party divisions in England, the more decisively they spilled over into colonial politics.

When, in the decade before the American Revolution, English factions each tried—albeit without success—to encourage local divisions within the colonies for their particular purposes, they were following a well-established approach. Whether they wanted colonial bases from which they might reconquer England from Oliver Cromwell, or colonial disturbances they might use to embarrass Sir Robert Walpole or Lord North, English minority factions had looked to the colonies as indirect sources of help in their domestic conflicts; from Edward Randolph to the subministers under Lord North, English colonial officials had appealed to ministers in power with the argument that the needs of momentarily submerged Anglophile sections of the colonies obliged the government to tighten imperial ties.

Up to 1765 these had been reasonable assumptions; after that they were not. Colonial politicians, increasingly suspicious that they were merely pawns in the politics of English factions, developed a cynical disregard for the Rockingham and Chatham parties who professed to espouse the colonial 'cause'.

Moreover, Anglophile minorities in the various colonies now despaired of using imperial connections to protect themselves from local pressures. Up until the 1760s their position in the Empire had given legitimacy, safety, and even political prospects to minority groups or 'outs' opposing the provincial governments. Imperial machinery provided a place to which they could appeal against adverse local legislation; English connections in London and officials in the colonies informally protected the existence of minority groups; the quotation of English writings that had escaped censorship as the source of their ideas shielded opposition factions from charges of sedition there. Even after the disillusionment of the 1730s 'country' parties in the colonies continued to find in the ideas and mechanism of imperial politics some hope for the redress of local grievances.

After 1765 this was no longer possible. Colonial leaders, it is true, rallied around the slogans of John Wilkes, but Wilkes's imprisonment destroyed the colonists' general ability to use the ideas of the contemporary British opposition as a shield in local politics (it may well have reminded them—though they never mentioned it—of the long-time colonial association with English lost causes: Shaftesbury, Bolingbroke, a host of lesser colonial models had had to flee the country); the ignominious treatment of the colonial agents eliminated the usefulness of imperial administration in handling local appeals; the weakness of English officials in the face of the colonial mobs destroyed any prospect of their rallying Anglophile sentiments against the Assembly majority; these, along with the assumed selfishness of the factions of Rockingham and Chatham, meant that the imperial machinery, which previously had provided a way for colonial opposition to blow itself off without becoming violent, had now lost its safety valves.

It was not the Stamp Act that made this clear; it was the deterioration of British politics afterwards. What the Stamp Act did was to reveal the power of popular pressure groups in the colonies and force the colonial politicians to think out their positions accordingly. That they reacted differently from colony to colony is testimony to the differences in local party politics from one colony to another; that they reacted in the same general context is testimony to the homogenizing effect of the imperial experience—an effect essential for the founding of the new nation.

Index